Richard Nixon

REAL PEACE

NO MORE VIETNAMS

With a New Introduction
by President Nixon

A TOUCHSTONE BOOK
Published by Simon & Schuster Inc.
New York   London   Toronto   Sydney   Tokyo   Singapore

Touchstone
Simon & Schuster Building
Rockefeller Center
1230 Avenue of the Americas
New York, New York 10020

Copyright © 1983, 1984, 1985, 1990 by Richard Nixon

1   3   5   7   9   10   8   6   4   2

Library of Congress Cataloging in Publication Data
Nixon, Richard M. (Richard Milhous),
[Real peace]
Real peace ; No more Vietnams / Richard Nixon.
p.   cm.
"A Touchstone book."
Reprint (1st work). Originally published: New York, c 1983.
Reprint (2nd work). Originally published: New York : Arbor House,
c 1985.
Includes bibliographical references.
1. Peace.   2. International relations.   3. United States—Foreign
relations—Soviet Union.   4. Soviet Union—Foreign relations—United
States.   5. Vietnamese Conflict, 1961–1975—United States.
I. Nixon, Richard M. (Richard Milhous), No more Vietnams.
1990.   II. Title.   III. Title: Real peace.   IV. Title: No more
Vietnams.
JX1963.N66   1990
327.1'72—dc20   90-9516
CIP
ISBN 0-671-70620-9

CONTENTS

INTRODUCTION

I published *Real Peace*, my fifth book, in a private edition in 1983. It was my first and only experience as a publisher. It was also the only case in which I was able to approach writing an entire book in the way I had always wanted, which was to envision it as a long speech. I wanted it to have the impact of a book but with the clarity, simplicity, and immediacy of a spoken address.

Real Peace was written five years after *The Real War*. During his first years in office President Reagan had vigorously addressed the crisis in superpower relations I had described in the earlier book. He had undertaken a massive defense buildup and was taking a more assertive line against Soviet aggression. Now I felt our goal as a nation should be a realistic strategy for preserving and extending peace around the world while reducing the chances of a suicidal nuclear war.

My advice to anyone undertaking a major writing project is to do what I have done throughout my political career, whether with speeches, articles, or books: Make an outline. You do not have to be bound strictly by it. But unless you begin by ordering your thoughts coherently, your writing will meander rather than march, sag rather than sing. Always remember, too, that while you may think all your words are pearls of wisdom, shortening the string during the editing process will keep you from getting tangled in your own rhetoric. Publishers often want big, fat books they can label as "sweeping" or "definitive." Sometimes a subject requires such length and detail, but all too often it does not. Shorter is frequently better, because shorter texts are usually more powerful and always more read.

I began making notes over the Independence Day weekend in 1983. I finished the seventeen-page outline, written out in longhand on a yellow legal-sized pad, at 12:30 in the afternoon on July 4th, just before leaving my home in Saddle River to go to Yankee Stadium to see New York play the Boston Red Sox. The young Yankee pitcher, Dave Righetti, threw a no-hitter, his first, and mine as well. I decided this was a good sign for *Real Peace*!

Five weeks later, I had finished the manuscript. Any author will tell you that when he has completed a project he wants to see it in print as quickly as possible. But publishers require as much as six months' lead time to get a book into bookstores. I decided to cut out the middle man and asked Marin Strmecki, who had helped research the manuscript and prepare it for publication, to produce the book instead. He found a printer and designed the book and the jacket, and by September it was finished. Without a publisher's giant publicity apparatus to depend upon, I mailed copies of page proofs, and later, finished books, to key columnists and opinion leaders around the world. Their responses made *Real Peace* my most critically acclaimed book, and soon Little, Brown asked permission to publish a regular commercial edition.

Many praised the book because they thought I was being critical of President Reagan's hard line. But my most hard-hitting passages were about the myths of peace, the naive and fatally flawed nostrums being put forward by his harshest critics. I also returned to a theme I have repeatedly emphasized ever since Mrs. Nixon and I took a seventy-day trip around the world in 1953: the need to develop a more effective policy to promote freedom and prosperity in the Third World. "The people in these countries have terrible problems," I wrote. "The communists at least talk about the problems. Too often we just talk about the communists." Today the Berlin Wall has come down and most of the nations of Eastern Europe have begun to break free of Soviet domination. But in the developing world, the grinding poverty and misery that provide such fertile soil for communism persists and will do so for generations. The Soviet Union still spends $15 billion a year to prop up anti-American regimes in Vietnam, Syria, Cuba, North Korea, and Afghanistan. The Cold War has ended in Europe, but it is still being waged in the Third World.

During the 1980 Presidential campaign, Ronald Reagan proclaimed the war in Vietnam a noble cause. His critics called it a gaffe. I call it the truth. Of all the books I have written, *No More Vietnams* is the one that I felt I had an obligation to write—for the sake of the three million Americans who served, for the sake of the 56,000 who died, for the sake of the millions of people of Indochina still suffering under communism because of our failure, and for the sake of history.

Vietnam is the most lied-about war in our nation's history. In the wake of the Vietnamese gulag and the holocaust in Cambodia in which two million people were killed by the communist Khmer Rouge we had tried to keep out of power, those who opposed our efforts—including columnists, authors, and movie directors—have spent the last fifteen years scrambling to justify their anti-war position. Many of them still argue that we were on the wrong side. In this book I demonstrated not only that we were on the right side but that after our fighting men had won the war, the United States Congress lost the peace by slashing aid to our South Vietnamese allies at the same time the Soviet Union was dramatically expanding its aid to the communists in the North.

When I wrote the book in 1985, I was suffering from what my doctor described as the worst case of shingles he had ever seen. In spite of this ordeal, or perhaps as a way of distracting my attention from it, I was able to do some of the best writing

I have ever done. But I erred on one important decision: the title. The one I chose was based on this passage: " 'No more Vietnams' *can* mean we will not *try* again. It *should* mean 'We will not *fail* again.' " As I look back, the title seems too clever by half, as if I were trying to outsmart people by co-opting the anti-war critics' favorite bumper sticker. Titles, like texts, should be simple and direct. If I were making the decision today, I would choose a different title: *A Noble Cause*.

—RN
March 14, 1990
Saddle River, New Jersey

REAL PEACE

To the Peacemakers

THE MYTHS OF PEACE

There can be no real peace in the world unless a new relationship is established between the United States and the Soviet Union.

The two superpowers cannot afford to go to war against each other, at any time or under any circumstances. Each side's vast military power makes war obsolete as an instrument of national policy. The cost to both sides of a full-scale conventional or nuclear war would far exceed any conceivable benefits.

In the nineteenth century the German military strategist Clausewitz called war "the continuation of political activity by other means." At that time national leaders used war or the threat of war as a last resort to extract concessions from their adversaries.

Now, for the superpowers, using that last resort would be suicide. In the age of nuclear warfare to continue our political differences by means of war would be to discontinue civilization as we know it.

War is an option whose time has passed. Peace is the only option for the future. At present we occupy a treacherous no-man's-land between peace and war, a time of growing fear that our military might has expanded beyond our capacity to control it and our political differences widened beyond our ability to bridge them.

The situation is precarious, but the moment is precious. It is imperative that the leaders of the United States and the Soviet Union seize the moment to achieve a major breakthrough for peace—not a mythical perfect peace but a real peace, based on a joint recognition of the harsh reality that they have profound, irreconcilable differences but that their survival depends on their finding ways to manage their differences without war.

A world war, whether conventional or nuclear, must never again be allowed to take place. One of the most empty-headed and dangerous fallacies of the nuclear disarmament movement is that the world would necessarily be better off without nuclear weapons. Those who survived the trench warfare of World War I, the Allied firebombings in Germany and Japan during World War II, or the Soviets' recent use of chemical warfare in Laos can testify that conventional war brings its own unique horrors.

We must not allow our understandable fear of a nuclear war to blind us to the increasingly awesome destructiveness of conventional weapons. Conventional weapons killed 15 million in World War I and over 54 million in World War II. Casualties in a conventional World War III would be far greater. We must face up to the fact that in any conventional or nuclear world war there will be no winners, only losers. Charles de Gaulle recognized this when he observed during our meeting at Versailles in 1969, "In the Second World War, all the nations of Europe lost; two were defeated."

The United States' superiority in nuclear weapons, which we no longer have, was the indispensable factor in deterring the Soviet Union from launching a conventional war against Western Europe after World War II. While war has become obsolete as an instrument of policy the tools of war must continue to play a role in keeping the peace. Military deterrence, including nuclear forces, is an essential component of any lasting peace. When each side holds an equally good hand, a potential aggressor is likely to keep both his hands on the table.

Paradoxically, though war is obsolete, we live in a world that is perpetually at war. In this summer of 1983, fifteen wars and a score of minor conflicts are raging around the globe. Since World War II there have been 140 wars, resulting in the deaths of over ten million people. Many of these have been local conflicts in the Third World in which nations have fought over religion or territory, or in which people have risen up against unpopular leaders. But virtually all of them have been haunted by the specter of superpower confrontation.

In some cases the Soviet Union has initiated or exacerbated such conflicts; in other cases the U.S. has stepped in to protect its interests against communist aggression. As long as the superpowers view their interests and responsibilities on a global level, each small war is a world war in the making. Any guerrilla, no matter how obscure his cause or how remote his country, can fire a shot that will be heard around the world. A real peace between the superpowers must therefore take into account all conflict, everywhere in the world, and also those political, social, and economic tensions that lead to conflict.

Real peace will not come from some magic formula that will suddenly and once and for all be "discovered," like the promised land or the holy grail. Real peace is a process—a continuing process for managing and containing conflict between competing nations, competing systems, and competing international ambitions. Peace is not an end to conflict but rather a means of living with conflict, and once established it requires constant attention or it will not survive.

Confusing real peace with perfect peace is a dangerous but common fallacy. Idealists long for a world without conflict, a world that never was and never will be, where all differences between nations have been overcome, all ambitions forsworn, all aggressive or selfish impulses transformed into acts of individual and national beneficence.

Because of the realities of human nature, perfect peace is achieved in two places only: in the grave and at the typewriter. Perfect peace flourishes—in print. It is the stuff of poetry and high-minded newspaper editorials, molded out of pretty thoughts and pretty words. Real peace, on the other hand, will be the down-to-earth product of the real world, manufactured by realistic, calculating leaders whose sense of their nations' self-interest is diamond-hard and unflinching.

Those who make peace at the typing table rather than at the negotiating table have the luxury of being peacemakers without having to grapple with complex problems in the rough-and-tumble world of real international diplomacy. To them the only obstacle to peace is the regrettable lack of leaders who are as selfless and idealistic as they claim to be and who are willing to put aside parochial national interest in the interest of bringing peace to the world. They hope that this era will be the one in which self-interest, the force that has driven history since the dawn of history, will simply evaporate.

Perfect peace has no historical antecedents and therefore no practical meaning in a world in which conflict among men is persistent and pervasive. If real peace is to exist, it must exist along with men's ambitions, their pride, and their hatreds. A peace that fails to take these things into account will not last.

We will meet the challenge of real peace only by keeping in mind two fundamental truths.

First, conflict is a natural state of affairs in the world. Some nations are certain to be unsatisfied by what they have and will try to get more, for a variety of reasons and through a variety of means. Other nations will resist the designs of these acquisitive powers. One way or another nations in such positions will come into conflict, and if they cannot resolve their conflicts peaceably they will eventually try to resolve them violently.

Second, nations only resort to aggression when they believe they will profit from it. Conversely, they will shrink from aggression if it appears in the long run it will cost them more than it benefits them.

Short of changing human nature, therefore, the only way to achieve a practical, liveable peace in a world of competing nations is to take the profit out of war.

. . .

Most of the obstacles to peace today result from the Soviet Union's expansionist policies. But there are also those in the West who impede the peacemakers. A few, their allegiances and their motives clear, do so intentionally. Those who do so inadvertently are far more dangerous.

Lenin was fully aware of how helpful naive Westerners could be to the communist cause. He contemptuously called them "the useful idiots." More out of ignorance than by design, the useful idiots earnestly plug ridiculously simplistic answers to our most complex problems. They are the sloganeers whose idea of thoughtful analysis is often limited to what will fit on a t-shirt or a bumper sticker. "Make love, not war." "You can't hug your kids with nuclear arms." "Honk if you want peace." Much of this fatuous nonsense is harmless, but unfortunately not all the useful idiots occupy themselves by marching and honking for peace. Some teach in our universities; some write newspaper columns; others pontificate on television.

The complexities of the modern world are so baffling to them that they seek comfort in simple answers. What they fail to recognize is that for every complicated problem there is *always* a simple answer—and it's usually wrong.

Building a real peace will be arduous, frustrating work, and it is not surprising that some fall for shortcuts that promise to get them what they want quickly, painlessly, and cheaply. These shortcuts never work, and we should not expect them to work.

In his heart everyone knows that the only people who get rich from the "get rich quick" books are those who write them. But just as there are countless "get rich quick" schemes there is also a wide array of seductively appealing "get peace quick" schemes.

These are the myths of peace. Myths are fairy tales that people make up about things they otherwise would not understand. The ancients devised them to "explain" lightning and the changing of the seasons; today many concoct them to "explain" international relations. They are profoundly reassuring to those who otherwise would be profoundly confused by the complex dilemmas we face. But these myths are doubly dangerous: dangerous because they can distract and confound our leaders and clog decision-making channels, and also because of the chance that one of them might actually become official policy.

The Disarmament Myth. This is the granddaddy of peace myths, a favorite of generation after generation of idealists. Founded on a logical fallacy in which human intentions are equated with the means men use to carry out their intentions, the idea of disarmament has alternately seduced and disappointed peacemakers throughout history.

"Disarmists," those alarmists who think the world's greatest evil is the arms race, believe that it is the *existence* of arms that causes war rather than the political tensions which lead to their use. Because of this fundamental misconception, the disarmists' best hope for peace is a prescription for international disaster.

If we are to make any progress toward real peace we must accept the fact that war results from unresolved political differences, not from the existence of arms. Pursuing arms control talks without dealing with our other nation-to-nation problems at the same time would be the ultimate example of treating a symptom while letting the disease run its brutal course. It is like a doctor prescribing aspirin rather than penicillin as a cure for pneumonia.

One of the few arms control pacts of the twentieth century was concluded in 1922 at the Washington Naval Conference. The U.S., Britain, and Japan agreed to limit their naval forces by adopting a battleship ratio of 5-5-3; Japan had also signed a treaty with eight other powers agreeing to observe the integrity of China. But Japan's ambitions in the Far East and its resentment of the Western powers were both far greater than its commitment to the agreements it had signed. In 1931 it invaded China, and in 1941 it struck our naval forces at Pearl Harbor.

World War II resulted not from arms buildups but from the

territorial ambitions of Japan and Germany. Germany's and Japan's arms buildups were a result of these ambitions, not the cause of them. The current arms race is between a similarly ambitious Soviet Union and a free world that has determined not to be caught off-guard again. The root causes of that conflict must be addressed before arms control can have any purpose.

The one sure way to prevent a nuclear holocaust would be to eliminate all nuclear weapons. But complete nuclear disarmament is an impossible dream. The reason is simple: nuclear weapons are simple. The principles of physics that make them possible are widely understood by governments, by terrorists, even by college undergraduates. The materials for making them are within the grasp of virtually every modern nation.

Some, out of desperation or supreme naivete, have suggested that an international authority be established to banish nuclear weapons and make sure they are never built again. Because such an authority would by necessity be privy to the inner workings of every government in the world, it would itself be the most powerful and ultimately the most dangerous institution on earth. Incredible political force would have to be brought to bear to keep nuclear weapons from being built, and that force would be so vast as to change the character of life on earth. Like the seventeenth-century political philosopher Thomas Hobbes, the disarmists are in effect asserting that we must offer ourselves and our liberties up to some superstate so that it can protect us from being devoured by each other in the nuclear state of nature.

That the disarmists would propose some outlandish "world government" shows that most of them, to put the most charitable light on the matter, are living in a dream world in which problems between nations can be solved by some authority other than national governments. This delusion is a form of radiation sickness. If you look directly at an atomic blast you may go blind; apparently intellectual blindness can result from contemplating the nuclear weapons issue for too long.

Nuclear weapons will always exist. We must learn to live with what we know rather than wasting our energies in the pretense of not knowing it. But while we cannot eliminate nuclear weapons, we can do a great deal to prevent them from being used. It is only by learning to live in peace with our adversaries that we will learn to live with nuclear weapons.

The World Government Myth. After the cataclysm of World War II, in which 55 million people died, those who had served and survived returned home to the happy news of the United Nations conference in San Francisco. Everyone was hopeful that through this new organization we would debate about our disagreements rather than fight about them.

But as was the case with the League of Nations after World War I, the promise of the UN was illusory. The League of Nations and the UN were both noble but unavailing attempts to turn man's most idealistic impulses about peace into reality. Envisioned as the peacekeeper of the postwar world, the UN has been unable in most cases either to forestall war or to end a war once it was begun. One expert has concluded that of 93 separate conflicts between 1946 and 1977, the UN held limited debate on 40, did not debate at all about 53, and did not significantly contribute to the resolution of any.

Many nations are ably represented in the UN by dedicated, highly intelligent delegates, and the organization as a whole does important work in such areas as health and hunger relief. At its best the United Nations serves as a forum for the views and complaints of smaller nations that otherwise might be ignored in a world dominated by the superpowers. But at its worst it is more often than not a propaganda arm of the Soviet Union and its satellites and shills, a hall of distorting mirrors where peace-loving Russian armies are "invited in" by their victims, where the aiding and abetting of terrorism is actually "supporting wars of national liberation"—where, as in the world of George Orwell's 1984, "war is peace" and "freedom is slavery." The UN has exacerbated many conflicts either by cavalierly blaming the U.S. or by ignoring the involvement of the Soviet Union. While 160 flags fly at the UN, the one that flies the highest is the double standard.

No major power will submit an issue affecting its basic interests to a forum in which it can be overruled by smaller powers. The UN's failure shows that international problems must be solved by negotiations between autonomous governments or they will not be solved.

The Myth of Peace Through Trade. Optimism, like hope, springs eternal, and from each generation of leaders spring the eternal optimists who say that trade between aggressive adversaries softens their belligerence. Five years after the Russian Revolution David Lloyd George, the British prime minister, said that trade with the Soviets would "bring an end to the ferocity, the rapine, and the crudity of Bolshevism surer than any other method." Many in the West, eager for what they called "peaceful coexistence" with the new communist government, agreed. Western businessmen scrambled for access to what they hoped would be rich new Soviet markets, and the Russians obligingly granted over 300 "concessions" to Western companies. Eventually all these manufacturing firms were expelled, but not before Soviet engineers had studied and copied Western industrial technology and methods and put them to work during Stalin's massive industrial buildup in the 1930s.

That first round of economic cooperation in the 1920s did not bring the West and the Soviets closer together. It did help turn the Soviet Union into a much stronger adversary.

Yet today there are many, especially in the Western business community, who share Lloyd George's view. Their optimism, though commendable, is again based on faulty logic. Peace-through-trade did not work before, and it will not work now. As Konrad Adenauer told me in 1967 just before his death, "Trade is trade." Nations enter into trading relationships in the hope of making a profit, and any nation with aggressive ambitions can be expected to use its profits in the pursuit of those ambitions.

In both world wars nations that had traded with each other fought each other. Before World War II Japan had trade ties

23

with the U.S. that had been painstakingly built up since the nineteenth century. Germany traded extensively with each of the countries it invaded.

In the end both nations' leaders found their grievances and territorial ambitions to be far stronger than their desire to remain at peace and engage in peaceful commerce with their neighbors. Believing that they could profit more from war than from peace, they went to war. Their choice proved that just as weapons are dangerous only insofar as they may be used to resolve political differences, commerce with an adversary contributes to peace only if it is part of a larger structure designed to reduce political differences. Otherwise, by trading with an aggressive, expansionist power you are fueling a fire that could eventually consume you.

The Myth of Peace Through Friendship. Some of the useful idiots put no faith in leaders. Others put far too much. The latter believe that if leaders would only meet and get to know one another, peace would follow as a matter of course. Since they think international conflict results primarily from misunderstanding and bad communication, they assume that friendships between nations and treaties and agreements designed to set the world right will inevitably result from friendships between national leaders.

This has never been the case, in our century or in any other. William Jennings Bryan, Woodrow Wilson's first secretary of state, believed war could be prevented if nations would agree to meet amicably to settle their disputes, and he signed treaties with 30 nations creating mechanisms for doing so. World War I followed fast on Bryan's heels. In the 1930s Imperial Japan's promise to observe the integrity of China did not prevent or delay its Invasion of Manchuria. In World War II Nazi Germany invaded the Soviet Union in 1941, thus violating the two-year-old Hitler-Stalin nonaggression pact.

History is a pathetic junkyard of broken treaties. Yet naive idealists persist in believing that summits, state dinners, windy toasts, tearful bearhugs and *abrazos*, and solemn signing ceremonies are the very essence of diplomacy. They put great faith in good relations among leaders, and their hearts swell when they turn on the evening news and see two "former" adversaries grinning and tipping glasses at each other.

The media frequently mistake such atmospherics for real diplomatic progress because they only scan the surface of events, accumulating photographs of smiles and handshakes to print and copies of agreements to excerpt and summarize. Following such a meeting the diplomatic correspondents count up all the smiles, handshakes, and agreements, scrutinize the texts of the dinner toasts, study how pleased the officials are with themselves on the flight home, determine how many souvenirs the diplomats' wives bought, and then, relying on a journalistic calculus known only to themselves, pronounce the event a success or a failure. In the end they and their readers will probably learn little or nothing about what actually happened when the leaders sat down by themselves and tackled the substantive issues. In front of the cameras the leaders had been friends joined in the pursuit of peace, but behind closed doors they reverted to their real selves: aggressor, victim, cat, mouse, hawk, chicken, winner, loser.

Handshakes do not change national ambitions or interests. "Friendship treaties" do not necessarily express or create friendship. When two leaders sit down to talk, they do not turn into philanthropists. They do not give away anything without getting something in return which they value as much or more. Good personal relations do not ensure good state relations. All leaders, not just communist leaders, put their nations' interests above their personal likes and dislikes.

Leaders go to meetings with adversaries in pursuit of good press back home, in search of leverage to use in relations with other nations, or in the hope of exploiting the other side's weaknesses or irresolution and coming out ahead as a result. International relations are not like lunch at the club or a round of golf with friends. They are more like entering a snake pit where good intentions and good manners, adhered to slavishly in the face of your enemy's malevolence, are bound to be distinct hindrances. No leader should meet with an adversary unless he is fully aware of his own strengths and weaknesses and those of his opponent; unless he has something he wants to bargain for and something to bargain with; and unless he is prepared to be worked over by professionals.

Face-to-face meetings between leaders of hostile powers always have been and will continue to be useful for only two reasons. First, they help the leaders get each others' measure and as a result help them avoid potentially disastrous miscalculations later on. Second, they provide a setting for the exceedingly delicate, difficult process of making agreements the observance of which will serve both sides' interests simultaneously. Unless agreements are self-enforcing they will not last. It is a reflection of the great difficulty of meaningful negotiation between adversaries that such agreements, amid all of history's friendship treaties and nonaggression pacts, have been few and far between.

In the long term we can hope that religion will change the nature of man and reduce conflict. But history is not encouraging in this respect. The bloodiest wars in history have been religious wars. Men praying to the same God killed each other by the thousands in America's Civil War and by the millions in World War I and World War II. Unless men change, a real peace must be built on the assumption that the most we can do is to learn to live with our differences rather than dying over them.

THE KEYS TO REAL PEACE

The door to real peace must be unlocked. Two keys are required to open it. The United States has one; the Soviet Union has the other. Unless the superpowers adopt a new live-and-let-live relationship, the world will not see real peace in this century. If we fail to work toward that end, suicidal war is inevitable. If we succeed in reaching it, not only does world war become avoidable, but world peace becomes possible. Working against each other, the superpowers will enter a spiral of escalating differences that could lead to war. Working together, they can be an irresistible force for peace not only for themselves but for others as well.

Never has real peace been so necessary and yet so difficult to achieve. The stark truth is that the ideologies and the foreign policies of the superpowers are diametrically opposed. The struggle between the Soviet Union and the United States is between an avowedly and manifestly aggressive power and an avowedly and manifestly defensive one, between a totalitarian civilization and a free one, between a state that is frightened by the idea of freedom and one that is founded on it.

The United States wants peace; the Soviet Union wants the world. Our foreign policy respects the freedom of other nations; theirs tries to destroy it. We are interested in peace as an end in itself; they are interested in it only if it serves their ends. The Soviets pursue those ends unscrupulously, by means short of all-out war. They lie, cheat, subvert governments, disrupt elections, subsidize terrorists, and wage wars by proxy. For the Soviets, peace is a continuation of war by other means.

Russians and Americans can be friends. But the governments of the Soviet Union and the United States can never be friends because their interests are irreconcilable. The peace we seek cannot be based on mutual friendship. It can only be grounded on mutual respect for each other's strength.

We will continue to have political differences that will drive us apart. We must also recognize, however, that the United States and the Soviet Union have two common interests that can draw us together. As the world's two greatest military powers, we both want to avoid a major war that neither of us would survive. As the world's two major economic powers— each with enormous resources and capable people—we can cooperate in ways that could benefit both of us immensely.

We must not delude ourselves into believing that the East-West struggle is the result of a giant misunderstanding that can be overcome if we sit down and talk it over. We can form Soviet-American friendship societies or tip vodka glasses with Kremlin leaders, but it will not lead to peace. That approach assumes the Soviets share with the West a "sincere" desire for peace. But as Ambassador Charles Bohlen told me in 1959, "Trying to determine whether the Soviet leaders are sincere about anything is a useless exercise." Pointing to a coffee table, he added, "They are pure materialists. You can no more describe them as being sincere than you could describe that table as being sincere."

If our differences are so intractable, is peace possible? Our differences make a perfect, ideal peace impossible, but our common interests make a pragmatic, real peace achievable. We are entering a new phase of the East-West struggle. In view of the verbal missiles rocketing between Washington and Moscow, we might conclude that the chances for peace are remote. But if we look beyond the rhetoric to the realities, we can be more optimistic. The table is set for a breakthrough toward real peace.

In working for peace, we must not pursue the unachievable at the expense of the attainable. Neither we nor the Soviets can compromise our basic values. Only if we recognize that we are not going to settle our differences can we avoid going to war over them. The most we can hope to achieve is an agreement establishing peaceful rules of engagement for our continuing conflict. If we cannot walk arm-in-arm down the road toward peace, we must try at least to walk side-by-side.

The enormous military strength and the aggressive policies of the Soviet Union lead many in the West to conclude that the prospects for peace are virtually nonexistent. Their concerns are justified, and I have addressed them in *The Real War*. But our analysis of the Soviet position cannot stop with their troop and weapons count. In designing our foreign policy, we must know not only our adversary's strengths, but also his weaknesses. We must not wallow in despair about Soviet might, for then we will fail to focus our attention on Soviet vulnerabilities.

No man knows the strengths and weaknesses of the Soviet Union better than Yuri Andropov. For fifteen years he was the head of the KGB, the Soviet espionage and police apparatus. There he received reports from the vast network of Soviet agents at home and abroad and travelled extensively throughout the Eastern bloc. We can be certain that as he steps up to bat, he knows the score, knows the other team, knows how to play the game, and is prepared to put more than pine tar on his bat.

The West knows little about Andropov himself. When he came into power, he was the subject of intense speculation in the West. Some media observers suggested that he was a closet liberal, a pussycat who would be easy to deal with because he liked American jazz and drank Scotch rather than vodka. Such commentators are forever confusing style with substance. They are suckers for style because style is their bread and butter. In the 1950s, they dismissed Nikita Khrushchev as a lightweight because he spoke bad Russian, drank too much, wore ill-fitting clothes, and had crude manners. They were wrong about Khrushchev, and they are wrong about Andropov. Anyone who claws his way to the top in the murderous jungle warfare of the Soviet hierarchy is bound to be a formidable adversary. Only the strong survive and reach the top in communist regimes.

We know this for sure about Andropov. He is an intelligent, dedicated, ruthless communist who shares the global ambitions of every Soviet dictator since the Bolshevik Revolution. Those who expect the Soviet Union to moderate its belligerence as soon as Andropov consolidates his power are deluding themselves.

Fortunately, however, he is a hard-headed pragmatist, not a madman. This makes him less dangerous in the short run but potentially more dangerous in the long run, unless we develop pragmatic policies that will affect his interests.

Andropov knows the strengths of the Soviet Union. He can point to some significant achievements over the past decade. Since 1974, over 100 million people have come under communist domination or have been lost to the West. Most ominously, the Soviets have gained superiority over the West in the most powerful and accurate nuclear weapons, land-based strategic and intermediate-range ballistic missiles.

Today the Soviets, through their Cuban and Nicaraguan surrogates, are threatening to make Central America the next East-West battleground. Through their Libyan proxies, they are advancing in Central Africa. They are inching, via Afghanistan, toward the Persian Gulf. Through their support of Syria and the radical Palestinians, they are trying to exacerbate the Arab-Israeli conflict. By supporting both Iran and Iraq they are positioning themselves to pick up the pieces after that war in the oilrich Persian Gulf. Their propaganda machine is operating at full throttle, helping fuel the disarmament movement in

Western Europe and thus continuing their 35-year-old campaign to divide the West against itself. The overall picture they present to the West is one of enormous power that backs up a menacing, expansionist foreign policy.

But Andropov is no fool. He is also aware of the profound weaknesses of the Soviet Union. Its economy is in desperate shape. Western economies have been through some rough seas, but the Soviet economy is dead in the water. The growth rate is plummeting. Productivity is dropping. Absenteeism, corruption, malingering, and drunkenness are rife. The standard of living is sinking, so much so that the life expectancy of Russian men is actually going down. The *average* wage of workers in the Soviet Union is lower than Brazil's *minimum* wage. Japan, with one-half the population of the Soviet Union, less arable land than California, no oil and very few natural resources, has a gross national product almost as large as that of the Soviet Union and a per capita income three times as high.

Andropov's vastly overblown military budget only increases the problem. It is twice as large as ours in terms of the proportion of GNP it consumes. That creates an enormous drag on the economy, reducing the incentives for individuals to produce goods and limiting potential future growth. After 60 years of big promises and poor performance, the stark truth is there for all to see. Soviet socialism does not work.

The ideology of communism has lost its appeal. Communists have never won a majority in a free election anywhere in the world. The crisis in Poland is only the most visible example of the popular discontent that is heating up just beneath the surface and threatens to boil over throughout Eastern Europe and in the Soviet Union itself. A scene I remember from my trip to Poland in 1959 illustrates this. Even now I can see the members of a crack Polish honor guard standing on a flatbed truck, cheering, and raising their hands in the "V-for-victory" sign as our motorcade left the Warsaw airport. The Kremlin's military planners are daydreaming if they are counting on the loyalty of Polish troops in the event of a war in Europe.

Never in history has an aggressive power been more successful in extending its domination over other nations and less successful in winning the approval of the people of those nations. As has been the case since the end of World War II, millions of refugees are on the move today. The traffic is all one way—from communism to freedom.

The costs of Soviet conquests are a massive drain on its desperately weak economy. The British may have been enriched by their empire, but the Soviets are being impoverished by theirs. Andropov must pour huge economic resources into his empire to keep his shaky political investments afloat. Cuba costs him $14 million a day. Angola, Ethiopia, Vietnam, and Nicaragua cost him over $5 million a day. Afghanistan has cost him millions of dollars and thousands of casualties. The resistance Soviet puppet regimes are meeting in Afghanistan, Angola, Mozambique, Ethiopia, and Nicaragua proves that the Soviet Union is increasingly unable to digest what it swallows.

On its Western front, the Soviet Union faces a newly united NATO. America's allies, without whom a comprehensive peace would be impossible, are acting with vision and strength under the leadership of conservatives like Margaret Thatcher and Helmut Kohl and anti-Soviet socialists like François Mitterrand and Bettino Craxi. The alliance is united behind a program to redress the European balance of power by deploying American Pershing II and cruise missiles. The Soviet propaganda campaign has failed. Andropov must now know that these deployments will begin by the end of the year unless he concludes an arms control agreement in Geneva.

On its Eastern front, the Soviet Union faces its greatest long-term challenge: Under the leadership of Yasuhiro Nakasone, Japan, an economic giant but a military pygmy, is beginning to address the question of improving its national defenses. China, still a potential enemy, is not a military threat to the Soviet Union today. But it looms as an awesome danger for the future because of its one billion people and enormous resources. As historical determinists, the Soviets look at events with the long term in mind. For them, threats in the future are problems in the present.

Andropov can boast of great gains for the Soviet Union in the Third World, but his position with the world's major powers must give him pause. Mao Zedong's military manual called for isolating the cities by capturing the countryside. Andropov's policy is right out of Mao's book. He seeks to strangle the industrial West by cutting off its supply of key resources from the Third World. This strategy might work in the long run, but its most profound immediate effect is to isolate the Soviet Union. Andropov has no allies among the major nations of the world. He faces potential adversaries in Western Europe, Japan, China, Canada, and the United States. Together these countries represent over 60 percent of the world's economy and present the Soviet Union with the grim prospect of having to face powerful enemies on two fronts.

When Andropov totals up the balance sheet of Soviet strengths and weaknesses, he cannot be encouraged. The debits are the tremendous problems he confronts both inside and outside his country. The assets are his military power. Great as they are, his assets are ill-suited to solving his problems.

Andropov is motivated by personal factors as well. He is a man in a hurry. He is ten years older than Brezhnev was when he came to power, eight years older than Khrushchev, 23 years older than Stalin. No one questions his mental alertness, but his physical health is suspect. And while he has taken the reins of the Soviet government, he is not yet firmly in the saddle. He needs a foreign policy initiative.

He has to be looking for ways to deal with his problems or at least to mitigate them. That fact makes the prospects for real peace great. Putting it simply, both sides want peace—the United States because we believe in peace, the Soviets because they need it.

The time is ripe for a deal.

. . .

If war in the nuclear age is so disastrous and if economic cooperation is so beneficial, it would seem that striking a deal for peace should be a natural. But that is not the case. The Soviet leaders are not the same kind of people we are. Their political system promotes individuals who view the world in a completely different way and who put an entirely different value on human life.

As Russians, they will weep over the millions of deaths their country suffered in World War II. But as communists, they will defend the actions of a government that killed millions of other Russian citizens. In meeting with Soviet leaders, I often thought of Dr. Jekyll and Mr. Hyde as the warm, friendly Russian of our social conversations transformed himself into a cold, heartless communist as we got down to business. Within minutes, someone who appears to be a warm-hearted pacifist turns into a ruthless thug.

There are many views about how we should deal with the Soviet leadership. At one extreme, we have the superhawks. They argue that because the Soviets are in deep trouble and are out to do us in by any and all means, we should build up military superiority and try to isolate them by cutting off all trade and negotiations. If we do that, they contend, the rotten Soviet economy will eventually collapse, bringing down the communist system with it.

That is an appealing scenario, but not a realistic one. The superhawks are correct in recognizing the Soviets for what they are. But while their premise is correct, their conclusion is wrong. The Soviet system will not collapse. The Kremlin leaders have never won a free election, but they are masters at getting and keeping power. They have ruthlessly squeezed their people with brutally austere economic policies before, and they will do so again if that is necessary to keep themselves in power. Confrontation and isolation can strengthen a dictatorship. Hard-headed negotiation and contact with the outside world can weaken it.

The superhawks also fail to realize that in a democracy it is impossible to sustain such a policy. The American people and our allies in Europe will shoulder the burden of armaments and bear the risks of military conflict only if they believe their leaders are actively trying to reduce international tensions. The people need to be given hope, for without hope the support for defense expenditures will crumble and the pressure for an ill-considered accommodation with the Soviets will build.

Even if we assume that the superhawks' policy would work and would command the sustained support of the American people, we would still be wrong to adopt it. It is irresponsible for the world's two greatest military powers not to have maximum communication with each other and not to try to negotiate their disputes. This would put our relations in a highly combustible atmosphere of semi-belligerency, with both sides building up armaments without restraint while firing salvos of hot rhetoric. Our interests would inevitably rub together in the powder kegs of the world like the Middle East, possibly sending off the spark which would ignite a nuclear war.

Sir William Slim, a Governor-General of Australia and one of Britain's greatest generals in World War II, made this point in a conversation with me 30 years ago. He was a dedicated anti-communist, but he was also a realist. He believed even then, when the United States had overwhelming nuclear superiority over the Soviet Union, that we should move from confrontation toward negotiation. He told me, "We must break the ice. If we don't break it, we will all get frozen into it so tight that it will take an atom bomb to break it."

In contrast to the superhawks, we have the superdoves at the other extreme. They argue that the Soviet Union fears the United States and arms only because we arm. They excuse virtually every instance of Soviet aggression, from the Cuban missile crisis to the invasion of Afghanistan, on the basis of the Kremlin's need to feel safe from an aggressive West. They contend that if we reassure them that we want peace, they will cease to prepare for war. They say that if we set a peaceful example—by cutting our defense budget—the Soviets will do likewise.

They are wrong. By portraying the Soviet Union as a defensive power beset by foes on all sides, they are doing the same thing Abraham Lincoln wryly accused his political opponents of doing when they twisted his policy statements to serve their purposes: "Turning a horse chestnut into a chestnut horse." A major nuclear power is not threatened by Afghan tribesmen and a country fearful of invasion by its European neighbors does not project its military power into southern Africa and the western hemisphere.

President Carter, with the best of intentions, followed the advice of the superdoves until the Soviets invaded Afghanistan. He cancelled, delayed, or cut back one after another of our arms procurement programs and made a series of conciliatory gestures toward the Soviets. The Kremlin leaders reacted by increasing their arms programs and pushing forward with their armed conquests.

Unlike the superhawks, the superdoves do not recognize the Soviets for what they are. Their argument is flawed at its premise and leads to a dangerous conclusion. We do not have to convince the Soviet leaders that we want peace. They know that. What we need to do is convince them that they cannot win a war. If we take the superdoves' advice, war would become more likely because the risks for an aggressor would be less.

There is also a third group—the defeatists. They argue that we are "better red than dead." They look with horror upon the awesome power of nuclear weapons, see communism as the wave of the future, and conclude that we are better off capitulating quietly. They have little faith in the strength of Western ideals, and value them still less.

What they fail to recognize is that there is a third choice. We can be alive and free.

To keep the peace and defend our freedom, we need to adopt a policy of hard-headed detente. "Detente" has become a notorious codeword. The debate over the word has become so charged with emotion that substance gives way to semantics.

We must therefore be clear about what hard-headed detente is and what it is not.

Hard-headed detente is a combination of detente with deterrence. It is not an entente, which is an agreement between powers with common interests, nor is it a synonym for appeasement. It does not mean that the United States and the Soviet Union agree. Rather it means that we profoundly disagree. It provides a means of peacefully resolving those disagreements that can be resolved, and of living with those that cannot.

Hard-headed detente must be based on a strength of arms and strength of will sufficient to blunt the threat of Soviet blackmail. This should be combined with a mixture of prospective rewards for good behavior and penalties for bad behavior that gives the Soviet Union a positive incentive to keep the peace rather than break it. We must make it clear to the Soviets through our strength and our will that when they threaten our interests, they are risking war. If we simultaneously engage them in a process of resolving our differences where possible, we can turn their attention toward the promise of peace.

There are those who say that detente was merely an attempt to contain the Soviet Union by tying it down in "a delicate web of interdependence." Hard-headed detente as we practiced it did not rely on anything so flimsy. We were prepared to stop Soviet aggression, direct and indirect, not only with diplomatic pressures, but also military ones. We did not reassure those who were threatening our interests that we would not use force unless attacked. Instead, we told them that we would do whatever was necessary to defend our interests and those of our allies. What was even more important, they knew we had the will to back up our words. We did not wring our hands when it became necessary to use military force or the threat of force. Our record established our credibility, and the Soviets respected it.

As we practiced it from 1969 through 1974, hard-headed detente worked. During that period, we used a combination of military and diplomatic pressures to block Soviet advances. We were prepared, if necessary, to give direct or indirect military aid to any country they threatened. We also undertook negotiations with the Soviets on a broad range of issues. Some, like arms control and the settlement of World War II debts, were of mutual interest. Others, like the granting of Most Favored Nation status and the purchase of American grain, were of particular interest to the Soviets. That gave us leverage over them. When they threatened our interests, we slowed or suspended those negotiations. When they relented, we proceeded with them.

As a result, not one nation was lost to the Soviet bloc during this period. Under pressure from us, the Soviet Union in 1970 retreated from its attempt to establish a nuclear submarine base at Cienfuegos in Cuba and from its effort, through Syria, to topple King Hussein of Jordan. It backed away from its support of India's attempt to gobble up West Pakistan in 1971. It abandoned its threat to send Soviet forces into the Middle East during the Arab-Israeli war of 1973.

On the eve of the summit meeting in 1972, we ordered the bombing and mining of Haiphong in order to stop the North Vietnamese offensive. Those who did not understand hard-headed detente thought it would torpedo the summit. They were wrong. It strengthened our hand and helped pave the way for a broad range of agreements.

After this initial success, detente is widely thought to have failed. Detente did not fail, but Congress between 1974 and 1977 and the Carter Administration between 1976 and 1980 failed to implement it in a hard-headed way. Detente without deterrence is a sure-fire recipe for retreat and defeat.

In Southeast Asia, the Congress cut Administration requests for military aid to South Vietnam by half in 1974 and another third in 1975. Also, by passing the War Powers Act and resolutions banning the use of American air power in Indochina, the Congress denied the President the power to enforce the Paris peace accords. The Soviet Union at the same time increased its military aid to North Vietnam. Indochina was lost because the Congress would not allow the United States to do as much for its allies as the Soviet Union did for theirs. This pattern was repeated in Angola in 1975.

Between 1968 and 1975, the Congress cut a total of $40 billion from the defense budgets submitted by the White House. Beginning in 1977, the Carter Administration compounded the problem by unilaterally cutting back on U.S. weapons programs. During this same period, the Soviet Union continued and accelerated its arms buildup. It was inevitable that the Soviet Union would move from strategic parity with the United States in 1974 to a position of decisive superiority in land-based nuclear weapons, the situation that confronted President Reagan when he took office in 1981.

President Carter had tried to practice detente without deterrence. The results were a disaster. The Soviets expanded their domination in the Arabian Peninsula, in southern Asia, in Africa, and in Latin America. The lesson is clear. We can influence Soviet policies but only if we recognize that they will react to our policies. If we block their advances, they will choose restraint and negotiate. If we give an inch, they will take a thousand miles.

The Soviet Union and its apologists are quick to blame the United States for the demise of detente. There is fault on both sides, but far more on the Soviet side.

The practice of hard-headed detente requires the use of both the carrot and the stick. When the Congress refused to grant the Soviet Union Most Favored Nation status, it took away the carrot. Its cuts in the defense budget coupled with President Carter's cancellations and delays of major arms programs left us with a weak stick.

But it was the Soviets who put the nails in the coffin of detente. They destroyed detente by their support of the North Vietnamese offensive in South Vietnam that violated the Paris peace agreements and by their expansionism throughout the Third World. When they invaded Afghanistan, the Soviets made it impossible for President Carter to get SALT II approved by the Senate, and at the same time gave those who opposed detente an effective political issue.

President Reagan has restored the policy of deterrence. He has initiated a major buildup in our military forces in order to reestablish the balance of power, and he has made it clear that he will intervene with those forces to defend our interests and those of our allies and friends. The Soviets as a result have made no geopolitical gains since he came to office.

The President has won Soviet respect with his actions. By standing up to the Soviets, he has made them eager to sit down with him at the negotiating table. This puts him in an ideal position from which to open a new relationship with the Soviet Union that will advance the cause of real peace.

This new relationship must address the two dangers confronting us. We must avoid war, and we must avoid defeat. Defeat can come in war, but the greater danger is that it will come without war, through Soviet adventurism, intimidation, and blackmail. If we lull ourselves into a sense of security while the Soviets take over one country after another, we will wake up one day to find the global balance of power weighted fatally against us.

War can come from five principal sources. It could result if the military superiority of an aggressive power were to go unchallenged. It could result if a leader were to miscalculate what actions by him would provoke a military response from his opposite number. It could result if the major powers were drawn in on opposite sides of a war between minor powers. It could result if a nuclear missile were to be launched accidentally. It could result if a madman were to capture power and embark on an aggressive war.

There is little that we can actively do to prevent the last danger from coming about. But a renewed policy of hardheaded detente can reduce the other dangers greatly. Today, hard-headed detente requires us to restore fully the military balance of power and at the same time to negotiate meaningful arms control agreements. It requires us to use the West's economic power, through strictly regulated East-West trade, to give the Soviets an incentive for peace. And it requires us to establish a process of negotiation and summitry that will weave these strands together into the fabric of real peace.

Restoring the military balance. Our first goal must be to take the profit out of war. Aggressors wage war if they think they can gain something by it. To deter war we must remain powerful enough so that potential aggressors will conclude that they stand to lose far more than they could possibly gain from war. Thus it is essential that we restore the military balance of power.

There are those who say that in the nuclear age it does not matter if one side has a margin of superiority over the other. This reasoning overlooks the diametrically opposed purposes of the United States and the Soviet Union. The United States is a defensive power. When we have used force or threatened to use it, we have done so for defensive, not offensive purposes. If we had so chosen we could have ruled the world immediately after World War II. Instead, we helped rebuild it. Since then, we have gone to war twice, in Korea and in Vietnam. Both times it was for the purpose of defending other nations from aggression by the Soviet Union and its allies.

The Soviet Union is an admittedly and avowedly offensive power. Its leaders' stated goal is world domination, and they have been pursuing that end by every means at their disposal. The Soviet Union does not arm itself for defensive reasons. The leaders in the Kremlin stand behind the aggressors in virtually every one of the world's hotspots and have instigated every postwar confrontation between the superpowers.

This divergence in our aims puts the question of whether military superiority matters in a new light. Winston Churchill understood that difference. In 1946, when only the United States knew how to make the atomic bomb, he commented, "No one in any country has slept less well in their beds because of this knowledge, and the method and the raw materials to apply it are at present largely in American hands. I do not believe we should all have slept so soundly had the positions been reversed and if some communist or neo-fascist state monopolized for the time being these dread agencies."

History has borne out the truth of Churchill's insight. For 30 years, from the end of World War II to the mid-1970s, the United States had nuclear superiority. This was the principal factor that deterred the Soviets from launching a war in Europe. When our superiority was great, it also served as a powerful deterrent to Soviet aggression and adventurism in other regions. Superiority in the hands of a defensive power is a guarantee of peace; superiority in the hands of an offensive power is a threat to peace. The danger of defeat without war also increases because the means for nuclear blackmail are given to those who would use it.

Today the United States no longer has the credible nuclear superiority to deter Soviet aggression. While we are still ahead in sea- and air-based missiles, the Soviet Union has in the last ten years acquired decisive superiority in the most powerful and accurate nuclear weapons—land-based missiles. They have a first-strike capability—the ability to destroy virtually all of our land-based missiles in a first strike while having enough left over to destroy our cities. The United States does not have a first-strike capability and has no plans to obtain one.

There are those who say that any such advantage in the nuclear age is meaningless. After all, they argue, even if the Soviet Union destroyed all of our land-based missiles in a first strike, the United States could retaliate by launching its submarine- and bomber-based missiles. Therefore the Soviets would never launch the first strike to begin with.

This overlooks the perilous situation in which an American President could find himself. After a Soviet first strike, the United States would not have the capability of taking out the Soviet Union's remaining land-based missiles. Very few of our strategic bombers can get through Soviet air defenses. Our sea-based missiles can only be used against cities because they do not have the power or accuracy to take out Soviet land-based missiles.

The President's only possible response to a first strike would be to take out Soviet cities. But the Soviets, knowing that they could retaliate in kind, would hardly find such a threat believable. A threat to commit mutual suicide is not a credible policy, let alone a moral one.

However frightening that scenario might be, the real danger is more profound. There are two reasons why any Soviet leader would be reluctant to initiate a nuclear war. The Soviets have never tested their nuclear weapons under wartime conditions. They have a first-strike capability in theory. But the theory relies on the execution of their military plans with split-second timing and precision accuracy during the chaos of war. Military men, who are by nature cautious, would be hesitant to go to war if a minute technical error could lead to devastating defeat. And while the Soviets want to dominate the world, they want to do so without war. They do not want to rule a world of destroyed cities and dead bodies.

The greater danger is that, knowing we have no credible response to their clear superiority in land-based missiles, they will be emboldened at other levels. They will tend to be more adventurous in Asia, Africa, the Middle East, and Latin America and more intimidating in their approach toward Western Europe. They can use the threat of their potential power to dominate the world through nuclear blackmail.

We cannot expect to regain the nuclear superiority we had for 30 years, but the least we must do is deny superiority to the Soviets. The MX missile will help to achieve that goal. It is powerful and accurate enough to take out Soviet land-based missiles. The program President Reagan has asked Congress to approve will not provide us with a first-strike capability because we do not plan to build enough MX missiles to take out all of the Soviet Union's land-based missiles. But it at least begins to rectify the military balance of power. Equally important, if war comes, the MX missile will give an American

43

President some option other than an attack on Soviet cities.

The burden of building up our armed forces will not be light but it will be long. As the richest nation in the world, the United States can afford to spend whatever is necessary for our national defense. But restoring the military balance does not mean that what the Pentagon wants the Pentagon gets. We cannot and should not tolerate waste, duplication, and inefficiency in the military bureaucracy any more than we would in the social service agencies. Mismanagement not only erodes public support for necessary defense spending, but also reduces our ability to defend our national interests.

Some of America's ablest executives have served as secretary of defense in recent years—Melvin Laird, James Schlesinger, Donald Rumsfeld, Harold Brown, and Caspar Weinberger. They can testify to the fact that keeping Pentagon costs under control is an almost impossible task. The secretary of defense often finds himself in the unenviable position of being the ringmaster of a three-ring circus in which the services turn somersaults competing for the attention and dollars of the Administration and Congress. Each service chief understandably believes that what is best for his service is best for the nation. We need a strong Navy, a strong Army, and a strong Air Force. But the Congress and the taxpayers should not and will not support unnecessary duplication of missions and weapon systems.

As President Eisenhower, no dewy-eyed dove, once said, "This country could choke itself to death piling up military expenditures just as surely as it can defeat itself by not spending enough for protection."

Arms Control. The issue of arms control cannot be separated from the question of national security. They are intimately intertwined. Realistically conducted, arms control negotiations can contribute to real peace. Naively pursued, they can increase the risk of war.

Arms control can serve four major purposes.

A properly negotiated agreement can help create the strategic stability that could reduce the chances of war. Strategic instability results when either side or both sides deploy weapons with first-strike capability. This creates a temptation to use these weapons to gain a decisive advantage. The danger is greatest if these weapons themselves are vulnerable to a first strike because in a crisis a leader would be tempted to use his arsenal before he loses it. Any arms control agreement between the United States and the Soviet Union must be based on true equality and must assure strategic stability. Neither can be secure unless both feel secure.

An arms control agreement could reduce the costs of defense for both the United States and the Soviet Union. President Reagan's proposal in the Strategic Arms Reduction Talks calls for each side to dismantle part of its nuclear arsenal and to curb the deployment of even more accurate land-based missiles. If the Soviets accept this approach, it would stop not only the spiral of the arms race but also that of the defense budget.

Achieving arms control is a political imperative. Western leaders will be unable to mobilize public support behind the defense spending necessary to keep up our deterrent unless they have a credible policy of negotiating arms control. The current debate over the production of the MX missile demonstrates this vividly.

Arms control between the superpowers is the first step in controlling nuclear proliferation. Preventing the spread of nuclear weapons technology to other countries is in the interest of both the United States and the Soviet Union. If scores of minor powers acquire nuclear weapons, the chances are great that one will someday use them in a crisis in one of the world's hotspots. Nuclear proliferation could turn out to be the spark that explodes the global nuclear tinderbox. To stop it the superpowers must work together. Only if they succeed in capping their own nuclear buildup can they have any influence over smaller powers that are thinking of developing nuclear weapons.

But while weighing the potential benefits of arms control, we must recognize the hard reality that it will improve the chances for peace only under certain conditions.

An arms control agreement will not contribute to peace unless we reduce the political differences that can lead to war. Avid arms control proponents reject the concept of linking arms control negotiations to political issues. But linkage is a fact of international life. It was the Soviet invasion of Afghanistan that destroyed the chances for Senate approval of SALT II. This was linkage in action, not just in theory.

We should not pursue arms control as an end in itself. It is dangerous to assume that any arms control agreement is better than none. If an agreement is to reduce the risk of war, it must advance six goals.

First, it must create a true balance between the superpowers. All arms control treaties are not created equal, and any we sign must be based on equality. Equality in numbers is important, but numbers should not be the sole measure of equality. For the United States to have an equal number of weapons as the Soviet Union is not enough if the Soviets alone are allowed to retain their present first-strike capability. We should set the number and size of missiles and the number of warheads so that each side has the same military capability in both strategic and medium-range weapons.

Second, it must not allow either superpower to have a credible first-strike capability. If both were to have this capability, each would be strongly tempted in a crisis to preemptively attack the strategic forces of the other. What would be worse, if an agreement gave superiority in first-strike weapons to an offensive power like the Soviet Union, it would actually increase the danger of war and of defeat without war.

We should formally offer to share any technology we develop for a space-based missile defense system with the Soviet Union or any other nation that joins us in seeking meaningful arms control. If all nations could deploy the system at once, none would suspect another of wanting to use it as a shield for an attack.

Third, it must provide the means for each side to verify the compliance of the other. We have relied in the past on satellite photography and other national means of verification. But advances in military technology now require that we settle for nothing less than on-site inspection. The Soviets have always rejected such provisions. We must make them understand that the Administration will only be able to muster the two-thirds Senate majority needed for ratification of a treaty if we have absolute confidence that both sides will carry out its provisions.

Fourth, it must restrict the testing of new missile technology that would destabilize the strategic balance. Technology is advancing faster than the superpowers can negotiate controls on the weapons it produces. The danger is that missile accuracy will advance to the point that neither side will have a nuclear deterrent that can survive a first strike. If we limit the testing of new missiles, we can prevent their deployment, because no country would stake its survival on missiles that had not been flight-tested.

Fifth, it must reduce, not just limit, the nuclear arsenals of the superpowers. The United States has proposed such reductions several times, but the Soviet Union has always rejected the idea. The only conceivable reason for each superpower to maintain its nuclear stockpile at today's levels is that the other superpower is doing so. Through arms control agreements, we can retire the aging and obsolete missiles on both sides and reduce the numbers of new missiles as well.

Sixth, it should allow for the implementation of the Scowcroft Commission's recommendation to replace fixed, land-based, multi-warhead missiles with mobile, single-warhead ones. It takes at least two warheads detonated simultaneously to destroy a land-based missile in its silo. If both sides had equal numbers of single-warhead missiles, neither would have enough warheads to launch a successful first strike against the other. If these missiles were mobile, it would make the success of such an attack so doubtful that one side would never risk attacking the other.

The proposal to freeze the nuclear arsenals of the United States and the Soviet Union at current levels is fatally flawed because it fails to meet these six criteria. Its proponents say that their goals are to achieve meaningful arms control and to reduce the danger of war. Their intentions are good, but their judgment is not. If we were to negotiate a nuclear freeze, its effect would be just the opposite of what they expect.

A nuclear freeze would increase the danger of war because it would leave the Soviet Union, an offensive power, with an unquestionable first-strike capability. It would destroy any chance for meaningful arms reductions because it would eliminate the incentives for the Kremlin leaders to negotiate.

The history of the negotiations that led to the 1972 SALT I treaty limiting defensive nuclear weapons illustrates this point. The Soviets already had begun to deploy an anti-ballistic missile system. When completed, it would protect their command centers and missile bases from a nuclear attack. We countered this by asking the Congress to approve funding for an ABM system for the United States. Our critics charged that we were escalating the arms race and destroying the chances for an arms control agreement. Only after intensive lobbying were we able to get the Senate, by a margin of just one vote, to go along with the proposal.

The approval of the ABM program made SALT I possible. It was in the Soviets' interest to stop us from going forward with our system because our technology was better than theirs. They were therefore willing to pay a price to stop us. But if we had lost the Senate vote, I would have had to ask Brezhnev to give up his ABM system without getting anything in return. He would have just laughed in my face.

The Soviets are not philanthropists. Nor are they fools. They are tough, ruthless negotiators who will give nothing for nothing. In negotiating with them, we cannot get something from them unless we have something to give to them.

The greatest threat to peace today is the Soviet arsenal of strategic land-based missiles. It gives them a first strike capability. We have nothing in our arsenal to counter this. They will have no incentive to reduce that threat through arms control negotiations unless we have a weapons system in place or in production that would at least in part match their capability. That is why it is essential for us to go forward with the MX missile. Without it, we will never be able to reach an agreement based on any semblance of equality.

The nuclear freeze is a fraud. It is a simple answer to a complex problem. We cannot expect to achieve all our goals in one negotiation, but no agreement we sign should freeze them beyond our reach.

Negotiating an arms control agreement that will contribute to real peace will take years. It is fatuous to suggest that such an agreement could be struck through a quick telephone call between an American President and Andropov. We will not be able to reach all of our goals for restoring strategic equality, increasing stability, and reducing the size of the nuclear arsenals in time for a summit meeting in 1984. But we could negotiate a substantial first step toward one or more of these goals and an agreement in principle on the others.

If significant progress is made along these lines before a summit, Presidents Reagan and Andropov when they meet could agree on long-term goals for arms control and establish a step-by-step process for reaching them. New top-level representatives, who would report directly and periodically to the Presidents, should be given the responsibility for negotiating a specific timetable.

The pieces are in place for an arms control breakthrough. The Soviets dealt themselves a strong hand by relentlessly building up their nuclear weaponry in the 1970s. By modernizing our own we have improved our hand through the draw. But we also have an ace in the hole that gives the Soviets an incentive to strike a fair deal: if there must be a nuclear arms race, we will win it through our superior economic strength and advanced technology.

After an agreement is signed, the pundits inevitably speculate about who won and who lost. But for an arms control agreement to contribute to real peace, there should be no losers, only winners. If the agreement is not to our mutual advantage, it will become politically impossible for the losing side to implement it. Unless both sides reap benefits, the process will falter.

Once we conclude arms control agreements, we must do everything they allow us to because we can be sure the Soviet Union will do so. Opponents of arms control claim that SALT I allowed the Soviets to gain nuclear superiority. The facts prove the contrary. In 1972, programs were under way to develop the B-1 bomber, the Trident II submarine, and the MX, cruise, and Minuteman III missiles. It was the Congress, not SALT I, that delayed these programs. Forty billion dollars were lopped off Administration defense budgets between 1968 and 1975. This mistake was compounded by President Carter. In his first years in office, he cancelled the B-1, delayed the MX and cruise missiles, shut down the Minuteman III production line, and cancelled the neutron bomb. The Soviets, not surprisingly, did everything SALT I permitted, stretching some provisions in the process. If we had followed a similar policy, there would be no land-based missile gap today.

While we must seek arms control agreements, we must not overestimate what they can accomplish. A bad agreement will increase the risk of war. Not even the best agreement imaginable would solve all our problems. If the United States and the Soviet Union cut their nuclear arsenals in half, a goal that is beyond the wildest dreams of even the most optimistic arms control negotiator on either side, we would still have enough weapons to destroy each other many times over. If we were to make such drastic arms reductions, a nuclear war would be just as devastating as it would be today.

If we are to reduce the risk and danger of war, we must leapfrog the sterile arms control debate and go to the heart of the problem: the political differences between the United States and the Soviet Union and the policies we can initiate that will deter the Soviets from resorting to war to resolve those differences.

Incentives for Peace. Only when deterrence is assured can

detente be effective. If the Soviets realize that aggression will not pay, they will have no choice but to behave with restraint. We can then reinforce the effect of the fear of war by providing them with the rewards of peace. Real peace requires a policy that has incentives for peace as well as disincentives for war.

Our economic power dwarfs theirs because our economic system works and theirs does not. The NATO allies and Japan outproduce the Soviet Union and its Warsaw Pact allies by a ratio of over three to one. Trade between our systems can give them an economic stake in peace and lead to greater Soviet restraint.

The Soviets need us. We know this, they know it, and we should make use of it. They are more economically dependent on us than we are on them. We largely trade Western technology for Soviet raw materials. The Soviets need access to our know-how if their economy is to grow through the end of the century. If necessary, we can go elsewhere to buy their products, but they have no alternative supplier for ours. This gives us leverage over them. We should use it to further the cause of real peace by stamping our goods with a political price tag as well as an economic one.

We should have no illusions about what trade can accomplish. Trade by itself will not produce peace or prevent war. Some contend that if we trade more with the Soviet Union, they will be less aggressive. But the Kremlin leaders cannot be bought off by trade. In the late 1970s they showed us that they would both trade and invade. At the other extreme, some contend that the increase in Soviet-American trade in the early years of detente helped fuel Soviet expansionism. This claim is preposterous. The level of trade was minuscule then; it could not possibly have affected Soviet military power. Economic relations can never substitute for deterrence. If properly implemented, they can reinforce it.

Lenin contemptuously remarked that capitalists were so short-sightedly greedy that they would sell the communists the rope by which they themselves would someday hang. Unfortunately, some Western businessmen fit the bill. They would sell the Soviets not only rope, but also the scaffolding and a how-to book for the hangman. By refusing to look beyond the bottom line, they blithely ignore the military power the Soviets are massing on the front line.

Trade should be expanded only in ways that serve our interests. This means that we must not sell the Soviets goods and technology that directly contribute to their military capability. It also means that our trade must not be at subsidized prices or on easy credit terms. The rule should be "trade, not aid."

Beyond this, we should expand our economic contacts. We should sell them rope, if they want to buy it, but do so in a way that binds their hands and prevents them from reaching out to further their domination. The more we engage the Soviet Union in an intricate network of commercial relations, the more we increase its stake in peace—and also increase its incentive to maintain good relations with us.

When the Russians marched into Afghanistan, the United States was reduced to boycotting the Olympics in Moscow and imposing a grain embargo that was meaningless because other suppliers were ready to rush in to fill the gap. We would have had more leverage if we had been trading in more things the Russians wanted.

Our leverage with trade will be minimal unless our allies in Europe and Japan join with us in developing a common policy. Acting together economically, the West is a powerful giant. Acting separately, it is an impotent giant.

For economic leverage to be effective, it must be substantial. We must have something significant to give and also to take back. We need both the carrot and the stick.

The Soviet leaders want what the West produces, and they are willing to give up something to get it. The key is to make it very clear to them that there is an iron link between their behavior and the West's willingness to make the trade deals they hope for.

Soviet leaders reject explicit linkage, whether to trade or to arms control negotiations. They will not adopt the principle of linkage, but they will adapt to the fact of it. We must make them understand that linkage is a fact of international life. The American people will not support arms control and trade initiatives with the Soviet Union at a time when it is engaging in aggressive actions that threaten our interests.

For linkage to work, however, it must be done privately. We should not make statements or take actions that will make the Soviets lose face publicly. For example, Jewish emigration from the Soviet Union increased from 400 in 1968 to nearly 35,000 in 1973 as a result of the private pressure of our Administration. Congress then passed a law—the Jackson-Vanik amendment—which put the Russians on the spot publicly by tying trade to emigration policy. The number of Jews allowed to emigrate was cut in half the following year.

Peaceful trade is totally inconsistent with the Soviet Union's aggressive policies. I once heard President Eisenhower remark, "We should sell the Russians anything that they can't shoot back." When they use their economic ties with the West to finance their expansionist policies, the Soviets are in effect shooting back our assistance. The West cannot be so foolish as to subsidize its own destruction.

During World War II, the United States recognized the importance of economic power by setting up a Board of Economic Warfare. Today we need a Foreign Economic Policy Board to concert the use of our economic power. It should answer directly to the President because only he would be able to knock heads together when the bureaucrats in the various agencies involved with foreign economic policy engage in Washington's favorite sport: fighting for turf. Policies governing trade, foreign aid, loans, and support of international lending agencies must be coordinated to serve American foreign policy interests. A process should also be established for enlisting the cooperation of the private sector in serving those interests. It makes no sense for the government to cut off aid to hostile nations while American banks continue to make huge loans to those same nations.

Trade is not a panacea. It does not solve all our problems.

Nothing can remove the burden of deterrence from our shoulders. Our policies must be designed to take the profit out of war, but we should also put more profit into peace. On these two pillars—deterrence and detente—we can build a structure of real peace.

Summit Meetings. Summitry between the leaders of the superpowers is indispensable in the pursuit of real peace. It is at the summit that we bring together the various strands of hard-headed detente. This is a delicate exercise that we should undertake only if progress on resolving substantive issues is assured. No American President should go to the summit unless he knows what is on the other side of the mountain.

Rushing into a quickie summit just so the leaders of the superpowers can get acquainted would be a stupid and devastating mistake. Such a summit might temporarily improve the atmospherics of our relations, but little else. The famous "spirit of Geneva," as well as the spirits of other Soviet-American summits at Camp David, Vienna, and Glassboro, was illusory. When a summit is all spirit and no substance, the spirit evaporates fast.

Andropov is understandably reluctant to schedule a summit at a time when it might help President Reagan win reelection. But with the resurgence of the American economy and the President's rise in the polls, Andropov is caught between a rock and a hard place. If he deliberately delays a summit until after the election, he will find himself facing a President with a new mandate and a stronger bargaining position. Andropov needs a summit before the American election more than President Reagan does. We should not give it to him on the cheap.

The words coming out of Moscow seem to indicate that they would like a summit. Their deeds would indicate otherwise. Some pundits have seized upon certain "signals" they interpret as being positive. But permitting a half-dozen Pentacostalists to emigrate, making some semantic concessions on human rights at the Madrid conference, allowing progress toward expanded cultural and diplomatic ties, and lifting martial law in Poland while transferring most of its repressive features to the civil code are not actions that deserve serious consideration. Real peace is too important for tokenism. Unless substantial progress is assured on arms control and on reducing Soviet adventurism in Central America, we should not agree to hold a summit.

If the summit produces too little, there are two dangers. The first is disillusionment. The first Reagan-Andropov meeting will receive enormous worldwide attention. Expectations will be high. If the summit fails to live up to them, the letdown will be catastrophic. The disappointment could lead both sides to give up on the process of peace and increase preparations for war.

The second danger is euphoria. Sometimes simply the fact of a summit gives many in the West unrealistic hopes for the future. They mistakenly believe that we have reached the end of the journey to peace rather than just made a beginning. This makes it more difficult for Western leaders to gain public support for the decisive actions and strong military forces that are needed to make hard-headed detente work.

Summits must produce more than tokenism. They cannot make miracles, but they can make progress. As Churchill once said, "It would, I think, be a mistake to assume that nothing can be settled with Soviet Russia unless or until everything is settled."

The first Soviet-American summit in Moscow in 1972 was scheduled only after the Soviets agreed to the Berlin settlement in 1971. We believed that if we could reach an agreement on an issue that had plagued East-West relations for 30 years and had at times brought us to the brink of war, we could reasonably expect to make progress on other major issues.

Similarly, before we schedule the next summit, personal representatives of Presidents Reagan and Andropov should undertake a series of intensive, absolutely confidential negotiations to explore what progress can be made in reaching agreement on major issues. This would be the most promising forum in which to search for some form of accommodation that advances the general interests of both parties by compromising on the specific interests of each. It would allow the two sides to subtly feel out the differing degrees to which various elements of the other party's positions are negotiable, and to try varying combinations of give-and-take.

The summit agenda must be broad. It must include arms control, trade, and conduct in areas where our political differences collide, such as the Middle East, Africa, and Central America. In these preparatory talks, links should be forged between these issues. For example, the Russians must be made to understand that there is no way the Congress could or should approve arms control or trade agreements reached at a summit when Soviet surrogates continue to try to build another beachhead in Central America.

The Soviets will loudly object to such linkage, but they will understand it. After all, their paranoia about having "friendly" buffer states on their borders puts them in a poor position for objecting to our concern about what happens to our neighbors. President Kennedy drew the line when the Soviets tried to put missiles into Cuba in 1962. I drew the line when they tried to put a nuclear submarine base on Cuba in 1970. President Reagan has drawn the line in El Salvador. He is right to do so. We should make it clear to the Soviets that we will do whatever is necessary to prevent the establishment of another Soviet base in the Americas.

All discussions should proceed on the principle of strict reciprocity. We give them something they want only if they give us something we want. By not capitalizing on our economic power, we have been giving away enormous assets for free. And the Soviets, who are experts at the hoarding and exploiting of power, must certainly view our failure to use our assets as a sign of both stupidity and weakness.

Our primary goal should be to build a new relationship with the Soviets in which we will be able to prevail upon them to cease their aggression. This can only happen when the bilateral relationship with us becomes more important to them than their adventurism.

We must develop a process for annual summits between the

leaders of the United States and the Soviet Union. These meetings can both reduce the chances of war and help restrain Soviet behavior.

Regularly scheduled summits allow each leader to take the measure of the other and thus can reduce the possibility of miscalculation during a confrontation. In 1973, on the last night of my second summit with Brezhnev, we had a midnight meeting in San Clemente about the Middle East situation. He tried to push me into agreeing on a settlement that the superpowers would impose on Israel and the other nations of the region. I categorically and firmly resisted this pressure. We went at it toe-to-toe for three hours. After that confrontation, he had to know that we were not bluffing during the Yom Kippur War four months later, when we called an alert of our military forces in response to his threat to send Soviet combat troops into the Middle East.

If the leaders of the superpowers get to know each other, it does not mean they will like each other. But each controls such enormous power that it is vital that they take every possible step to reduce the possibility that either might underestimate the will of the other to defend his nation's interests.

Regular summits will tend to restrain Soviet behavior. As a meeting approaches the Kremlin leaders will be reluctant to do anything that might "poison" the atmosphere and therefore make it more difficult to reach the agreements they want. Brezhnev had an eye on the calendar when he agreed to join us in bringing about a ceasefire in the war between India and Pakistan in 1971. He would have preferred to embarrass the Chinese by allowing his client, India, to gobble up China's client, Pakistan. But he knew the cost would include the cancellation of a summit meeting he wanted. We had made that risk categorically clear to him.

Regular summits that produce concrete results will help the United States and our allies mobilize public support for necessary defense programs. While we should not have a summit simply because our allies and friends favor it, the fact that we will go to the summit when it is properly prepared reassures them. Hope for real peace is essential if the people of the United States as well as Europe are to continue to support the military strength necessary to maintain the foundation of deterrence on which detente rests. There may be occasional spurts of spending when the threat of Soviet aggression seems acute, but over the long haul the absence of hope for peace fuels the forces of appeasement.

Good or bad personal relations at a summit will not have a decisive effect on state relations. But the two cannot be separated. We should not assume that better personal relations will automatically improve bad state relations. Still, poor personal relations will make it more difficult to improve bad state relations, and could even aggravate them.

In negotiating with the Kremlin leaders, an American President should be cordial in personal matters but unyielding in policy matters. As Franklin Roosevelt learned, with tragic consequences for the people of Poland and the other nations behind the Iron Curtain, any President who believes he can get the men of the Kremlin to change their policies by charming them or simply through personal persuasiveness is due for a rude awakening. But while mushy sentimentality should be avoided, a President achieves nothing—by bluster and belligerence. The Russians are masters of the bluff and can usually detect that tactic when it is used against them. Bluster and bad manners may intimidate the weak but never the strong. Talking softly while carrying a big stick is the most effective way to deal with the Soviets.

While not decisive, personal relationships can be marginally important when dealing with the leaders of the Soviet Union. Before my meeting with Khrushchev in 1959, British Prime Minister Macmillan told me that the Soviet leaders desperately wanted to be "admitted to the club"—accepted and respected as major world figures in their own right and not simply because they control the great military power of the Soviet Union. The Russian people are a great people, and the Soviet Union is a great power. We should agree to admit the Soviet leaders into the "club," but only if they agree to abide by the rules. It is a cheap price to pay if it helps restrain Soviet conduct.

We must make the Soviets understand that there is no way that we would or should admit them to the club if they continue to act as the moral outlaws of the world. When they shot down the Korean jetliner, they also shot down the prospects for quickly improving our relations in mutually beneficial ways.

Our initial response was to express our outrage in the strongest moral terms. We should not mince words in venting our anger because it clarifies the moral issue that is at the heart of the East-West struggle. But we must not delude ourselves by thinking that our statements about morality will have any effect behind the Kremlin walls. Condemning the Soviet leaders with statements based on Western ideals about the sanctity of human life is like making faces at the Sphinx.

Some have understandably urged us to make a stronger response. They advocate that we break off our diplomatic relations with the Soviet Union, halt all our bilateral negotiations, and impose an array of trade sanctions. But they are overlooking one of the important lessons of this tragedy. As a vivid example of the danger of accidental war, it points out the fact that in the nuclear age there should be more communication between the superpowers rather than less.

While this is not the first atrocity committed by the Soviets, the West should seek to make it their last by seizing the moment to implement a strategy for dealing with them. We must develop a policy of hard-headed detente that will convince the Kremlin leaders that they stand to lose far more than they could possibly gain by threatening our interests. We can succeed only if we use the unity the world has found in its moral outrage to forge a strategy for real peace.

A major communist head of state in Eastern Europe recently remarked to me that the last 60 years have seen a curious reversal in the rhetoric of East and West. The communists used to say that capitalism was collapsing, and now the capitalists are saying that communism is collapsing. He then observed, "Perhaps both are wrong."

He was right. We have differences with the Soviets that we will never overcome. We will never condone their conquests and will always oppose their expansionist policies. But we cannot wish them away. They are there, so we have to deal with them. How we deal with them will determine whether we achieve real peace.

We should avoid hot rhetoric, but we should not mince words. If the world is to have real peace, the Soviets must change their aggressive ways. Their persistence in expanding their influence and control by violent means will sooner or later end in war. And the chances are good that such a war will end the world.

Winston Churchill once said, "I cannot forecast to you the action of Russia. It is a riddle wrapped in a mystery inside an enigma; but perhaps there is a key. That key is Russian national interest." Hard-headed detente is not a magic wand that will with one wave instantly make over the ruthless men in the Kremlin. It is a policy that will lead them to cooperate in the search for real peace because it is in their interest to do so.

Hard-headed detente gives the Kremlin leaders a choice between aggression and restraint. If they choose the first, the danger of war will escalate and the burden of arms will become unbearable. The world will be an increasingly perilous place to live in. If they choose the second, we can reduce the risk of war and reap the fruits of real peace. We will still have our conflicts, but these will not lead to war. If we act together, the United States and the Soviet Union can contribute to peace for ourselves and for others. If we continue to act against each other, peace has no chance.

NATO AND JAPAN

In considering the role the United States and Soviet Union must play, we must always bear in mind that other nations, particularly those of Western Europe and Japan, must be part of any effective effort to build a real peace. After all, the struggle between East and West for 35 years has in large part been a struggle over the fate of Europe and Asia.

Given the Soviets' ambitions and strength, Europe cannot have peace and freedom without the United States. But by the same token the U.S. cannot build a lasting peace without Europe. As Franklin Roosevelt said to his war-weary people in 1945, "We have learned that we cannot live alone, in peace." We learned that lesson from lighting the bloodiest war in history, and it is even more true today.

The U.S. is linked with its European allies on a variety of levels. We are largely a composite of European peoples and European ideals. We share values, faiths, and cultural and philosophical heritages with Europe. But what links us most fundamentally is our reverence for liberty, and we realize that the greatest evil of Soviet totalitarianism is that it smothers liberty. Our military alliances and our close economic and cultural relationships are expressions both of our common heritage and our mutual awareness of a common external threat.

That is why Japan, while an Asian rather than a European nation, is as central to the Western alliance as any NATO member. Strategically, along with China it holds the eastern ramparts. Economically, its might is indispensable if we are to have an effective Western economic policy. And practically, it has much to gain from an alliance with the West because it has just as much to lose as the U.S. and the Europeans from further Soviet advances.

The postwar Japanese economic miracle was the result of an unprecedented synthesis of East and West. Japanese creativity, drive, and skill, channelled through Western systems of government and free enterprise, made Japan one of the economic giants of the modern world. The Japanese have reaped the rewards of liberty, and not surprisingly they have shown a growing willingness to defend what they have built.

Americans sometimes have a certain messianic, "We'll save the world" attitude. We believe in our system and way of life and are eager to share both with the rest of the world. Woodrow Wilson did not call on the American people to fight in World War I just to save *America* but to serve the greater goal of making the *world* safe for democracy. We have always been confident that the sheer rightness of our ideals will win out in the end.

We believe the American ideal is still the world's best hope. But the economic and military power of the United States in the world is not as commanding as it once was. After World War II the U.S. economy accounted for more than half of the world's industrial production. The figure is now less than a third—in part because with our help Japan and West Germany, our adversaries in war, have become our strongest competitors in peace. Our military dominance is also gone. We have lost the strategic edge in land-based missiles to the Soviet Union. To meet the Soviet military challenge we need European forces, deployed through NATO; as well as our own.

The U.S. has played the starring role in the Western alliance for so long that our allies sometimes act as if it is a one-man show. Too often when crises have erupted—in Iran, in Afghanistan, in Central America—our allies have sat back and waited for the U.S. to step forward and respond. This cannot continue. The Europeans and the Japanese need the U.S., and the U.S. needs them. If hard-headed detente is to work, each nation in the industrialized West must realize that we live in a new world which the superpowers alone could destroy in a nuclear war, but in which we need the full participation of all our allies to build a real peace.

NATO, as it prepares for its thirty-fifth anniversary next year, faces an urgent task: it must achieve no less than a new birth of purpose and function. It was formed in 1949 as a deterrent to a Soviet attack across the central plain of Europe, and since then it has been the most successful military alliance in modern history. But what was adequate in 1949 is not adequate to meet the challenges of 1983.

As a military alliance NATO has precise, narrow perimeters. Today it must grow in order to survive: grow not in the sense of adding more members, but by expanding its geographical horizons, deepening its military strength along the front lines, and pulling itself together in the way it uses its economic power, one of its strongest weapons.

Just as a house divided against itself cannot stand, an alliance cannot stand if its periphery is threatened, its military forces inadequate, its members divided on the question of how to use its economic power. NATO is weakened by all of these maladies, and to overcome them it must take a good, hard look at itself. It must refocus, rethink, reappraise, and renew.

A common error in military planning is to prepare for the wars of the future with the strategies and the weapons of the past. Alliances are as prone to making this mistake as are generals and nations. To avoid the pitfall NATO must acknowledge the passing of an era, one in which the greatest likelihood of a Soviet attack was in Europe, and acknowledge the coming of a new era. Today the Soviets, directly or through proxies, have the ability to act virtually anywhere and on virtually any level of military force, from guerrilla insurrection through nuclear attack. We must be able to respond accordingly.

If it is to meet the challenge of the new era, NATO must grow in three distinct ways.

It must strengthen its military power.

America's historic guarantee of Europe's security is questionable today because of our lost strategic superiority. The strategy of the Atlantic alliance was based on the proposition that the U.S. and Europe were militarily linked—that a Soviet attack against Europe would be senseless because of the certainty of a U.S. nuclear response. We now lack a credible deterrent to a Soviet attack on Europe for the same reason we lack a credible deterrent to an attack on the United States. Mutual suicide, again, is not a viable foreign policy.

The so-called trip-wire—the likelihood of massive U.S. nuclear retaliation against a Soviet conventional attack in Europe—is dangerously frayed. Nothing has yet taken its place. With their multiple-warhead SS-20s trained on every military target in Western Europe, the Soviets could hold NATO hostage to the possibility of a successful nuclear first strike. As NATO's new missiles are deployed beginning late this year the theater balance will be gradually corrected. The MX program will begin to restore the strategic balance. But this will still leave a yawning gap in the West's defenses: our substantial weakness in conventional forces.

There is a dangerous military imbalance in Europe that must be corrected across the board, at both the theater nuclear level and the conventional level. The West needs a seamless web of military power in which the fabric will be just as strong wherever and however our opponents try to penetrate it.

Some say a balance between NATO and the Soviet Union in theater nuclear weapons will obviate the need for a conventional buildup. Others say that if NATO restores the conventional balance the new medium-range theater missiles, the Pershing II and the cruise, need not be deployed in Western Europe.

Both these contentions are wrong. The Soviet threat exists at both levels, nuclear and conventional, and the threat must be countered with equal effectiveness at both levels.

Once East-West nuclear forces are stabilized, the incentive for Soviet aggression in Europe using conventional forces will vastly increase because of the Warsaw Pact's decisive advantage on the ground. As matters stand now, NATO could hold out only for a matter of weeks, perhaps days, against such an attack. Combatants in war will always use the ultimate weapon to avoid defeat. Any conventional war stands a good chance of escalating to the nuclear level.

NATO's neglect of its conventional forces has lowered the nuclear threshold and increased the chances of nuclear war in Europe. But the damage is not irreparable. According to a recent study published in the London *Economist* NATO would only have to spend a relatively modest four percent more a year to beef up its conventional forces to levels which could deter a Soviet conventional attack. By thus raising the nuclear threshold, it's worth every cent it would cost.

However, developing the capability to deter a Soviet conventional attack does not mean that NATO could safely accept superiority in nuclear weapons by cancelling deployment of the new Pershing II and cruise missiles.

Even with sufficient NATO forces on the ground, we need theater-level nuclear equality with the Soviet Union. The Russians think of war as war; they do not make polite distinctions between the use of nuclear weapons and conventional weapons. What has been called the "unusability of nuclear weapons" makes them more usable to the Soviet Union than to the West. The Soviet Union has no domestic restraints from a population paralyzed by media reports about the terror of nuclear weapons. It can manipulate the fear of nuclear weapons in the West without being too concerned about the fear of nuclear weapons in the Soviet Union.

If because of NATO's increased conventional forces the Russians launched an attack on the ground and that attack was repulsed, they would be tempted to use their SS-20s against

Europe as long as NATO lacked the capacity of striking back at the Soviet Union with medium-range missiles such as the Pershing II and the cruise.

In the short term, before the Warsaw Pact-NATO conventional balance is achieved, renouncing a first strike or cancelling the new medium-range missiles would sound the death knell for NATO. Keeping 200,000 American soldiers in Europe at a time when the Soviet Union had superiority at both the conventional and theater nuclear levels would leave them fatally vulnerable to attack.

Failing to restore the theater nuclear balance would force the President of the United States to withdraw our forces from Europe. Without American troops NATO would disintegrate, leaving to the Soviets the morsel that has tantalized them since World War II: West Germany, a non-nuclear power that could not by itself resist a Soviet attack even for a few days.

Since the end of World War II Germany has been the Soviet Union's primary target in Europe. That is why Andropov's insistence on counting French and British nuclear weapons against his SS-20s is such a patent sham. Both Britain and France maintain their forces for their own defense, not for the defense of others. Nuclear weapons under U.S. control are West Germany's only deterrent against massively superior Soviet conventional forces. Without that deterrent West Germany would be nothing but blackmail bait for the hungry Russian bear.

For 30 years after World War II American strategic superiority, the trip-wire, was enough to deter the Soviets from an attack in Europe. Those days are over. NATO must pick up the slack.

Its first steps in that direction have been costly and controversial. While fear of the Soviet Union helps hold NATO together, fear of a nuclear holocaust among a growing number of Europeans threatens to tear it apart.

Ultimately fear of the Soviets is not enough to sustain the Western alliance. The essence of deterrence is the *belief* in deterrence and the hope that the West's military power is being used as part of an overall plan to prevent military confrontation. Without hope of progress toward real peace NATO's will to resist could collapse. Hard-headed detente will provide that hope; so too will the softening of harsh East-West rhetoric that will inevitably result as the superpowers begin to substitute negotiation for confrontation.

The Western alliance must realize that Soviet advances in the Third World threaten the lifeline of every Western industrial nation. Whether this takes place in Afghanistan, Yemen, Ethiopia, or Angola, it is as much an attack on the Western alliance as would be an assault on Europe itself.

In the third of a century since NATO was founded there have been enormous changes in the nature of the Soviet challenge. In the early postwar years the Soviet Union was dangerous to those on its borders, but it was not yet skilled in the projection of power. As the Soviet Union has grown stronger, however, it has also grown immensely more sophisticated in making its power felt far beyond its borders.

NATO remains a traditional military alliance, its forces deployed to deter a Soviet blitzkrieg across the Elbe but dangerously unprepared for a Soviet thrust toward the Persian Gulf or a maneuver by Cuban proxy forces in Africa. In effect we have built a Maginot Line of nuclear and conventional forces along Western Europe's border, while the Soviet Union has learned to use its forces to go under and around borders. As a result the West is in grave danger of being outflanked.

When NATO was founded Europe was weak at the center but strong on the perimeter. The continent itself had been devastated by World War II, but the great European empires were still in place. Today Europe is strong at the center but vulnerable on the perimeter. If the perimeter is breached, the center will collapse. Soviet advances anywhere around the globe—in Asia, the Persian Gulf, or resource-rich Africa—are as potent a threat to Europe as any conventional attack. The industrialized West, including Japan, will be choked to death if the sources of oil and minerals essential to its economies fall into hostile hands.

Some, including many in Europe who continue to expect the U.S. to carry the ball in crisis after crisis, think it ridiculous to suggest that the West could be defeated in the hinterlands rather than on the front lines. If it were, however, it would not be unprecedented. In the American Civil War some thought the North would win by capturing the capital of the Confederacy. But wiser hands knew differently. The Union would defeat the South not simply by pressing "On to Richmond!" but by cutting it off from the rest of the world by blockading its ports, seizing the Mississippi River, and thus stemming the flow of resources for the Confederate war effort.

This was called the "Anaconda Plan." Although it was derided at first, eventually it helped the North win the war.

The Russians know that there are other ways to defeat Europe besides "On to Bonn!" or "On to Paris!" Theirs is an Anaconda Plan on a much grander scale. Like a giant octopus they might wrap one coil around the oil jugular at the Persian Gulf; another could reach into Africa and cut off the flow to Europe of key raw materials. The West depends on the resources of the developing world to keep its economies and its armies functioning. The Soviets know that depriving the West of these resources could injure it as mortally as a direct military assault.

There are those who say that since the U.S. is the Soviet Union's principal adversary, countering Soviet aggression, especially in the developing world, is Washington's problem. This is a fatal delusion. The U.S. is far more self-sufficient in resources than Europe. While we could get along without the oil of the Persian Gulf, Japan and Europe, with the exception of Britain and the North Sea countries, could not. Europe and Japan have a far greater stake in what happens in Afghanistan, Ethiopia, Yemen, and other Soviet targets in the Gulf than has the United States.

Recently, because of such programs as the rapid deployment force, the United States has improved its ability to act quickly in crises on the other side of the world. While the rapid deployment force is a good idea, too much such power would be too much of a good thing. It might encourage our allies in their tendency to think that the U.S. can do it all. The Europeans have generations of experience in dealing with the nations of Africa and the Mideast. If a crisis that threatens the alliance's interests erupts in the Europeans' backyard, they should be prepared to act on behalf of the alliance. France's playing the lead role in Chad, for instance, is an indispensable factor in stopping the Soviets, through their Libyan proxies, from muscling into central Africa.

The idea that the United States could or should act as the policeman of the world is obsolete. Peace is everybody's business. And real peace will not be built unless everyone does his share in building it and keeping it in good repair.

The United States, Europe and Japan must consolidate and learn to use their economic power. Together we could use our strategic economic edge in the same way the U.S. once used its military edge: to deter Soviet aggression around the world. Separately we are isolated nations the Soviets can deal with individually and even play off against one another. Together we out-produce the Soviet bloc by over three to one. Separately any attempt to deter Soviet aggression with economic power is doomed to failure.

The pipeline fiasco proved this point. The United States' trade with the Soviet Union in 1982 was $2.5 billion; Western Europe's was $40.7 billion. Acting together, we could have had a massive impact on the Soviets. But when the Europeans refused to go along, we found that acting alone amounted to a woefully ineffective gesture.

At present NATO recognizes and is beginning to repair the rips in the fabric of its military deterrent. By failing to unite on economic questions in addition to military ones, the West is denying itself the advantage in an area where it still has superiority over the Soviet bloc. To be united militarily but divided economically courts disaster. But by concerting the use of their economic power the U.S. and its allies can develop a powerful weapon to deter Soviet adventurism, while forging an equally powerful instrument with which to encourage peaceful change within the Soviet bloc.

Economic power can be both our sword and our plowshare. Unfortunately, so far the profound differences that have existed between the members of the Western alliance over the use of economic power have made it a useless weapon in our strategic arsenal. In the future, however, we cannot afford to let any of our weapons go unused. The Soviet Union wages the contest across the entire board, militarily, economically, and ideologically. For the West, meeting the Soviets on each of these fronts is both an opportunity and a necessity.

A U.S. President who goes to the summit with the leader of the Soviet Union should carry with him the chits of the other major industrial powers. When he sits across from his Soviet counterpart it should be as if the leaders of all the nations of the Western alliance were arrayed at his right and left at the negotiating table.

When President Reagan meets Andropov the consensus statement in support of theater nuclear weapons that emerged from the recent Williamsburg summit guarantees that he will hold a stronger hand than he would have otherwise. Now that the economic picture in the United States and Europe is improving another meeting of the Western leaders might produce the agreement on unified economic policies that has proved so elusive in the past few years. Before meeting with our adversaries it is essential that we meet with our allies. The Western powers and Japan should schedule an additional summit before the Soviet-American summit.

Such a show of unity has two advantages. It makes it unmistakably clear to the Soviets that the alliance is sound. It also gives the Europeans a chance to help set the agenda.

The U.S. is far more powerful than it was two decades ago, but relative to the rest of the alliance it has proportionately less power than it once had. That means the alliance as a whole is more powerful than it used to be, but only if it acts as an alliance and not a mutual admiration society composed only of fair-weather friends.

Our alliance should not be like OPEC, a cartel whose fabric is in immediate danger of being rent whenever market conditions make it profitable for one or more members to bolt. The members of the Western alliance must accept that the only kind of action that will have an effect in the struggle with the Soviet Union is unified action—that in matters of East-West relations it is in *each nation's* interest to serve the *alliance's* interest.

This applies not only to the Europeans but to the United States as well. Europe's military contribution is as indispensable as ours; along with Japan its combined economy is greater than ours. Yet on matters affecting the whole alliance American Administrations have too often acted first and consulted with our allies second, and then only as an afterthought. By virtue of our position as the "leader of the Western world" we have sometimes treated the Europeans as poor relations who were expected to follow us meekly down any path we chose to take.

The Europeans have centuries of experience in leadership. Every one of our political institutions is based on European models or theories. They know the way the world works. The fact that we are the West's most powerful nation does not mean that we have a monopoly on wisdom. America needs Europe not just because of its economic power and potential military power but because of its brain power. Real peace is too important to settle for anything less than the best thinking the Western world can mobilize to achieve our goal.

CHINA

Before negotiating with our adversaries we should develop a consensus on key issues with our allies and friends. This is true of Japan and the nations of Western Europe. It is also true of the People's Republic of China. That is why, apart from other issues, President Reagan's meeting with Chinese leaders next spring is vitally important.

Our relationship with China is a key element of our strategy vis-a-vis the Soviet Union. Many in the United States opposed our China initiative 11 years ago because of their opposition to communism in any form. They contended that since both China and Russia are communist powers, we should treat both as potential adversaries. They failed to recognize a profound difference. The Soviet Union threatens us. China does not. If we had not undertaken that initiative and China had been forced back into the Soviet orbit, the threat to the West of Soviet communist aggression would be infinitely greater than it is today.

When I travelled to China in 1972 to meet Mao and Zhou, it was in the interests of both nations that we forge a new link based not on common ideals, which bind us to our Western allies, but on common interests. Both sides recognized that despite our profound philosophical differences we had no reason to be enemies and a powerful reason to be friends: our mutual interest in deterring the Soviet threat.

That threat is much greater today than it was then. The Soviet Union is ahead of the United States in strategic land-based missiles. In addition it has every major military installation in China targeted with its powerful SS-20s. The 50 Soviet divisions on the Chinese border, the Soviets' invasion of Afghanistan, and Soviet domination of Southeast Asia threaten China with the possibility of encirclement, a prospect it did not face in 1972.

Both China and the United States should increase their military strength to deter Soviet aggression in Asia. An important goal in any talks between the Reagan Administration and China's pragmatic new leadership should be to generate more action and less talk about joint defensive efforts. Public posturing about our military cooperation only irritates the Soviets. It does not frighten or deter them.

The relationship between the U.S. and China, however, must be more than simply a strategic and military one. Many, by speaking flippantly of "playing the China card," imply that one billion Chinese are just an ace in the hole for the U.S. to deploy against the Russians whenever it suits our interests. This trivializes a profoundly important relationship. If two nations treat their relationship like a game of cards, what they build will be a house of cards that will collapse when hit with the first ill wind.

I believed in 1972 and still believe that even if there were no Soviet threat, the world's most prosperous nation and the world's most populous nation must work together if we are to succeed in building a safer, better world.

Such a relationship, based on the prospects for long-term benefit rather than the dictates of short-term expediency, will require careful tending. It should not be allowed to founder on minor obstacles such as textile imports or the fate of Chinese defectors, or even more difficult ones such as the Taiwan question.

When President Reagan and the Chinese leaders meet they are certain to find that the interests that draw them together are infinitely more important than the differences that could drive them apart.

We should welcome and not fear China's attempt to reduce tensions with the Soviet Union. Those who cynically observe that it might serve our interests for the two communist giants to fight each other are out of their minds. A war between two major powers in the nuclear age would inevitably escalate into a world war. Consequently it is in our interests for China and the Soviets to try to reduce tensions between them which could result in war. It is equally in China's interests for the U.S. and the Soviet Union to try to reduce tensions between them which could result in war.

On the other hand, both China and the United States should approach any negotiations with the Russians with hard-headed realism. Neither China nor the U.S. threatens the other. When the Soviet Union adopts this same policy toward both of us, only then will progress be made in reducing tensions.

China and the United States are held together now by a common fear of the Soviet Union. But as is true in NATO or any other formal arrangement among nations, fear alone is not enough to sustain our new relationship. Fear is the result of the actions of other nations, such as the Soviet Union. When fear is our only incentive to stay together, in effect we leave our fate in the hands of others. A relationship will last only if we have compelling reasons to work together apart from fear of what others do. If our relationship is based on economic cooperation, our fate remains in our hands. If our relationship is to grow, in the next ten years Sino-U.S. economic cooperation can and should become at least as important as our military cooperation.

Our economic relationship is a natural one. China is still a developing nation; it needs rapid economic progress. The two areas where its need is the greatest are the two in which the United States is best able to provide: agriculture and technology. The progress in the first ten years of our new relationship has been substantial—our trade with China is twice as great as our trade with the Soviet Union. The increase in U.S.-China trade in the next ten years could be dramatically higher.

Closer economic ties between China and the U.S. have strategically significant implications. A weak China invites aggression. China cannot become stronger militarily unless it becomes stronger economically. A strong China will be a problem for the Soviet Union long before it is a problem for us. In the foreseeable future we have more to fear from a China that is too weak—and therefore subject to Soviet intimidation—than one that is too strong.

What is needed in our economic relations is not a Mao-style "great leap forward," which has connotations of unreality, but a *new* leap forward, based on the realization that increased Sino-U.S. cooperation could prove to be the decisive factor in ensuring the health and growth of our relationship in the future. Apart from the security aspect, China, with its enormous natural and human resources, will inevitably become an economic giant in the next century and potentially one of America's most important trading partners.

China's leaders have two often contradictory interests. The first is communist ideology. The second is survival, which means not only physical survival but also economic growth and development. Under Deng Xiaoping and his pragmatic colleagues, survival is in the ascendant over ideology. We can help keep it that way by making sure China's faith in the West is constantly renewed and strengthened. If China loses confidence in our military power and our will to use it to deter Soviet aggression, it will have no choice but to seek a rapprochement with the Soviet Union. By the same token, if China's hopes for economic progress through increased trade with the West prove illusory, they will be tempted to turn toward the Soviet Union, despite their distrust and dislike of the Russians. An enlightened, hard-headed U.S. and Western policy to meet China's needs for both security and economic progress will assure that China is not faced with that Hobson's choice.

Too many people assume that the United States has the primary responsibility for satisfying China's need for economic progress. Our role is significant. But Western Europe's trade with China in 1982 was equal to ours, and Japan's was twice as much. Europe and Japan have as great a stake as we do in helping China develop its economic strength so that it will be able to build the necessary military power to deter Soviet aggression.

The Sino-Soviet split in 1961 and the U.S.-China rapprochement in 1972 were the most significant geopolitical events of the post-World War II era. The West has no higher priority than to pursue policies which will convince the Chinese leaders that their hopes for security and economic progress will be realized if they turn West rather than turning to the polar bear in the north. There can be no real peace in Asia if China comes under Soviet domination.

THE THIRD WORLD

The greatest threat to peace comes not from the possibility of a direct conflict between the United States and the Soviet Union, but from the chance that a small war in the Third World will drag in the two superpowers and escalate into a world war. If our goal is real peace, we must address ourselves to the conditions in the Third World that bring about conflict and war.

Three and a quarter billion people live in the developing nations of Africa, Latin America, the Middle East, and Asia, the vast majority of them in abject poverty. Their average per capita income is $600 a year, compared with $10,000 in the United States. Their societies are starkly divided between the very rich and the very poor. Their governments are seldom democratic and often corrupt.

Poverty and bad government are nothing new. What is new is that millions who endure poverty and bad government can now know what they are missing. To see how the other half lives all they have to do is switch on their television sets. Their realization that those who live in the West are far more wealthy, far more comfortable, and far better fed has created enormous frustration and tension throughout the developing world.

This tension and frustration make revolutionary change inevitable. The question is whether change will come by peaceful means or by violence, whether it destroys or builds, whether it will leave totalitarianism or freedom in its wake.

Although the Soviet Union is the source of many of the conflicts in the Third World and profits from most of them, it is not the only cause. If the Soviet Union did not exist there would still be regional conflicts and civil wars. The Palestinian people would still fight for a homeland, Iran and Iraq would still be at war, and India and Pakistan, two of the world's poorest countries, would still be spending $8 billion a year on defense—not because they fear the Soviets, but because they fear each other.

Still, even in these conflicts the Soviet Union is sometimes an instigator, sometimes a facilitator, occasionally an observer waiting for the right moment for taking an active role. In virtually every region of the world—the Middle East, the Persian Gulf, Southeast Asia, the Asian subcontinent, Latin America—the Soviets are involved in one way or another in doing what they do best: making bad situations worse. Their long-term goal is to initiate or assist in the overthrow of any government that is not under communist domination, especially in the Third World where regimes are often temptingly unstable.

The stakes are high, for it is not just the Third World that is at stake. When the interests of the great powers collide in areas like the Middle East and the Persian Gulf, any small war between their respective allies can rapidly escalate into a world war. In the Middle East crises of 1956, 1958, 1967, and 1973, for example, the superpowers were drawn toward the precipice of direct conflict by the actions of their allies in the region. The world saw how easily the cradle of civilization could become its grave.

The most immediate threat to peace in the Third World is Soviet adventurism—not overt aggression across borders by

Soviet troops as in Afghanistan, but covert aggression under borders by Soviet proxy forces.

The Soviets are shrewd observers of the international scene who know what the geopolitical market will bear. They avoid promoting invasions across borders such as North Korea's invasion of South Korea. In that case communist aggression provided a clear rationale for response by a united West.

Since the West is moved to outrage in such matters of sharp black and white, the Soviets have learned to do much of their dirty work in gray areas. Theirs is a thoroughly modern technique of expansionism. They provide arms, training, and propaganda support to revolutionary forces within a country. Their recent victories—in Yemen, Ethiopia, Angola, and Nicaragua—have been sleights-of-hand, backdoor operations in which their involvement was hidden behind local forces or proxies.

Overt aggression across a border entails great risk and cost in terms of worsening relations with the West, as was the case following the Soviet invasion of Afghanistan. Aggression-by-proxy is a low-cost, low-risk enterprise that can therefore be carried out on a far vaster scale. An indication of the success of this tactic is that nine countries and 100 million people have come under Soviet domination since 1974. Until Afghanistan no Russian soldiers were lost in combat in the process of bringing these victories about. Such conquests cost only as much as the weapons do. And the risk to Soviet interests is minimal, because the West usually directs its response against the proxy forces, not the source.

The West has not yet found an effective way to combat indirect Soviet aggression, and our weakness in this regard is one of the Soviets' greatest strengths. Their policy is one of sheer, ruthless opportunism; the West, meanwhile, struggles to find ways to combat covert Soviet aggression that are in accordance with accepted rules of traditional warfare. As a result we have found ourselves outgunned and outmaneuvered time and time again in the Third World because we have been unwilling to do what is necessary to win.

It is not that we should "sink to their level" in combating the Soviets. It is simply that we should be just as aggressive in promoting our ideals and in assisting our friends in the Third World as the Soviets are in promoting and assisting theirs. At a time when the Soviet Union's entire strategy is based on using covert rather than overt tactics, for instance, it would be the height of stupidity for the United States to castrate our CIA.

Our first step in building real peace in the Third World should be to end our romance with left-wing revolution. The catharsis of violent revolution has been so common in this century that many have come to think of it as inevitable. If we are to play a productive role in the Third World, and if we are to stop playing into the Soviets' hands, we must stop assuming that violence is the only road to change that developing nations can take.

Revolutions can begin without outside support. But they cannot survive and prevail without weapons, logistical expertise, food, medical supplies, communications equipment, and training. These things must be provided from outside the country. The North Vietnamese could not have conquered the South without the support of the Soviet Union. In Nicaragua the Sandinistas would have been hard-pressed to take power without the backing of the Soviets and the Cubans. And while there would have been a guerrilla insurrection in El Salvador without outside support, the guerrillas could not survive without the weapons they receive through Nicaragua, again from the Cubans and the Soviet bloc.

One nation falls after another, often with the help of communist leaders in nations that fell before. But eventually all roads and supply lines lead back to Moscow. In recent months shipments from the Soviet bloc have been intercepted en route to Central America. Crates marked "medical supplies" have been found to contain arms. Here in a nutshell is the essence of the Soviet policy in the Third World: the weapons of war wrapped in the empty promise of peace; the promise of soothing misery, the reality of exacerbating it.

We are a nation of idealists, yet we are often blind to the cynicism of Soviet foreign policy. The Russians make revolutions, and they feed on them. Like a vulture hunting fresh carcasses the Soviet Union scans the globe for potential trouble spots, places where people are groping for a better way or suffering through periods of instability. Poverty and injustice do not produce communism; communism produces poverty and injustice. But the Soviets are skilled at exploiting peoples' grievances in order to bring about communist takeovers.

The Soviet challenge is total. Our response must be total. We must provide military and political support to governments threatened by Soviet-supported revolutionary forces. While this sometimes poses a difficult choice, it is rarely between a bad regime and a potentially good one. Rather it is usually a choice between an imperfect regime and a post-revolutionary regime that would be far worse. The liberal critics cannot bring themselves to recognize this stark fact of international life. Time and again they have glorified and celebrated revolutionaries, no matter how inflated their promises or how vicious their tactics. And yet when have the critics been right? Do they believe now that Iranians are better off under Khomeini than the Shah, that Cubans are better off under Castro than under Batista, or that the Vietnamese are better off under the communists than under Thieu?

Still, simply opposing violent, communist revolutions is not enough. We must be able to convince people that they should fight against insurgents not just because of the fear of communism but also because of the promise of freedom. The people in these countries have terrible problems. The communists at least talk about the problems. Too often we talk only about the communists. It is not enough for us to point out that going down the communist road is the wrong way. The only effective answer is for us to offer a better way.

That is our task today in Central America.

In the 1970s the United States failed a critical test in Indochina. Central America, which has triggered the most bitter American foreign policy debate since Vietnam, is also the most important test of American fortitude since Vietnam. We have had nearly a decade to study the lessons of our past failure. If we fail again there will be no excuses and little hope that we will ever again be able to defend our interests beyond our borders.

El Salvador is only today's crisis. As long as Soviet ambitions remain there will be other ones like it. This newest instance of Soviet aggression on our doorstep, however, challenges us to find both an effective way to counteract a Soviet-backed insurrection already under way and also to stop future such insurrections before they are hatched. How we meet these challenges in the Third World will decide whether we will preserve Western civilization or preside over its demise.

Two things are at stake in El Salvador: American interests and the interests of the people of El Salvador. As far as resisting communist aggression is concerned, our interests are identical.

America's new isolationists are living in a dream world when they contend that what happens in "little" El Salvador does not threaten our interests. Apart from our concern that in the event of a communist takeover hundreds of thousands of refugees would flood into high-unemployment areas of Texas and other border states, the U.S. has a vital strategic interest in the outcome in El Salvador. Nuclear missiles based there would take only eight minutes to get to Washington. If the Panama Canal were blocked by hostile forces American shipping would be paralyzed. If the communists, who now have a foothold on our continent in Nicaragua, extend that foothold into El Salvador they will have a secure basing station for further forays—both to the south into South America, and to the north into Mexico and beyond.

The refrain of the new isolationists is unchanging and unending. In the 1960s, after Castro's revolution, they asked: "What can little Cuba do to hurt us?" Cuba became a proxy of the Soviet Union, a supplier of crack shock troops for conquests in Africa and elsewhere. One of its victims was Nicaragua, and after the Sandinistas took power there in 1979 the new isolationists were again in full chorus: "What can little Nicaragua do?" The Sandinistas, having made a mess of their own country by replacing a right-wing authoritarian regime with a left-wing totalitarian one, began to export their revolution. One of their targets is El Salvador. And just as they were not satisfied with Nicaragua the communists would not be satisfied with conquering the 2.4 million people of El Salvador. If the communists win there they will look elsewhere: Honduras, Costa Rica, Guatemala, Panama—and eventually the Soviets' big enchilada, Mexico.

Like many who were born and raised in southern California and the Southwest, I have great respect and affection for Mexico and its people. I went to school with Mexican-Americans for 16 years. Mrs. Nixon and I spent two weeks in Mexico in 1940 on our wedding trip. Our daughters' second language in college was Spanish. We have been back to Mexico many times for both public and private visits. As Vice President-elect in 1952 I attended the inauguration of President Adolfo Ruiz Cortines. He made a profound impression on me as being one of the free world's ablest and wisest statesmen.

Mexico's people are able, hard-working, and proud. But as a nation Mexico is dangerously unstable. It is a prime candidate for communist subversion. Over half a century of one-party government has left it awash in corruption. As a result of short-sighted economic policies and in spite of its position as a major oil-exporting country, its economy is in shambles. The strength of its currency has hit a record low. The Cubans, meanwhile, already have a beachhead in Mexico. The two countries have signed 27 major formal agreements on trade and other forms of cooperation. The Mexican far-left is fanatically pro-Castro.

We have learned over and over again that once they establish a beachhead, the communists always want more. Mexico and the other countries that follow El Salvador on the Kremlin's shopping list are the ones that have the most to fear both from the revolutionaries and from any hesitancy on our part about stopping them. For the moment the U.S. could endure a communist government in El Salvador. To its neighbors such a development would be an immediate, mortal danger.

Resisting the communists is in the interests of all the nations of Central America. It is also in the interests of the people of El Salvador. There is no question but that El Salvador needed a revolution. Of the more than 80 countries I have visited I can think of none in which the gap between rich and poor was greater than in the El Salvador I visited in 1955. For generations the oligarchs had been squeezing the people dry. Reform on all levels of Salvadorean society was desperately needed.

In recent years, however, peaceful revolution has been under way in El Salvador. The current government, empowered as a result of a free, fair election in which 77 percent of the country's eligible voters participated, is working to bring justice and progress to a nation that has seen little of either. But it must also contend with a murderous insurrection by an 8,000-man guerrilla army, dominated by Marxist-Leninists and armed with Sovietbloc weapons channelled through Nicaragua.

American media coverage is blatantly biased against the Salvadorean government. Virtually every day we hear or read of guerrillas and civilians being killed by government troops. The fact that in the past year alone the guerrillas have killed or wounded 7,000 government soldiers and murdered hundreds of innocent civilians receives only passing notice.

The senseless killing on both sides must stop. We should support efforts by the nations in the area to end the war by negotiation, but with two caveats.

We talk to bring peace. As we learned in Vietnam, the communists use talking as a screen for continued fighting.

Also, under no circumstances should we support the guerrillas' demand that they should hold high posts in a popular front government. A popular front would be a front for the guerrillas' ongoing revolution. Communists usually enter negotiations or coalition governments not to achieve peace but to achieve the same objective they had sought on the battle-field: total victory.

The choice is clear-cut. Should ballots or bullets determine what kind of government El Salvador will have? If the communists have so much faith in their system, why do they resist letting the people decide the question in a free, internationally supervised election? It is time to let the people of El Salvador decide whether they will have a better chance to get reform and economic progress under a Nicaraguan- or Cuban-style communist government, or under one supported and influenced by the United States.

Nicaragua is a tragic example of the kind of government El Salvador will get if the guerrillas win. When the Sandinistas took over many in Washington said we should just leave them alone. Keep the economic aid flowing, the revolutionaries' apologists assured us, and Nicaragua will flower into a functioning democracy.

Instead it is degenerating into a Castro-style dictatorship. A quarter-million refugees have fled the country. The villages of the Miskito Indians, who refused to be assimilated into the revolution, were burned to the ground. The free press was closed down, religious leaders were harassed, and citizens were taught to spy on each other Stalin-style through neighborhood "defense" committees. Children receive Marxist indoctrination in school. Meanwhile, real wages are down by 50 percent, unemployment is rising, and there are shortages of key foodstuffs.

With their people and their economy on the ropes, the Sandinistas turned away from problems at home to expansion abroad, building up a 138,000-man army, larger than the armed forces of all the other nations of the region put together, and prosecuting their "revolution without borders" in El Salvador and elsewhere—with the assistance of Soviets, Cubans, East Germans, and Libyans. As these foreigners flooded in thousands of Nicaraguans, including former Sandinistas, flooded out, vowing to return and oust those who betrayed their revolution.

In Nicaragua the U.S. policy of hands-off and handouts—including $120 million in aid to the Sandinistas from 1979 to 1981—didn't work. A policy designed to encourage the Sandinistas to allow more democracy only encouraged them in their belief that they could get away with less. A policy designed to leave them alone to mind their country's business only freed them to meddle with impunity in their neighbors' business. That is why the Reagan Administration began its covert support of anti-Sandinista rebels based in Honduras.

The Administration's Central America policies are designed to achieve three goals.

The purpose of our support of anti-Sandinista forces is to help the elected government of El Salvador by cutting off military supplies to the guerrillas: As British M.P. Julian Amery recently observed, "Experience has shown that a guerrilla movement can generally be beaten only if the base from which it operates is destabilized."

Our policy of economic and military aid to El Salvador is designed to strengthen the anti-communist government forces so that they can stop the communist-dominated revolutionaries, thus derailing Soviet hopes of subverting other governments in a strategically vital region.

A third goal is to quarantine Cuba and Nicaragua by preventing them from infecting their neighbors with their tyranny and their misery. In that connection the United States should not be defensive about our military presence in the area. We should not make threats as to what we *will* do. But even more important, we should not proclaim what we will *not* do. In attempting to reassure our own people we should not reassure our potential enemies. We should leave no doubt in their minds that we have the capability and the will to do what is necessary to stop the flow of arms from Cuba and Nicaragua into El Salvador.

The question now is whether Congress will support the President's policies or cut the authority and the funds he needs to continue them. In considering that question the critics should bear in mind that President Reagan did not create the crises in Nicaragua and El Salvador. He inherited them.

The specter of American men dying in Vietnam is being raised to defeat the Administration's military aid and training program. The comparison does not bear analysis. American troops were sent to South Vietnam because communist North Vietnam invaded South Vietnam. As the North Vietnamese have since admitted, they instigated, supplied and controlled the guerrillas in South Vietnam from the beginning. That was why President Kennedy sent the first American combat troops to Vietnam in 1962. Crack North Vietnamese regulars, not barefoot peasants, rode Soviet tanks triumphantly into Saigon in April 1975. Had there been no outside forces in South Vietnam, American troops would not have been needed.

There are as yet no outside troops in El Salvador. As long as this is the case no American combat troops will or should be sent there. Our policy in El Salvador and in other countries similarly threatened by revolutionary forces should be to provide arms and economic aid only. They must provide the men. If when adequately trained and armed they lack the will and the ability to defeat the revolutionary forces, we cannot do it for them. Even if we were to win, the victory would be temporary. As soon as we withdrew the revolutionaries would take over.

The doves who oppose military aid contend that the primary problem in El Salvador is poverty. Since poverty causes communist revolution, they assert, then we should deal with the cause by providing economic rather than military aid.

I first heard this argument in 1947, when President Truman asked the Congress to provide military and economic aid to Greece and Turkey. Thousands of postcards inundated our congressional offices. The message was simple: "Send food, not arms." Fortunately, a bipartisan majority resisted the pressure and supported the Truman Doctrine. If we had not done so and the U.S. had sent only food and not arms, Greece and Turkey would probably be communist today.

Both military and economic aid are essential. Either one

without the other will fail to do the job. That is why the U.S. is sending El Salvador three dollars in economic and humanitarian aid for every dollar of military aid, a fact the critics persistently ignore.

The hawks contend that our primary emphasis should be on military aid rather than economic aid. This course would also be folly. Helping a government stop a violent revolution without helping it deal with the economic conditions that helped spawn the revolution would also buy only a short-lived victory. After one revolution was put down, another would take its place.

The critics—both hawks and doves—fail to recognize a fundamental truth about nations in the developing world: they cannot have progress without security, and they cannot have security without progress.

If there is one justifiable criticism of U.S. Latin American policy which applies to all Administrations since World War II, it is that we have consistently provided too much military aid and not enough economic aid for our friends and allies in the area.

But the worst mistake we could make in El Salvador or in any country under siege from Soviet-backed guerrillas would be to provide just enough military aid to keep them fighting, but not enough to win. If the Congress refuses to support President Reagan's policy with the funds he feels are necessary to prevent a communist victory, he will have no choice but to get out and let the communists take over. This would be tragic for the people of El Salvador and for us, but it would be worse to half try and to fail. We cannot afford another Bay of Pigs, where we sent a brave but pathetically undersupported force to be cut to pieces on the beaches of Cuba. And we cannot afford another Vietnam, where Congress was unwilling to follow through with the commitment we had made in the 1973 Paris peace agreements to provide the same amount of support to South Vietnam that the Soviet Union was providing for North Vietnam.

Such setbacks are bad enough for the people we let down. The legacy of our failure in Vietnam was over 100,000 boat people and three million Cambodians slaughtered by the communist Khmer Rouge government. But if it happens again the world may decide that failure is endemic to America, that our idealism and our good intentions, since they spell defeat for us and our friends time and time again, are burdens rather than blessings. Leaders everywhere will conclude, as did President Ayub Khan of Pakistan when he learned of U.S. complicity in the coup that led to the murder of President Diem of South Vietnam, "It is dangerous to be a friend of the United States; it pays to be neutral; and sometimes it helps to be an enemy."

The "how not to do it" pundits and congressional critics dominate the dialogue on Central America. What they fail to recognize is that while our current policy is not an ideal one, it is the least we can do under the circumstances. In the future, however, the United States should act *before* Soviet puppets such as the Sandinistas take power, *before* communist guerrillas can assail another freely-elected government such as El Salvador's.

To put it charitably, U.S. policy toward Latin America since World War II, while well-intentioned, has been inadequate, inept, and, worst of all, plagued by fitful starts and stops. Because of its proximity, Latin America should be our first foreign policy priority. But as I observed when I returned from Caracas in 1958, the only time Latin America receives front-page attention in the U.S. media is when "there is a revolution or a riot at a soccer game."

For decades the U.S. has been smothering Latin America with slogans. Foreign aid programs such as the Alliance for Progress and Good Neighbors raised high hopes in Latin America, and when the hopes were unfulfilled they raised hackles. Despite our good intentions we have broken our promises to the Latin Americans over and over again. Most of the billions of dollars we have sent to their governments have been sucked up by corrupt officials or wasted on poorly conceived or poorly managed projects.

Meanwhile we have left the impression that we become actively involved in Latin America only when our interests are threatened by communist aggression. We must now develop policies which also address *their* interests. Even if there were no communist threat millions of Latin Americans would justifiably demand reforms to lift the burdens of poverty, injustice, and corruption that have been their lot for generations. In addressing these concerns we will serve the interests of the people of Latin America and serve our own interests as well by depriving the communists of the issues they exploit to gain power and impose a new tyranny.

A top Carter Administration official recently said that after the flurry of high-level concern in the U.S. government as Somoza was falling to the Sandinistas in Nicaragua in 1979, Latin America was once again put on the back burner—until the crisis in El Salvador erupted.

It would be unfair to single out the Carter Administration for this tragic error. All postwar American Presidents, understandably busy with innumerable current crises far away, have not had the time or the inclination to focus on potential ones close to home. The tendency is understandable, but it must stop. We can no longer afford it. Since so many crises in Latin America and the other parts of the Third World are either instigated or encouraged by the Soviets, a modus operandi based solely on crisis management will give our adversary the advantage of always making the first move.

To stop the Soviets from reaping further grim victories, we must scan the globe just as they do. When all is quiet in the Third World, all is not necessarily well. The potential for unrest in a country often smolders just below the surface. Up until now we have only moved in to put out the fires of revolution once they start. In the future we must learn to keep them from igniting at all.

We need an early warning system for pinpointing these potential Third World hot spots. Once we identify them we must offer an active, workable alternative to communism.

Our goal is not to prove to people that our system is better than communism. They know that. Communism is something a country is infected with, not something it chooses. We must help those countries whose immune systems are low, build up those countries the Soviets and their proxies are apt to find most susceptible to their tactics. The West must learn how to practice preventive political medicine. More economic aid now could reduce the possibility that we would be called on for more military aid later.

The United States' responsibility in this effort should be principally, but not exclusively, our own backyard: Latin America, both Central America and South America. Since every Latin American country is a potential target for the communists, every country should be a target for us.

Our efforts, while directed primarily toward Latin America, should not be restricted to our hemisphere, and our allies' efforts should not be restricted to theirs. The Soviets' front lines in the fight for the Third World circle the globe. Their challenge is unified and centrally managed, and we will not meet it effectively if we simply divide the world into exclusive spheres of economic influence.

Soldiers wearing the uniforms of many NATO nations serve on the front lines in West Germany because each member of the alliance recognizes that what happens there affects its interests. We must grapple in the same way with the Soviet threat in the Third World. In the effort to strengthen the economic base of the developing world each alliance nation should act in the areas with which it is most familiar—the Europeans in Africa, for instance, and the Japanese in Asia. But each Western nation must also recognize that its interests are directly affected by events on the other side of the world, such as those in Central America. Likewise, European and Japanese efforts in Africa and Asia should not preclude the U.S. from assisting in these regions.

There is no reason why prosperity should necessarily exist north of the equator but not south of it. The West must find ways to teach what it knows. It will take an international effort involving both the public and private sectors; businessmen, government officials, educators, technical experts all must participate. If we are to protect what we have from our aggressive adversaries, we must share what we have with our less fortunate friends. Otherwise, it is through them that our adversaries may eventually get at us.

We need dramatic new initiatives to break the vicious cycle through which underdeveloped nations with authoritarian governments and some hope for the future are transformed into underdeveloped nations with totalitarian governments and no hope for the future. The West has been on the defensive for 35 years on all fronts—in Western Europe, in Asia and Southeast Asia, throughout the Third World. We must now go onto the offensive—not just in Central America but worldwide. We and our allies must be as bold and as generous in helping poor Third World countries get started on the road to economic progress as the U.S. was in helping Europe and Japan recover after World War II.

Obsessed with the idea that there is a limit to what we can do in the world, we have failed to press as hard as we could right up to that limit. In the Third World the Soviets exploit and extend human misery. It is our responsibility to confine and ease human misery. This is true of every nation of the Western alliance. The U.S. can show the way, however, by its actions in Latin America.

The threat of communist aggression is far more immediate to the nations of Latin America than it is to us. These nations' leaders are also far better acquainted with their peoples' problems and needs than we are. We should encourage and welcome their guidance and initiatives. They, in turn, should encourage and welcome ours.

Some Americans, believing we can duplicate our success in helping the nations of Western Europe rebuild after World War II, have called for a "Latin American Marshall Plan." The goal is excellent, but in pursuing it we must bear in mind that the Marshall Plan was officially called the European Recovery Program. In Latin America and the rest of the Third World the issue is not *recovering* but *getting started*. The Europeans were experienced in running sophisticated industrial economies. Most developing nations are not. Any economic aid program for Latin America will cost far more and take much more time to achieve results than was the case with our aid to Europe and Japan after World War II.

The debate over U.S. foreign aid is confined by two extremes. Some say we should cut government-to-government aid and increase private investment in Latin America. Others insist that more government-to-government aid rather than more private investment is the answer. In fact neither will work without the other.

Government-to-government aid should be used as fertilizer, to prepare the ground for private investment and thus for economic growth. Such aid is only worth the investment if growing conditions are right. If the government is repressive, the aid won't work. If the government is corrupt, the aid won't work. If the government has policies that penalize private investment, the aid won't work. If the government is so unstable that businessmen, workers, and consumers have no peace of mind, the aid won't work. Most important, since aid will not work without trade, we must expand the array of trade preferences we offer to our Latin American neighbors.

The Reagan Administration's Caribbean Basin Initiative is an excellent step toward achieving these goals. It should be substantially increased and extended to other nations in South America.

A massive increase in both *financial* aid and *human* aid—in which Canada, Europe, and Japan carry their fair share and the great bulk of which will be provided through private investment rather than government grants—is the best investment the West could make for peace, progress, and stability in the Third World.

While the Soviet promise is an empty one, we cannot beat it with nothing. We can beat it by recognizing and using the enormous economic advantage the West has over the Soviets. Our system works; theirs doesn't. Marxist economic policies produce poverty rather than progress. The only economic success stories since World War II have been written in the free countries of Europe, North America, and non-communist Asia. The Soviets can only brandish their power. We can give the gift of progress by helping poor countries up the first, most difficult steps of the ladder of economic development.

We can offer advice and even prescribe solutions to economic problems. But as far as political systems are concerned, we should be far more restrained and patient. While democracy works for the nations of the West, instant democracy is neither possible nor desirable for most of the Third World. We should hold fast to our ideals of human rights, but at the same time understand that a regime that provides some human rights is better than one that will provide none. The answer to those who contend that the U.S. loses in the court of world opinion because we support repressive anti-communist governments is that the most repressive governments in the world are communist ones.

The West has a long tradition of democratic government that most of the rest of the world does not share. But even the U.S., as prone as we are to hurling moralistic lightning bolts at regimes that do not come up to snuff on human rights, gave the vote to women only 63 years ago and guaranteed civil rights to blacks only 20 years ago. We must learn to be less harsh judges.

On the other hand, neither good moral sense nor good strategic sense compels us to subsidize an authoritarian regime's practice of repression. By its very nature such a regime will inhibit rather than stimulate economic growth, and without growth and stability a nation remains vulnerable to violent revolution—and therefore Soviet meddling. Just as we can deter Soviet misbehavior by establishing economic ties the Russians would be loath to give up, we can influence friendly but authoritarian regimes if we quietly but unmistakably let them know that our friendship will be even more profitable to them once they adopt less repressive policies.

If we give our friends nothing but public lectures on political morality, we create resentment and thus widen rather than narrow the gap between us. But if we give them economic support to help create stability and military support, in the form of aid and advice, against forces that threaten them with chaos, we will be sowing the seeds of democracy. Democracy is inevitably the first casualty of unrest and war. It is also an inevitable product of peace and prosperity.

To build real peace in the Third World, we must be patient with those who do not yet come up to our standards of political behavior. We must be loyal to those nations that choose not to threaten us. And we must be generous in sharing what our prosperity has given us.

In the countries where it has been established, Marxism has produced poverty, not progress; tyranny, not liberation; repression, not justice. Communism's performance has belied its promise. In the 1950s and 1960s, many leaders of nations emerging from colonialism understandably mistook Soviet successes in forced industrialization as the wave of the future. But the failure of socialism in the Soviet Union and in the Third World has been exposed in ways all can see. Eighteen countries in the world have communist governments. None came to power in a free election. And there is no country in the communist world whose leaders will risk having a free, democratic election. Today Marxism-Leninism is only a recipe small groups of ruthless men use to gain power and stay in power.

The Soviets have lost the ideological battle in the Third World. But this does not mean the West has won it. In the Third World, where change is inevitable, the West too often finds itself on the side of the status quo. If the choice is between the status quo and communism, the latter will prevail if only by virtue of the shrewd, cynical opportunism of the Soviet Union.

To win the ideological battle, the West must be opportunistic, too. It must aggressively seek opportunities to channel the energy of inevitable change in the Third World toward peaceful revolution rather than violent revolution. Today, the only kind of revolution on the market is too often the kind that the Soviets and their surrogates sell. Tomorrow, we can put them out of business.

PEACEFUL COMPETITION

In World War I, the slaughter in the trenches prompted many to call the conflict "the war to end war." Yet 20 years later world war again engulfed the globe, leaving unprecedented destruction in its wake and killing almost four times as many people. When World War II ended the nuclear age began, and the potential destruction of war increased exponentially. Today it is no longer an exaggeration to say that the next war would be "the war to end war" because it would also end civilization as we know it.

We must not court confrontation or flirt with war, but neither should we let ourselves be seduced by the idea of peace at any price. Mao Zedong elliptically expressed concern about this danger in my last meeting with him in 1976. He asked me, "Is peace your only goal?" I replied that our goal was peace, but a peace that was more than the absence of war. I told him, "It must be a peace with justice." If I had answered Mao's question with a discourse that emphasized only the need for peace and friendship, he would have considered me to be not only wrong but also a fool. After all, if peace really is our only goal, we can have it any time we wish simply by surrendering. The peace we seek must be coupled with justice.

To pursue peace with justice, the West must adapt its policies to the realities of the world today. Our policy must combine deterrence with detente. Detente without deterrence leads to appeasement, and deterrence without detente leads to unnecessary confrontation and saps the will of Western peoples to support the arms budgets deterrence requires. Together, they will lead to the containment of and peaceful competition with the Soviet Union.

Hard-headed detente requires us to concert our actions on several fronts. We must erect a shield of military power that will deter Soviet aggression at all levels. We need to make progress on arms control agreements that will reduce the burden of defense, reestablish the balance of power, and increase strategic stability in crises. We have to provide the Soviets with an economic stake in peace as a further incentive to stop their aggression. We must create a process for settling those differences between the superpowers that can be resolved and for preventing our irreconcilable disagreements from leading to war.

Peace and justice require nothing less of us. We do not oppose communism simply because our economic system is capitalist. We oppose its spread because of what it does to the people forced to live under its rule. Communism is an ideological bubonic plague. Wherever it has spread, it has made a nightmare out of the common man's dreams of a better life for himself and his family. It has broken up millions of families and has turned millions of others into refugees. It has killed tens of millions of innocent people and has enslaved nations. The first requirement of justice is that we block the further expansion of communism.

But containment is not enough. It would be wrong to hold a second Yalta conference, carving the world into spheres of domination and tacitly accepting the Brezhnev Doctrine that whatever is communist must remain so. It would be the height of injustice to purchase peace at the price of condemning forever to communism the millions behind the Iron Curtain. The Soviets will never accept the status quo in the West. We must never be satisfied with the status quo—East or West. We must never accept their rules for "peaceful" competition: that the Soviet bloc is a privileged sanctuary and that the West is their happy hunting ground.

The Soviets' goal is to dominate the world. They want to win, but without war. We also must try to win, but through peace. Our goal should be to engage them in a peaceful competition between our systems that will foster peaceful change in theirs.

Establishing a process for peaceful competition will require creative statesmanship of a high order. We must make the Kremlin leaders understand that aggression, direct and indirect, will lead to war. We must not object to their attempts to spread communism as long as they use peaceful means to do so. In one of our heated exchanges in Moscow in 1959, Nikita Khrushchev shouted, "Your grandchildren will live under communism." I replied that we had no objection to his *saying* this but that we would firmly resist if he tried to bring it about by force.

Regardless of the progress we make in reducing tensions that could lead to war, the United States and the Soviet Union are destined to continue to be all-out competitors. What the Soviets must understand is that, if the game is to have any winners, they must abide by rules of engagement in areas short of war.

Our strategy for peaceful competition affects all of our global relationships. We must unify the economic power of the industrial democracies so that we can gain political concessions from the Eastern bloc in exchange for our economic cooperation. We must continue to develop constructive ties with China so that it chooses to align itself with us rather than with the Soviets. We must seek to alleviate poverty and repression in Third World countries so that they do not become tempting targets for Soviet adventurism. Above all, we must not stand aside and let events control us. If we ride the hurricane, we will become part of it.

Our most difficult problem in this competition is finding a

way to go over, under, and around the Iron Curtain to carry it on in Eastern Europe and the Soviet Union itself. We have no perfect solution, but this should not stop us from applying partial ones. We must recognize that the superiority of local Soviet military forces puts us at a disadvantage in the short run but that the superiority of our system and ideals gives us just as great an advantage in the long run.

We must not treat the countries of Eastern Europe as if they were part of a monolithic Soviet bloc. Those who insist that we do so make the same argument as some did when we opened the door to China in 1972. They say that all these nations are communist, that communism is evil, and that they are therefore all potential enemies and should be treated as such. They fail to recognize the profound truth of British historian Paul Johnson's dictum: "It is the essence of geopolitics to be able to distinguish between different degrees of evil."

The extent of Soviet control, though great, is not total. The countries of Eastern Europe are allied with the Soviet Union in the Warsaw Pact, and East European communists and Soviet ones share the same ideology. The presence of Soviet military forces within and on the borders of these nations severely limits the scope of independent action their leaders can take domestically and internationally. But the governments of Eastern Europe have developed personal, national, and even some ideological differences. Some East European leaders have exploited these to eke out a small degree of maneuverability. This should not be overestimated, but we should encourage it through the bilateral relations we develop with each country.

The crisis in Poland exemplifies our dilemma. Our hearts tell us to give all-out support and encouragement to the Solidarity labor union and the anti-Russian and anti-communist sentiments of the vast majority of the Polish people. But our heads tell us that we cannot play a military role in Poland. We learned that lesson from the uprising in Hungary in 1956, when we appeared to offer support to the freedom fighters only to be proven helpless when the Red Army moved into Budapest. The Soviets will not permit an independent, hostile

Polish government to take power, and they have the military power to prevent that outcome. We are left with the painful conclusion that it is better for Poland to be ruled by Polish communists than by Soviet communists, even though internally the two are usually indistinguishable by their actions.

This does not mean we are acquiescing to the Brezhnev Doctrine. The Soviets always assert that what is theirs is theirs and what is ours is negotiable. Unfortunately, the realities in Eastern Europe force us to accept the *fact* of Soviet hegemony, but we must never agree to the *principle* of it. We cannot set the liberation of the captive nations as our short-term policy goal, but we must never cease to proclaim it as our long-term goal.

Although Soviet power makes the cards in our hand seem weak, the magnetism of the West stacks the deck in our favor. How do we play out our hand? Their strong suit is in military power. Our strong suits are in economic power and in the power of ideas. If we play our cards wisely, the Soviets will be left holding theirs.

Increased trade and contacts can advance peaceful change within the Soviet bloc. There are those who argue that we should isolate these countries and let economic necessity force them to reform. They are wrong. The pull of a magnet is greatest nearby it. Similarly, the more contact we have with the East, the more we open it to the force of Western example. This will inevitably add to those internal forces that are generating change. During the long, chilly years of cold war confrontation there was little change in the countries of Eastern Europe. There has been substantial change since then. As I saw on a recent trip to four Eastern European countries, the stirrings of greater freedom are there—economic freedom in some, political or social freedoms in others. And conditions are ripe for further change.

The changes taking place in Hungary today prove the point. Situated on the frontier of the Soviet empire, Hungary is exposed to unjammed Austrian radio and television broadcasts and has become thoroughly infected with the tastes and ideas of the West. General-Secretary Kadar, whom Khrushchev appointed after crushing the uprising in Budapest in 1956, is a dedicated communist but also prides himself on being a patriotic Hungarian. His country languished until he implemented economic reforms during the years of detente. His production figures, while not high by Western standards, are now the envy of the Eastern bloc. Yet he faces a dilemma. Progress requires more freedom for enterprise; more freedom means less control for the state. He must constantly ask himself how much power he can afford to give up without endangering his rule, but for now the reforms continue. Isolating Hungary because of our differences with the Soviet Union would snuff out the prospects for more reform.

Our other strong suit is in the realm of ideas. A visitor to nineteenth-century Russia said that "one word of truth hurled into Russia is like a spark landing in a keg of powder." Today, the fact that the Soviet system lives on lies makes it extremely vulnerable to the truth. Truth can penetrate borders. Truth can travel on its own power, wherever people and ideas of East and West meet. Russia has heavy censorship, but its people are starved for the truth. Sending the West's message through every totalitarian barrier—whether by exchange of visitors, or books, or broadcasts—will give hope to millions behind those barriers and will gradually eat away at the foundations of the Soviet system just as seeping water can erode the foundation of a prison.

We should not shrink from the propaganda war, either within the Soviet empire or in the rest of the world. It is not enough to condemn the evil of communism. We must also proclaim the promise of freedom. We should strengthen Radio Free Europe and Radio Liberty and set up counterparts of them to compete directly with Soviet propaganda in those areas of the Third World that the Kremlin leaders have targeted for aggression. Even in peace, the war of ideas will continue. We must be sure it takes place on both sides of the Iron Curtain.

One great benefit of a summit meeting in Moscow would be that President Reagan would have the opportunity to address the Soviet people on television. Not only could he dispel his image in the Soviet press as a reckless warmonger, but he could also present our point of view as the free world's most effective spokesman. Some scoff at the thought that such a speech can accomplish anything. After all, the Kremlin leaders are hardly concerned by their Gallup rating. But I had the opportunity to address the Soviet people in 1959, 1972, and 1974, and if the level of official anxiety over these broadcasts was any measure of their power, it was not insignificant.

Khrushchev often challenged the West to competition with communism. We should accept that challenge and broaden it, bringing to bear the spiritual and cultural values that have distinguished Western civilization. Whether or not the Soviets choose to compete in these areas, we should compete with all the vigor at our command. The Soviets need contact with the West. They need our technology and our trade. They cannot keep out our radio broadcasts today and may not be able to keep out our satellite television broadcasts tomorrow. They cannot seal themselves off totally from the world. When they crack open the door to reach out for what they want, we should push through it as much truth as we can.

Winston Churchill once observed, "Russia fears our friendship more than our enmity." Churchill's insight showed a deep understanding of the Soviet leaders. They understand that one of the greatest dangers to the Soviet system is contact between their ideas and ours, their people and ours, their society and ours. This proximity invites unwelcome comparisons. It plants the seeds of discontent that will someday blossom into peaceful change. But if instead we isolate the East and reduce its contacts with us, we would be casting away one of our most effective weapons against the Kremlin leaders.

If peaceful change turns the attention of Soviet leaders toward their internal problems, real peace will have a chance to take hold in the world. It will at best take generations for such a resolution to come about. This is plainly unsatisfactory for a people as impatient as Americans, who are accustomed to solving their problems overnight. But history seldom accommodates the hurried. As with anything that is truly worth having, real peace will take time, effort, and above all patience.

In the meantime, there is no substitute for vigilance. We must restore without delay the military balance of power at the strategic, theater, and conventional levels.

We must also continue to build up our economic strength. Ironically, those who fault President Reagan's foreign policy but praise his domestic policy may one day look back and recognize that his greatest contribution in foreign policy *was* his economic policy. A democratic country with a weak economy will have a weak foreign policy. By wringing inflation out of the American economy, President Reagan has established a solid base for a sustained and long economic expansion. A strong American economy will strengthen the economies of our friends and allies abroad. It will enable him to win congressional approval for the defense and non-defense spending that is necessary to achieve our foreign policy goals. It will put him in a stronger position in negotiating East-West trade deals. It will help him fight off forces that advocate protectionism. And it will buoy the world economy and thereby strengthen the vulnerable states that are on the target list of the Kremlin leaders.

We must engage the Soviets in a process of peaceful competition. If they could sell communism in the marketplace of ideas, if they could make their system deliver on its promises, then they would deserve to win the global ideological struggle. But they cannot, and they never will. Thirty years ago, many saw communism as a way to progress, but now its performance has caught up with its promises. It is not enough that the Soviet Union has lost the battle of ideas. It is essential that the West launch an offensive to win it. If we succeed in winning this battle on both sides of the East-West divide, we will lay a firm foundation for building real peace in the years ahead.

Without one key ingredient, none of this is possible. Sir Robert Thompson, the great British strategist, once trenchantly described national strength as manpower plus applied resources times will. We have the manpower. We have the resources. But do we have the will to act as a great power with the vision to move the world toward real peace?

There is no question that if there is to be an arms race, we can win it. There is no question that if there is to be an economic race, we can win it. There is no question that if there is to be a contest for the "hearts and minds" of the world's people, we can win it. But there is a question whether we can win the contest we are actually engaged in today: a test of will and determination between ourselves and the most powerfully armed aggressive power the world has ever known.

Real peace requires that we resolve to use our strength in ways short of war. There is today a vast gray area between peace and war, and the struggle will be largely decided in that area. If we expect to win without war, or even expect not to lose without war, then we must engage our adversary within that area. We need not duplicate his methods, but we must counter them—even if that means behaving in ways other than we would choose in an ideal world.

National will involves far more than readiness to use military power, whether nuclear or conventional. It includes a readiness to allocate the resources necessary to maintain that power. It includes a clear view of where the dangers lie, and of what kinds of responses are necessary to meet those dangers. It includes also a basic, crystalline faith that the United States is on the right side in the struggle, and that what we represent in the world is worth defending.

If the Soviet leaders look westward and see an American leadership that eyes their moves in a measured way, that refuses to bow, that walks without faltering, that knows what it is doing, that is determined to do whatever has to be done in order to prevail, then those Soviet leaders will not be tempted to gamble all in high-stakes throws of the dice. They will make their cost-benefit analysis and postpone or abandon any aggression that will not be worth the effort or the risk.

As we look to the future, we should do so with confidence. I do not believe there will be a world war. I believe there can and will be progress in building more peaceful relations with the Soviet Union. I believe our geopolitical competition will continue. But if we muster the will, we need not be pessimistic about the outcome. As one generation succeeds another, we will begin to see the process of peaceful change take hold in the Eastern bloc as it is already doing to a small degree in Hungary and China. In that change lies the ultimate solution to the riddle of peace. We will win in the long run, and win without war.

But we must avoid soft-headed overconfidence. History tells us it is not enough to be on the right side. The pages of history are strewn with the wreckage of superior civilizations that were overrun by barbarians because they awoke too late to the threat, reacted too timidly in devising a strategy to meet it, and because they lacked the will to make the necessary sacrifices to win.

The history of the world is a narrative of man's struggle to become free and remain free. Freedom has not come cheaply, and keeping it is not easy. We hold a responsibility to the future unique to our time and place. Nothing that today's generation can leave for tomorrow's will mean more than the heritage of liberty.

No people have ever had a more exciting challenge. Yet the American people sometimes become deeply disillusioned about playing this role in the world. The loss in Vietnam was traumatically painful. The burden of building the defenses of the free world is great. The fact that countries to which we give billions of dollars in aid vote against us consistently in the United Nations is maddening.

Without the United States, there is no chance for peace and freedom to survive. Without the United States, the dawn of the twenty-first century would open a new age of barbarism on a global scale.

But we must assume this burden not just for others but for ourselves. We have a spiritual stake in not walking away from a great historical challenge. President de Gaulle wrote, "France is never her true self except when she is engaged in a great enterprise." This is true of individuals; it is true of nations; it is particularly true of Americans. Only by participating in a great enterprise can we be true to ourselves.

There could be no greater enterprise than to build a structure of real peace. The struggle to protect freedom and build real peace can raise the sights of Americans from the mundane to the transcendent, from the immediate to the enduring.

During a meeting with Brezhnev in the Crimea in 1974, I jotted down this note on a pad of paper: "Peace is like a delicate plant. It has to be constantly tended and nurtured if it is to survive; if we neglect it, it will wither and die." Peace has barely survived in the rocky soil of the twentieth century. The violence of two world wars and scores of smaller wars has nearly uprooted it time and again. It has managed to survive, but is far from safe. It is not a grim burden but an inspiring challenge to build and sustain real peace. Given the alternative of suicidal war, we must not fail.

No More Vietnams

To those who served

THE MYTHS OF VIETNAM

No event in American history is more misunderstood than the Vietnam War. It was misreported then, and it is misremembered now. Rarely have so many people been so wrong about so much. Never have the consequences of their misunderstanding been so tragic.

Vietnam has been the subject of over 1,200 books, thousands of newspaper and magazine articles, and scores of motion pictures and television documentaries. The great majority of these efforts have portrayed one or more of the following conclusions as facts:

- The Vietnam War was a civil war.
- Ho Chi Minh was a nationalist first and a Communist second and had the support of a majority of the people of Vietnam, North and South.
- Ngo Dinh Diem was a puppet of the French colonialists.
- The National Liberation Front was a revolutionary movement independent of North Vietnam.
- The Viet Cong won the hearts and minds of villagers through humanitarian policies.

- The Geneva Declaration of 1954 legally bound Diem's government and the United States to unify the two halves of Vietnam through elections.
- The agreements in 1962 "neutralizing" Laos prevented the widening of the war.
- The Buddhist protests in 1962 against Diem resulted from religious repression.
- The Johnson administration was the first to send American troops into combat in Vietnam.
- Most American soldiers were addicted to drugs, guilt ridden about their role in the war, and deliberately used cruel and inhumane tactics.
- American blacks constituted a disproportionate number of the combat casualties.
- The United States lost the war militarily.
- The Communist Tet Offensive of 1968 was a military defeat for the United States.
- U.S. secret bombing in 1969 and ground attacks on the Communist bases in Cambodia in 1970 were responsible for bringing the Communists into power in Cambodia in 1975.
- It was a calculated policy of the United States to bomb civilian targets in North Vietnam.
- The percentage of civilian deaths in the Vietnam War was higher than in other wars.
- American POWs were treated humanely by the North Vietnamese.
- The antiwar demonstrations in the United States shortened the war.
- The Paris peace agreements of 1973 were a cynical attempt to provide the United States with a "decent interval" between the withdrawal of its forces and the collapse of South Vietnam.
- The United States could have struck the same deal in 1969 as it did in 1973.
- The domino theory has been proved false.

- Life is better in Indochina now that the United States is gone.

All of these statements are false.

Ten years ago in April 1975, a violent peace engulfed Vietnam following the withdrawal of the Americans and the victory of the Communists. The North Vietnamese soldiers who steered their Russian-made tanks into the streets of Saigon were harbingers of tyranny and misery for the people of Indochina, of aimlessness and impotence for the United States, and of victory after victory for the Soviet Union in its relentless campaign of conquest and domination over other Third World nations. The spectacle of desperate men, women, and children who had depended on us dragging their household possessions before the Communist invaders was an unprecedented example of American betrayal and failure.

The American withdrawal and the Communist victory were an unmitigated tragedy for the 40 million people of Vietnam, Cambodia, and Laos. Before our withdrawal, they had a chance for a better life under governments supported and influenced by the United States. Today, because we failed to meet our commitment to them, they suffer under one of the most brutal regimes in the world.

Antiwar activists had proclaimed that there would be no bloodbath in South Vietnam if the Communists won. But while the blood may not be on their hands, they cannot sleep comfortably at night as they think of the 600,000 Vietnamese who have drowned in the South China Sea attempting to escape Communist tyranny; of tens of thousands more imprisoned in "reeducation" camps; and of the unhappy lot of millions of others condemned to live under Communist rule. There was some freedom of the press before the Communists came to power; now there is none. There were some opposition political parties; now there are none. There was some attempt to have free elections; now there are none. There was some hope for a better life; now there is none. The per-capita income of the South Vietnamese was $500; now it is less than $200 in Vietnam, one of the lowest in the world.

Even more tragic is what has happened in Cambodia, one of the fallen dominoes of Southeast Asia. When we withdrew our support from the anti-Communist Cambodian government in 1975, 7 million people lived in Cambodia, about the same number who live in Austria today. Three years later, Pol Pot's new Communist government had murdered or starved to death over 2 million.

The massacre of almost a third of the population of Austria would provoke an outcry in the civilized world that would resound for decades. After the Cambodian holocaust, there was only a whisper. Two million lost souls went unmourned while the self-proclaimed humanitarians in United States antiwar circles thrashed around desperately in their efforts to find someone to blame besides themselves. They claimed that the corruption and repression of the anti-Communist Lon Nol government led to the Communist takeover. Even today they continue to make the ludicrous charge that U.S. forces, who were fighting to *prevent* the Communist conquest of Cambodia, transformed peaceful Cambodian peasants into ruthless communist murderers.

They cannot bear to look in the mirror, because if they do, they will see who must share the blame: those who opposed the U.S. war effort and in doing so gave support to the Cambodian communists—who, once they came into power, pulled the triggers and dug the mass graves.

To dwell on Indochina as it is today is to think of how it might be if the Communists had not won. Would the people of South Vietnam, Cambodia, and Laos be better off? Would aggressors in other trouble spots around the world have encountered more resistance from the West? Was the effort to stop the Communists in Indochina a just effort?

The answer to each of these questions is yes, and so the questions are rarely posed. We must pose them now if freedom is to survive and real peace is to be achieved in the world.

. . .

The American failure in Vietnam was a tragedy for the people of Indochina. It was an even greater tragedy for the United States and for millions of people in the world who, without our help, may be deprived of any chance for freedom and a better life.

Vietnam was a crucially important victory in the Soviet Union's war for control of the strategically critical Third World. It was an important victory not so much because it gave the Soviets dominance over Vietnam but because it left the United States so crippled psychologically that it was unable to defend its interests in the developing world, the battleground in the ongoing East-West conflict that is best characterized as Third World war.

Our defeat in Vietnam sparked a rash of totalitarian conquests around the world as we retreated into a five-year, self-imposed exile. In crisis after crisis in Africa, the Mideast, and Central America, critics of American involvement abroad brandished "another Vietnam" like a scepter, an all-purpose argument-stopper for any situation where it was being asserted that the United States should do something rather than nothing. While we wrung our hands and agonized over our mistakes, over 100 million people were lost to the West in the vacuum left by our withdrawal from the world stage.

The Vietnam War has grotesquely distorted the debate over American foreign policy. The willingness to use power to defend national interests is the foundation of any effective foreign policy, but our ineptness in Vietnam led many Americans to question the wisdom of using our power at all. As recently as last summer, a correspondent of one of the major networks concluded a retrospective report on the war by saying, "We do not know yet if [Vietnam was] a turning point, if we have abandoned violence or turned away from solving our problems militarily." Many of our leaders have shrunk from any use of power because they feared it would bring another disaster like the one in Vietnam. Thus did our Vietnam defeat tarnish our ideals, weaken our spirit, cripple our will, and turn us into a military giant and a diplomatic dwarf in a world in which the steadfast exercise of American power was needed more than ever before.

This fear of "another Vietnam" was a disaster for our friends around the world because it contributed to a renaissance of the isolationism to which the United States is so prone. The post-Vietnam isolationism was a particularly virulent strain brought on by the combination of our new fear of failure with the old, familiar piousness that makes some Americans reluctant to support friends and allies whose systems are less admirable than ours.

"No more Vietnams" is the battle cry of opponents of the use of American power on the world scene, especially when it takes the form of military aid to governments that are not popular in the editorial columns or the salons of the intelligentsia. It is also a prescription for continued retreat and defeat for the West.

Until we shake this Vietnam syndrome, the United States will court failure in any international initiative it undertakes— in the Third World, in East-West relations, even in relations with our friends. Behind the champagne glasses and polite smiles, every leader and diplomat we encounter in Washington and abroad wonders whether we can be counted upon in a crisis or if we will cut and run when the going gets tough. They carefully analyzed the spasmodic opposition to our small Grenada operation in key media and intellectual circles. They puzzled over the difficulty the Reagan administration encountered in trying to obtain the approval of the Congress for adequate military and economic aid to those fighting Communist aggression in Central America. From these events they cannot help but conclude that we have not recovered from the Vietnam syndrome.

They are half right and half wrong. The American people remain committed to the cause of freedom around the world. In their hearts they understand that American power plays a crucial role in that cause. Throughout the Vietnam War, a majority never stopped believing that the Communists should be prevented from winning. But their willingness to help South Vietnam resist Communist aggression was sapped by the length and seeming futility of the war, by the shrill voices of dissent, and by the trauma of Watergate. Eventually, in 1974 and 1975, when we could have kept South Vietnam afloat by keeping our commitment to provide military aid at a level commensurate with Soviet support of the North, Congress refused. The American people, by then exhausted, discouraged, and confused, tacitly accepted a congressional decision that led to a defeat for the United States for the first time in our history.

The American people have begun to emerge from the shadow of the Vietnam disaster; their election and reelection of President Reagan proved as much. But an alarming number of those political and intellectual leaders who belonged to the so-called leadership elite remain in the darkness, muttering to one another the tired old verities of the 1960s, the reassuring but thoroughly fatuous myths of Vietnam.

The twenty-year story of the Vietnam War is a long, complicated one with many characters and a wide variety of subplots. The drama is replete with missed cues and lost opportunities. Many must share the blame for missing those opportunities: the military commanders and political leaders who made political, strategic, and tactical errors in waging the war; those in the Congress who refused to do as much for our allies in South Vietnam as the Soviet Union was doing for North Vietnam; and those whose irresponsible antiwar rhetoric hampered the effort to achieve a just peace. In the end, Vietnam was lost on the political front in the United States, not on the battlefront in Southeast Asia.

Some tag the media or the antiwar movement, and frequently both, for the loss of Vietnam. It is true that some of those who covered the war so distorted the truth that it became impossible for Americans to figure out what was happening. But while the antiwar movement—a brotherhood of the misguided, the mistaken, the well-meaning, and the malevolent—was a factor in our eventual defeat, it was not the decisive factor. There have been antiwar movements for as long as there have been wars; they existed, for example, in the United States during both world wars. What overwhelms them is victory in a just cause. Those who began and escalated the war in Vietnam in the 1960s did not give the American people victories and did not effectively explain the justice of what we were fighting for. In the resulting political vacuum, the antiwar movement took center stage and held it until the curtain fell on one of the saddest endings in modern history.

Those who parrot the slogan "No more Vietnams" in opposing American efforts to prevent Communist conquests in the Third World base their case on four articles of faith:

- The war in Vietnam was immoral.
- The war in Vietnam was unwinnable.
- Diplomacy without force is the best answer to Communist "wars of national liberation."
- We were on the wrong side of history in Vietnam.

The time has come to debunk these myths.

Myth I: The Vietnam War was immoral.

The assertion that the Vietnam War was an immoral war was heard more and more often as the years dragged on. This said less about the war than about the construction that critics were putting on the idea of morality. Like all wars, Vietnam was brutal, ugly, dangerous, painful, and sometimes inhumane. This was driven home to those who stayed home perhaps more forcefully than ever before because the war lasted so long and because they saw so much of it on television in living, and dying, color.

Many who were seeing war for the first time were so shocked at what they saw that they said *this* war was *immoral* when they really meant that *all* war was *terrible*. They were right in saying that peace was better than war. But they were wrong in failing to ask themselves whether what was happening in

Vietnam was substantively different from what had happened in other wars. Their horror at the fact of war prevented them from considering whether the facts of the war in Vietnam added up to a cause that was worth fighting for. Instead, many of these naive, well-meaning, instinctual opponents of the war raised their voices in protest.

Sadly, their voices were joined with those of others who did not like the war because they did not support its aim: resisting Communist aggression in South Vietnam. These critics' outrage was thoroughly premeditated. It was not that the war was immoral, but rather that their pretensions to a higher morality dictated that the United States should lose and the Communists should win. Except for a small minority, these critics were not Communists: Some believed the Vietnamese would really be better off under the gentle rule of Ho Chi Minh and his successors. Others knew this was not true but didn't care that Ho was a totalitarian dictator. Their immorality thesis was that we were fighting an indigenous uprising in South Vietnam and therefore opposing the will of the Vietnamese people; that the people of Vietnam would be better off if we let the South Vietnamese government fall; and that our military tactics were so harsh that we needlessly and wantonly killed civilian Vietnamese.

This thesis was false on all counts.

Antiwar activists portrayed the National Liberation Front as the soul of the Vietnamese revolution, an indigenous nationalist movement that had risen spontaneously against the repressive Diem regime. This made powerful propaganda in the West, providing both rallying point for antiwar forces and apparent evidence for the frequently made contention that the United States had intervened in a civil war. In reality the National Liberation Front was a front for North Vietnam's effort to conquer the South, and as such was just another weapon in Hanoi's arsenal. Many Viet Cong had infiltrated from the North, and all took their cues from the North. When the war was over and Hanoi had no further use for it, the National Liberation Front was immediately liquidated. Instead of being awarded positions of power in the new Vietnamese government, many of its members were sent to "reeducation" camps, along with hundreds of thousands of other South Vietnamese, by those who had directed the war effort from the beginning and who now ruled all of Vietnam: the warlords in Hanoi.

In fairness to some of the antiwar activists, it could be contended that they could not have foreseen the reign of terror the Communists have brought upon the people of Vietnam, Cambodia, and Laos. While they could be charged with naivete for overlooking Ho's murderous policies in North Vietnam, some deserve credit for condemning, however belatedly, the genocide in Cambodia. Certainly today the record is clear for all to see: A Communist peace kills more than an anti-Communist war.

The claim that United States tactics caused excessive casualties among civilians must have seemed bizarre to those who were actually doing the fighting. Our forces operated under strict rules of engagement, and as a result civilians accounted for about the same proportion of casualties as in World War II and a far smaller one than in the Korean War. Many American bomber pilots were shot down, ending up dead or as POWs, because their paths across North Vietnam were chosen to minimize civilian casualties.

For example, the two weeks of bombing in December 1972, which ended American involvement in the war by convincing the North Vietnamese that they had no choice but to agree to peace terms, caused 1,500 civilian fatalities, by Hanoi's own estimate, compared with 35,000 killed in the fire-bombing of Dresden during World War II. But by 1972 the war that was being reported in the United States bore scant resemblance to the war being waged in Indochina. Most American media reports conveyed the impression that our pilots, some of whom died in the air in order to save lives on the ground, were war criminals who had caused civilian fatalities comparable to those at Dresden, Hamburg, and other German cities where civilian targets were deliberately bombed for the purpose of breaking the enemy's will to resist. By then intellectual America was so possessed by its obsessive self-hatred that, despite all evidence to the contrary, it believed the worst about the United States and the best about our enemies.

Myth II: The Vietnam War was unwinnable.

This was a favorite argument of those who did everything in their power to prevent the United States from winning. They reasoned that if the Vietnam War was proved unwinnable, then all battles against totalitarian aggression were unwinnable. If we concede their point, we are giving a green light to Communist aggression throughout the Third World.

The Vietnam War was not unwinnable. A different military and political strategy could have assured victory in the 1960s. When we signed the Paris peace agreements in 1973, we had won the war. We then proceeded to lose the peace. The South Vietnamese successfully countered Communist violations of the cease-fire for two years. Defeat came only when the Congress, ignoring the specific terms of the peace agreement, refused to provide military aid to Saigon equal to what the Soviet Union provided for Hanoi.

But the myth of unwinnability was based on a more subtle assumption.

During Vietnam many decided that wars such as the one being waged against the North Vietnamese were unwinnable because victory by Communist revolutionaries was inevitable. They believed that a liberationist surge was sweeping the Third World and that there was nothing the Western world could do, or should do, to stop it. The supposed primitiveness of our adversaries was a status cymbal they crashed loudly and proudly; that our "brutal" modern tactics were apparently ineffective against barefoot peasants in black pajamas was only further proof that their cause was right and ours was not. We were bullies, imperialists, blustery militarists armed to the teeth and fighting out of sheer bloodlust. The Communists, in contrast, were dedicated servants of principle, armed with lit-

121

tle more than the joyful conviction that they were fighting for country, freedom, and justice.

The assertion that our very bigness is badness has infested our culture to a surprising and troubling degree. The creator of the phenomenally successful *Star Wars* series recently explained that the climactic scene in one of his movies—in which the evil "Empire's" giant war machines are destroyed by fuzzy little good guys with wooden bows and arrows—was inspired by the Vietnam experience. No matter that in Vietnam the Communist "good guys" packed Soviet automatic rifles and, in 1975, rode state-of-the-art Russian tanks across the South Vietnamese border. The propaganda of disproportionate forces in Vietnam, the myth of small/good versus big/bad, did enough damage to help lose the war for the United States and the people of South Vietnam. Today it is one symptom of the Vietnam syndrome to the extent that it makes Americans ashamed of their power, guilty about being strong, and forgetful about the need to be willing to use their power to protect their freedom and the freedom of others.

Myth III: Diplomacy without force to back it up is the best answer to Communist "wars of national liberation."

As with all the myths about the Vietnam War, it is important to distinguish between those who *believe* them and those who *use* them in pursuit of their own ends. Some do not want the U.S. to help non-Communist governments because they think it would be better if the Communists took power. Others believe that the use of military power by the U.S. has become irrelevant in Third World conflicts because we used power so ineptly in Vietnam. After all, they argue, since we were defeated by a tiny country like North Vietnam, we must have forgotten *how* to win.

As a result, in the post-Vietnam 1970s, while rhetoric about the limits of power and the promise of creative diplomacy clouded the American political landscape, the Soviet Union and its proxies licked their chops and gobbled up South Yemen, Ethiopia, Angola, Mozambique, Afghanistan, and Nicaragua, and the Ayatollah's mullahs plunged Iran into the Middle Ages. Each of the 100 million people who were lost to the West during our five-year geopolitical sabbatical is a living symbol of the sterility of arguments about peaceful diplomacy. Any nation that decides the way to achieve peace is to use only peaceful means is a nation that will soon be a piece of another nation. Its enemies will quickly take advantage of its good intentions.

Some critics believe we should never use our power to help a friend who faces aggression. Others believe we should help only those who come up to our rigorous standards of political conduct. We face such a challenge in Central America today. As was the case in Vietnam, totalitarian Communist aggression, which could not survive without the backing of the Soviet Union, is being brought to bear through both covert and direct means against local governments that are far better than the Communist alternative but which cannot pass muster in the rarefied atmosphere of intellectual America.

Increasingly the world balance of power will be determined by who wins these key conflicts in the Third World. To play an effective role, the U.S. must at times side with authoritarian governments that do not come up to our standards in protecting human rights in order to keep from power totalitarian regimes that would deny all human rights. Frequently, however, critics in the Congress and the media pass up the role of world policeman in favor of the role of kindergarten teacher, slapping the wrists of those who throw paperwads in the classrooms and ignoring those who are throwing Molotov cocktails in the streets. The United States must learn to accept the fact that there may be occasional lapses in the behavior of its friends or it will find itself surrounded by enemies.

Many of the high-minded critics of our association with less-than-perfect regimes are probably irredeemable. However, those who want the United States to play a major role on the international stage but are afraid that we will fail again need only be shown that failure in Vietnam was not inevitable.

Myth IV: We were on the wrong side of history in Vietnam.

British historian Paul Johnson has written that the essence of geopolitics is the ability to distinguish between different degrees of evil. He might have added that it is also the *willingness* to be objective enough to weigh the motives and actions of both sides in any conflict with an equally critical eye. Vietnam proved that, at least for many American intellectuals, this is virtually impossible to do. During the Vietnam era, an astounding number of otherwise thoughtful people gave our side the white glove test while eagerly seeking to justify the far more brutal actions of the enemy.

Often statements by American and South Vietnamese military authorities were assumed to be lies by the same reporters who printed North Vietnamese lies without question. A hue and cry was raised against the United States when an isolated incident of mass murder by American forces at My Lai was revealed; yet when the West learned of the massacre by the Communists at Hue, where twenty-five times as many civilians as at My Lai died in what was anything but an isolated incident, Amnesty International indulgently chalked the crime up to "the merciless tradition of the war" rather than to the merciless bestiality of the Viet Cong. Those who can always see the faults of our friends on the right are too often blind to the faults of our enemies on the left.

It was not that these critics necessarily disliked the United States. It was that they were sapped, as many before them had been, by the Communist PR blitz, the intellectual dream machine that, ever since the Russian Revolution in 1917, has been tricking Western intellectuals into looking at slavery and seeing utopia, looking at aggression and conquest and seeing liberation, looking at ruthless murderers and seeing "agrarian reformers," looking at idealized portraits of Ho Chi Minh gazing beneficently upon the children gathered around him and seeing a mythical national father figure rather than the brutal dictator he really was.

Many who opposed the war sincerely believed, since the Communists told them so, that South Vietnam would be happy and free under the Communists and that the Americans were simply out of touch with the reality of life in Indochina. Events since 1975 have proved instead that the ones who were out of touch were the bighearted, freedom-loving reporters, editorial writers, academics, and politicians who could not bring themselves to believe that the United States was doing exactly what it said it was doing in Vietnam from the beginning: trying to save the South from being conquered by forces that would enslave it.

Three years ago, writer Susan Sontag appeared before a conference hastily assembled in New York by a leftist coalition that hoped to save some face in the wake of the Soviet Union's brutal crackdown against the Polish labor movement. But when she stepped to the podium, she outraged her colleagues by stating that communism was a form of fascism and that those who read the conservative *Reader's Digest* knew more about the true nature of communism than those who read the ultraliberal *Nation*. The statements themselves, while true, were not particularly novel. What was most revealing was the vilification to which Sontag was subjected in the weeks that followed. It was further evidence of the capacity of the American left—even after the deaths of hundreds of millions under Lenin, Stalin, Mao, and now Cambodian Communist Pol Pot—for self-deception. It reminds us that among those who say the nations of the West are on the wrong side of history in the fight against communism are people who actually write the history. Unfortunately, they will continue to exert tremendous influence in foreign policy debates.

The war against the Vietnam syndrome, then, must be waged on two fronts. First, we must resist the laudable but often excessive idealism in the American character that prevents us from being as skeptical about the actions and motives of "forces of national liberation" as history teaches us we should be. Second, we must recover our confidence in our ability to wield power effectively.

Examining the Vietnam experience can help us on both these fronts. It shows us the true nature of our adversaries in Third World war and how effectively they can hide their intentions behind a dense screen of propaganda and shrewd political manipulation. And it teaches us that it is not wars such as Vietnam, but rather waging them ineffectively and losing, that leads inevitably to tragedy.

Everyone hopes the United States will not have to fight another war like the Vietnam War. The best way for us to avoid such a war is to be unmistakable in our will and sure of our ability to fight one if we must. But getting over the Vietnam syndrome means more than standing ready to use American military forces. It means being willing to provide military aid to friends who need it; being united, with each other and with our Western allies, in our responses to Soviet-backed aggression around the world; and, above all, having the wisdom and the vision to support nonmilitary programs to address the poverty, injustice, and political instability that plague so many Third World countries.

The antiwar movement did not have a decisive effect on the outcome of the war from a military standpoint, but it has had a decisive impact on the political battles that have been waged ever since. The protesters' rioting and bombing, all undertaken in the name of peace, ended with our withdrawal from Southeast Asia. Most of the physical damage has been repaired. The intellectual and psychological damage, however, still poisons our foreign policy debates. Ten years later the same distortions about the war that made antiwar activists into heroes on the campuses are still accepted as fact on television, in newspapers, and in college classrooms. Before we can cure ourselves of the Vietnam syndrome, we must purge our diet of the intellectual junk food that helped make us sick to begin with.

HOW THE VIETNAM WAR BEGAN

The Vietnam War began when World War II ended. The war in the Pacific radically changed the geopolitical landscape of Southeast Asia. It marked the end of Japan's regional hegemony and, most significantly, the beginning of the end of colonialism.

The great powers were totally at odds on the future of the European empires. President Roosevelt insisted on rapid decolonization. Prime Minister Churchill and General de Gaulle demanded a return to the status quo *ante bellum*. General Secretary Stalin, while talking of national independence for the colonies, consolidated his grip on Eastern Europe and began scanning the world for possible Communist conquests like a vulture searching for fresh carcasses.

Churchill had once proclaimed that he had not become the King's First Minister in order to oversee the dissolution of the British Empire. But this was his heart and not his head speaking. As a realist, he knew that independence for the colonies was inevitable. Nationalism was fermenting beneath the surface in all of them. It was not a question of whether movements for independence would arise, for they already had, but rather whether they would win power by peaceful or violent means and whether they would be controlled by true nationalists or by Communists who would impose a new colonialism far more oppressive than any that had come before. Would the colonies trade their old masters for new ones—or would they finally become their own?

France had ruled all of Indochina—Laos, Cambodia, and Vietnam—for over half a century. The French first had controlled only southern Vietnam, but local politics, geopolitical competition from China, and imperial ambition soon led them to conquer the entire region. Some popular histories portray French colonial rule as an unrelieved reign of terror. That picture is less a truth than it is a caricature. Like other imperial powers, France was often guilty of economic exploitation of its colonies, but the French also instituted social programs, particularly in education and land development, that greatly improved the lot of the average Vietnamese. The hospitals, schools, and other public facilities Mrs. Nixon and I visited in French colonial Hanoi in 1953 were among the best we saw on our official visits to over fifty Third World countries during the Eisenhower years. However, although in many respects Vietnam did benefit from their presence, the French failed in the most critical respect: They lacked the vision to prepare the Vietnamese for eventual self-rule and to set up a process to ensure stable government during the transition.

Vietnam was destined to be independent. In the 1920s and 1930s, Vietnamese resentments over colonial rule, coupled with a deep sense of nationalism, led to a ground swell of opposition to the French. The fashionable view that only Ho Chi Minh's Communist party sought independence is a myth. Scores of political groups organized to alter Vietnam's status as a colony. These included the Constitutionalist party, the Vietnam People's Progressive party, the Journey East movement, the League of East Asian Peoples, the Vietnam Restoration, the Vietnamese Nationalist party, the Vietnam Restoration Association, the Greater Vietnam Nationalist party, and two militant religious sects. Some sought self-determination within the French Community. Others wanted to break all ties with France and pushed for open warfare. Still others favored collaboration with Japan.

The turning point was World War II. The Japanese conquests of Southeast Asia shattered the aura of invincibility that the European powers had enjoyed as colonial masters. After the war, Europe's former subjects no longer held them in awe and would not tolerate foreign rule indefinitely. The Europeans found that they could either grant independence to their colonies voluntarily or be driven out militarily. Some, like the British in Malaysia, saw the writing on the wall and provided for a peaceful transition to independence. Others, like the French in Vietnam, asserted that they had come, as one French general put it, "to reclaim our inheritance" and delayed serious consideration of independence until it was too late to do so without bloodshed.

For France the result was the first Vietnam War. From 1946 to 1954, the French battled Vietnamese insurgents in a vain attempt to stay in Indochina. The United States from the outset urged France to give the colonies their independence. Roosevelt, Truman, and Eisenhower all pushed for decolonization. But it took over $5 billion in military expenditures and 150,000 casualties before the French government was forced to follow that advice.

France's principal enemy was the Communist Viet Minh, led by Ho Chi Minh. During World War II, Ho had taken carefully calculated steps to position himself to strike for power afterward. At the war's end, his opportunity came. Through ruthless and adroit infighting, he had eliminated his nationalist rivals as significant military forces. When the sudden surrender of Japan produced a vacuum of power in Vietnam, Ho moved quickly to exploit it. In 1945 he seized power in northern Vietnam and declared the creation of the Democratic Republic of Vietnam.

In 1945, when the French returned, they easily reestablished their control in southern Vietnam and extended their rule to northern Vietnam through the March 6, 1946, agreement with the Viet Minh. The French controlled all important cities but had no sound strategy to retake the countryside. They poured resources into building fortifications and spread themselves too thinly in widely scattered outposts. After relations between the French and the Communists broke down, the Viet Minh adopted the tactics of the weak—constant skirmishes, hit-and-run attacks, ambushes along jungle roads, always avoiding anything approaching an even test of strength. They also built a parallel government alongside the French colonial administration to organize those who supported them and to subdue or liquidate those who did not. Despite these efforts, the French continued to hold the upper hand through the 1940s.

The Vietnamese people had divided allegiances. Some, including many who were not Communists, joined the Viet Minh because it was the only group offering military resistance to the French. Others, including many nationalists, supported the French, apparently preferring foreign rule to Communist rule. The fact that 200,000 Laotians, Cambodians, and Vietnamese joined the French-controlled Armed Forces of the Associated States of Indochina suggested the Viet Minh Communists were even more despised than the French colonialists. But the vast majority of the Vietnamese people remained neutral. Mindful of the costs that backing a loser can carry in Asian politics, they patiently waited to see which way the prevailing winds would blow.

The United States kept the French war at arm's length. Truman wanted non-Communist governments in Cambodia, Laos, and Vietnam, but he did not want to taint American policy with colonialism by cooperating with the French in their war against the Viet Minh. He understood that the Indochinese needed to be given a stake in the battle against communism; they would not fight indefinitely in order to keep Indochina for the French, but they would do so if they were defending their own governments. Still, Truman believed he had little leverage to force the French to decolonize. His priorities were in Europe, where he needed French help to ward off a bellicose Soviet Union, and therefore he was reluctant to antagonize France over Indochina.

The fall of China to Mao's Red Army in 1949 swept away previous assumptions. The French, who had planned to grind down their weak opponent, now had to fight an enemy who, as a result of assistance from the Chinese, was better armed and supplied. Ho, who had waged a poor man's war, now could turn up the heat on the French. Truman, who had considered the war a colonialist misadventure, now saw it as a necessary element in his strategy to contain the expansion of communism. And when Communist Chinese troops intervened in the Korean War in late 1950, Truman came to regard the French in Indochina as the means to draw at least some Chinese forces away from the Korean peninsula.

Chairman Mao became Uncle Ho's godfather. He overhauled the Viet Minh's primitive forces, training its troops at Chinese bases and providing them with combat advisers, trucks, artillery, and automatic weapons. With six 10,000-man divisions, Ho had an army that could engage the French in positional warfare. Over the next three years, the Viet Minh cleared the French out of the areas adjacent to China but failed to take any major population or agricultural centers. In 1954, Ho's forces retreated toward Laos, but the French pursued them, establishing their principal base at Dien Bien Phu.

The French decision to entrench their forces there was a cataclysmic strategic miscalculation. Those who supported it were defending the defense of the indefensible: Dien Bien Phu was an isolated island of French power in a sea of Viet Minh territory. The French base invited attack. Supplies could reach it only by air, and it was situated in a basin dominated by surrounding high ground held by the Viet Minh. Ho would have been a fool not to hit it with all the force he could muster. Ho was no fool.

The battle began in March 1954. The Viet Minh captured the outlying defensive positions in the first two weeks and then used its five-to-one advantage in troops to launch massive human-wave attacks. They surrounded the 16,000-man French garrison and then inexorably tightened the noose. They pummeled French positions with artillery shells, expending over 350,000 rounds by the end of the siege, and encroached on the fortress with a network of trenches reminiscent of World War I. With their airstrip pockmarked with artillery craters, the French were prisoners in their own fortress. They could not evacuate the wounded. Supplies and reinforcements had to be dropped in by parachute, and when the weather turned bad, little got through at all. By early April, the situation looked hopeless.

The battle of Dien Bien Phu dealt a death blow to French morale. Because only about 5 percent of French forces in Indochina were involved, even total defeat at Dien Bien Phu could not have been decisive in the outcome of the war. But it had taken on symbolic importance out of proportion to its significance and proved to be a mortal psychological defeat. Ho Chi Minh had once said, "You can kill ten of my men for every one I kill of yours. But even at those odds, you will lose and I will win."

He turned out to be right. The Viet Minh suffered over three times as many casualties as the French did at Dien Bien Phu, but it was the French will to resist that was broken. Opposition to the war had been building in France. Now it snowballed. In the end, the war was lost on the home front in France rather than on the battlefields of Vietnam. No one dreamed that the same thing would happen to the United States twenty years later.

Our primary interest in Vietnam was to prevent the fall of Indochina to the Communists. We wanted to prevent the loss of Vietnam because we believed it would lead to the fall of the rest of Southeast Asia. This came to be known as the "domino theory." It was first set forth during the Truman administration in 1952. A National Security Council memorandum stated that in Southeast Asia "the loss of any single country would probably lead to relatively swift submission to or an alignment with communism by the remaining countries of this group." Dominoes would continue to fall because "an alignment with communism of the rest of Southeast Asia and India, and in the longer term, of the Middle East . . . would in all probability progressively follow. Such widespread alignment would endanger the stability and security of Europe."

John F. Kennedy, then a senator, expressed the domino theory even more vividly two years after the fall of Dien Bien Phu, when in a speech he described Vietnam as "the cornerstone of the Free World in Southeast Asia, the keystone to the arch, the finger in the dike. Burma, Thailand, India, Japan, and obviously Laos and Cambodia would be threatened if the red tide of communism overflowed into Vietnam."

Many would scoff at the domino theory in later years. But it is revealing to note that the siege of Dien Bien Phu was made possible only by the fall of Asia's largest domino—China. With the French war effort in imminent danger of collapse, the United States had to decide what it would do to stop the next domino from tumbling over.

When France asked the United States for help at Dien Bien Phu, its request was for air strikes, not ground troops. Only if the French were to withdraw from Vietnam would ground troops be needed. Having visited Vietnam the previous November, I made the point in a National Security Council meeting that our choice was to help the French now or be faced with the necessity of taking over the burden of preventing a Communist takeover later. Admiral Arthur Radford, the chairman of the Joint Chiefs of Staff, suggested that we use sixty B-29 bombers in the Philippines in night raids to destroy the Viet Minh positions. He also devised a plan, known as Operation Vulture, for accomplishing the same objective with three small tactical atomic bombs. This option was never seriously considered. President Eisenhower later spoke of possibly using diversionary tactics, such as a naval blockade, against the Viet Minh's patrons and principal source of military supplies, the Communist Chinese. This plan was also abandoned.

Both Eisenhower and Secretary of State John Foster Dulles

were reluctant to take any of these steps. Like Truman, they believed any direct intervention to help the French would gravely damage our relations with newly independent countries. The President also insisted that we had to have congressional approval before acting. When the administration tested the waters, it found significant opposition to the idea of another military involvement in Asia, especially so soon after the Korean War. Eisenhower concluded that he could bring the Congress along only if the United States acted in concert with its allies.

The proposal for united action ran into a roadblock in Britain: Prime Minister Churchill refused to cooperate. Eisenhower sent Radford for consultations. Churchill bluntly told the American admiral that if the British would not fight to stay in India, he saw no reason why they should fight to help the French stay in Indochina. Eisenhower steadfastly opposed a unilateral American intervention. The French were therefore left to fend for themselves.

On May 7, 1954, after fifty-five days of gallantly defending a territory that had been reduced to the size of a baseball field, the French garrison at Dien Bien Phu was overrun by human-wave assaults. The defeat signaled the beginning of a complete and rapid withdrawal of the French from all of Indochina and left the United States as the only power capable of blocking further Communist expansion in Southeast Asia.

Our first critical mistake in Vietnam was not to have intervened in the battle of Dien Bien Phu. The military situation was tailor-made for the use of our air power. The Viet Minh's siege required them to concentrate huge stores of matériel and hordes of soldiers in a relatively small area, and the terrain restricted them to only a few supply routes. The French air force in Indochina, which consisted of only 100 tactical bombers, was too weak to exploit this vulnerability. But if we had sent in fleets of heavy bombers to drop conventional explosives, we could have crippled the Viet Minh in a matter of days.

The French were in a much stronger position in Indochina

as a whole than the plight of their isolated garrison indicated. In his memoirs, Nikita Khrushchev wrote that in 1954 the situation for the Viet Minh was "very grave" and that "the resistance movement in Vietnam was on the brink of collapse." Khrushchev also reported that Zhou Enlai had said that unless the Geneva Conference concluded a cease-fire soon, the Viet Minh would not be able to hold out against the French. According to an official North Vietnamese history published in 1965, the Communists were seriously worried about the effect a possible American intervention would have on the balance of power in the war. Mao's support of the Viet Minh had kept his friends' hopes alive. We could have dashed them permanently if we had given our friends the support they needed at a pivotal moment.

By standing aside as our ally went down to defeat, the United States lost its last chance to stop the expansion of communism in Southeast Asia at little cost to itself. We should have intervened alone if necessary to help the French because they were the strongest regional power fighting Communist aggression. If we had saved Dien Bien Phu, the French still probably would have withdrawn and finally given their colonies independence, as we had urged for so long, but they would have done so in a deliberate and responsible manner rather than in a headlong rush for the door.

An obsessive fear of associating with European colonial powers blinded successive American administrations to a very simple fact: Communism, not colonialism, was the *principal* cause of the war in Indochina. Colonialism complicated the prosecution of the French phase of the war, because it allowed the Communists to obscure the issue, but the war itself originated in Ho Chi Minh's willful push for total power and was sustained by Communist China's massive support of the Viet Minh. Our mistake was failing to understand that the issue was not whether colonialism would succeed, but what would succeed colonialism.

. . .

The Geneva Conference of 1954 temporarily settled the question of who would be the successors to the French. Its declaration divided Vietnam into two countries: Communist North Vietnam and independent South Vietnam. But the long-term fate of Vietnam and of America in Vietnam was intertwined with the destinies of two leaders: Ho Chi Minh and Ngo Dinh Diem.

If Ho Chi Minh's popular image is any indication, he must have had the world's best public-relations organization working for him. Madison Avenue at its cleverest can only bow in deference. The typical line on Ho runs like this: Ho, though he was a Communist, was first and foremost a nationalist. He was variously described as a charismatic Vietnamese George Washington who led his people against French colonialists; an Asian Tito who turned for help to the Soviet Union and Communist China only after being spurned by American administrations obsessed with the Cold War; and a humanitarian Uncle Ho who preached about the need for liberation, literacy, and land reform.

In fact, Ho Chi Minh was a brilliant fraud who spent his life pretending to be exactly the opposite of what he really was. He was a nationalist only in the sense that he could not establish a Communist state in Vietnam if it was part of the French Empire. His only loyalty was to winning power for himself and his ideology. That made tactical calculations simple. He reasoned that if the French were in power, it meant he was not in power; and that if the French would not put him in power, they would have to be removed from power to make room for him.

There is almost nothing in Ho's biography to indicate that he placed nationalism above communism. In 1911, at the age of 21, he left Vietnam. While most Vietnamese nationalists exiled themselves to Japan, he went to France. Nine years later, he was a founding member of the French Communist party. He once wrote in the party's newspaper, L' Humanite, that nationalism, if left uncontrolled, was a "dangerous phenomenon" that could threaten the spread of communism in colonial areas. In 1923, the Soviets brought him to Moscow, where he was trained and indoctrinated as an agent of the Communist International. The Comintern, as it was called, demanded absolute fidelity to the Soviet Union, even if this required its members to betray their native lands. He spent the next two decades either in Moscow studying the science of revolution at Lenin University or in Southeast Asia practicing it for the Comintern.

Ho formed alliances with virtually all of Vietnam's nationalist groups, but he never put the common interest above his own. He cooperated with true nationalists only if he could advance his ambitions by doing so. When their interests collided with his, he destroyed them. In 1925, he betrayed Vietnam's most prominent nationalist, Phan Boi Chau, to the French secret police. Communist histories state that Phan walked right into a trap. But they do not mention that it was Ho who had set it up, for a payoff of 100,000 piasters. At the time, Ho justified his treachery by telling his comrades that Phan was a nationalist, not a Communist, and that as such he would have been a rival in the future.

Those arguing that Ho was a nationalist always point to the appeals he made to the United States on behalf of Vietnam after World War II. Many know that he repeatedly offered to ally himself with us in exchange for our recognizing an independent Vietnam under his leadership. But few know the entire story. His actions were actually nothing more than an ingenious ruse to propel himself to prominence and power in Vietnam.

Ho was virtually unknown to the Vietnamese people during World War II. He knew that to win the postwar struggle for power, he first had to win the support of a foreign power, whether it be the United States, China, or France. He ingratiated himself with several American intelligence officers stationed in Vietnam, plying them with information, charm, and flattery. His tactic worked. They supplied Ho with American weapons, which came in handy when he seized power in

Hanoi shortly after the war. They also bombarded Washington with memoranda urging that the United States back the Viet Minh.

On September 2, 1945, when Ho delivered the speech proclaiming the creation of the Democratic Republic of Vietnam, his newfound American friends loyally stood by his side and even saluted the Communist flag. In his remarks, Ho quoted from the Declaration of Independence: "We hold these truths to be self-evident, that all men are created equal, that they are endowed by their Creator with certain unalienable Rights, that among these are Life, Liberty, and the pursuit of Happiness." But Ho's actions spoke louder than his words. Three days later, his government outlawed Vietnam's largest nationalist political parties. Nevertheless, one O.S.S. officer later remembered Ho as "an awfully sweet guy."

Some believe Ho really wanted to be on our side. But the truth is that Ho wanted it to appear that *we* were on *his* side. Our association with him had a decisive impact on events. For the Vietnamese people, who trusted and believed in the United States, our officials' presence at Ho's speech conferred a degree of legitimacy and prominence that no other figure possessed. He proceeded to play this to the hilt. Emperor Bao Dai, who headed the French puppet government in the South, abdicated within days, later saying that he did so because he had heard the United States had thrown its support behind Ho. No other group could soon overcome the political momentum Ho gained by flim-flamming those pathetically gullible O.S.S. officers.

The postwar occupation forces of Britain, the United States, and China soon left Vietnam, and France returned. While nationalist groups refused to cooperate with the French, the Communist Viet Minh chose to collaborate. Ho signed the so-called March 6 agreement that brought the French army back into northern Vietnam. His greetings were effusive: "I love France and French soldiers. You are welcome. You are all heroes." Some say Ho compromised with the French to force the Nationalist Chinese to withdraw. But one week earlier, China had pledged to remove its army in a separate agreement with

France. As to the real motivation of the Communists, Ho's right-hand man, Le Duan, later said it was to "wipe out the reactionaries." For the Viet Minh, this included all nationalists.

Ho and the French together massacred hundreds of leaders and thousands of rank-and-file members of nationalist groups. The French gave the Viet Minh military equipment, troops, and even artillery support to carry this out. In July 1946, Ho's forces stormed the headquarters of all the remaining nationalist groups while French armored personnel carriers cordoned off surrounding areas. Most of the few remaining opposition leaders were arrested and later killed. When the French turned on the Viet Minh in November 1946, it was no accident that Ho became the leader of the only significant resistance. He had killed almost all the others.

The idea that Ho Chi Minh was primarily a Vietnamese nationalist has no basis in fact. Instead of cooperating with nationalists to win independence, he spent his entire career eliminating all independent nationalists, even if this meant openly collaborating with colonial France. Though he used the rhetoric of nationalism, Ho was first and foremost a Communist totalitarian. He used nationalism to serve communism rather than the other way around.

Ho's reputation in the West as a popular humanitarian is equally unfounded. When he took over half of the country under the Geneva Declaration, the Vietnamese people were given sixty days to resettle on either side of the line dividing North and South Vietnam. One million northerners out of a total population of 13 million moved south, while only 90,000 southerners went north. The number of refugees leaving North Vietnam would have been several times greater had the Communists not impeded their departure. Two years later, in 1956, Mrs. Nixon and I visited a refugee camp in South Vietnam. Thousands of people lived there in crowded tents with only those few possessions that they had been able to carry on their backs. It was a heartrending sight that recurred often during the war. The Vietnamese people voted with their feet, and the result was a landslide against the Communists.

It was easy to see why. Land reform stood at the top of Ho's agenda for North Vietnam. He had promised the peasants a program of "land to the tiller," but he delivered one of terror to the tiller. Ninety-eight percent of northern farmers cultivated their own land in 1954, but this did not stop the Communists from finding criminal "landlords" to fill the ever-escalating quota set by Hanoi. One witness said, "At least five percent of a village's population had to be branded as 'landlords.' " A North Vietnamese army officer who had served in the land-reform campaign and later defected said that "these crimes were only fabrications that the cadres said had been committed."

Ho's men first tortured the victims to extract a confession. Some were hung by their feet from ropes thrown over a rafter and then were beaten or violently pulled up and down. Others had their thumbs placed in a vise that was steadily tightened; with each turn of the screw, the interrogator repeated his question. Still others were put in a water-filled bamboo barrel and then immersed for a couple of minutes at a time until they confessed. A rigged public trial usually followed the confession.

These exercises were brutal travesties. During this period, one grade-school teacher asked her students to write an essay on "a scene of struggle in our village." The children obediently composed essays that combined the usual high praise of the Communist party with graphic accounts of arrests, beatings, and tortures. Officially, the party disclaimed responsibility for the terrorism, so the teacher criticized her pupils for their "inaccuracy." But in their youthful innocence, the students asserted that they themselves had witnessed these scenes, and some even said they had seen party members arranging the trials.

These so-called trials commonly ended in a sentence of death. Throughout the terror of the land-reform program, Ho

Chi Minh's party dutifully acted according to one maxim: "It is better to kill ten innocent people than to let one enemy escape." Estimates are that 50,000 Vietnamese were executed and that another 100,000 were sent to forced-labor camps.

The torment of Ho's policies did not end there. The families of convicted "landlords" then faced a government-inspired policy of social isolation. Ho knew his regime had earned the permanent enmity of the families of his victims. In his mind, they were possible future opponents and therefore had to be liquidated. Orders were handed down that no one was to talk with them, contact them, or give them work. One witness said, "Like leprous dogs, they became creatures at whom children were encouraged to throw stones." These outcasts usually died of starvation. It is estimated that between 300,000 and 500,000 peasants either committed suicide or died as a result of the policy of isolation.

There are those who say that Ho temporarily lost control of the revolution and that local peasants acting on their own chalked up this toll of terror. That is a fatuous claim. He knew exactly what he was doing. The policy was not improvised. It was imported. The whole program, from blueprints through training manuals, was stamped "Made in Communist China." He knew very well that these same policies had led to a reign of terror that killed millions of Chinese peasants, but he adopted them nevertheless. He wanted excessive violence and deliberately planned for it. "To straighten a curved piece of bamboo," he told key party members, "one must bend it in the opposite direction, holding it in that position for a while. Then, when the hand is removed it will slowly straighten itself."

Behind Ho Chi Minh's cruel policies was a brutally simple motive: He wanted to demonstrate with searing clarity that there was no alternative in North Vietnam to life under communism.

But there *was* an alternative: It was in South Vietnam. Ngo Dinh Diem had built a state that was substantially free, but, by American standards, not completely free. Like most post-colonial leaders, he governed in a manner that drew its inspiration partly from European parliamentary models, partly from traditional Asian models, and partly from the dictates of necessity.

Unlike Ho, Diem was an authentic nationalist. He came from an important family in the imperial capital of Hue and was renowned for his vehement opposition to French colonialism. A devout Catholic, he studied for two years at a Maryknoll academy in the United States. In 1933, he agreed to serve as Minister of the Interior of Annam in central Vietnam on the condition that the French undertake certain reforms, including the creation of a national assembly to govern the country. After three months of French inaction, he resigned in anger. But his prominence led to a long succession of offers. The French, who both respected and feared Diem, alternately courted him with offers of public office and threatened him with arrest. He turned down a post in Japan's wartime occupation government. After the war, Bao Dai, France's puppet head of state, repeatedly beseeched his help.

Even Ho respected Diem's patriotism—enough in fact to have him imprisoned and one of his brothers killed in 1945. Ho exiled Diem to a village near the Chinese border, where he nearly died of malaria. After six months, the Viet Minh leader summoned his future rival to offer him the Ministry of Interior in the new Communist government. Diem rejected it in a stormy exchange and was released. A Communist official later said, "Considering the events that followed, releasing Diem was a blunder." Soon after, Ho, yet again showing his respect for Diem's abilities, sentenced him to death in absentia.

Ho's respect for Diem was fully justified. In 1954, after the partition of Vietnam, Bao Dai appointed him Prime Minister with full powers. Diem faced a bewildering political task. Properly speaking, there was no state of South Vietnam, only a state of anarchy. Pro-French elements hostile to Diem ran the military and the civil service. Binh Xuyen bandits controlled the Saigon police and openly defied him. Two armed religious sects, the Cao Dai and the Hoa Hao, and rural ethnic Montagnards were in constant revolt. Before moving north, the Viet Minh had left behind a powerful infrastructure to subvert the government. A million refugees from North Vietnam, who had increased South Vietnam's population by 10 percent almost overnight, awaited resettlement.

Most observers did not expect Diem to survive in power for even a year. But within two years, he had purged disloyal army officers and government officials, seized control of Saigon's police force, divided and subdued the militant sects, routed the Viet Minh, defeated Bao Dai in a presidential referendum, and was looking forward to the election of a Constituent Assembly to draft a new constitution. When I visited Saigon on the first anniversary of his presidency in 1956, I was surprised and impressed by the progress he had made in bringing order out of chaos and in gaining broad support from the Vietnamese people.

Diem understood that the first task of government is to establish order. Without a strong ruler, South Vietnam's inherent anarchy and factionalism would have shattered the country's fragile stability. Diem's actions were all legitimate acts of government. But they were not without costs. Several thousand South Vietnamese were killed on all sides of the many internecine conflicts between 1954 and 1959. That toll was regrettable, but almost certainly would have been higher if the Communists or another of Diem's rivals had been in power.

By our standards Diem took excessive actions. He often used his power arbitrarily to suppress critical newspapers and to persecute political opponents, failing to distinguish between enemies of the state and opponents of his government. When I spoke to him of these excesses in 1956, he defended his actions by pointing out that in dealing with Communist violence and armed insurrection, ordinary peacetime rules of conduct would lead to Communist victory. "We are at war," he said, "and in war it is necessary to use wartime measures." In 1955, Diem conducted a ruthless nationwide purge of Communists and their sympathizers, shipping off tens of thousands of South Vietnamese to harsh ideological reeducation camps.

Many were part of the Communist network, two-thirds of which was uprooted, but a large percentage were innocent. Once the assault on the Viet Minh underground was completed, political repression in South Vietnam was minimal by East Asian standards. Under Diem, there were at most 300 political prisoners in 1960, while in Burma and Indonesia they numbered in the tens of thousands.

Diem, having imposed order, faced the second task of government: securing the consent of the governed. It was an almost impossible job given the fractious nature of South Vietnamese politics, and his record was mixed. His high-handed style of governing squandered much of the goodwill with which he began, and his willful actions earned him more than his share of enemies, many of whom had friends among the American press in Saigon. But among simple Vietnamese in the countryside, he was a legitimately popular figure.

Some of his popularity derived from his political reforms. Diem's government provided far more freedom than had the French. He also took the first tentative steps toward electoral democracy in a country that had never held an election. Like most Southeast Asian politicians, he tampered with the ballot box. In 1955, for example, the results of the presidential referendum showed him taking a preposterous 98.2 percent of the vote. A fair tally would have been lopsided—with Diem polling perhaps 90 percent—because his opponent, Bao Dai, had never been one to win popularity contests. But even against a strong opponent—Diem undoubtedly would have won a properly conducted election—probably with no less than 65 percent of the vote—because his popularity had reached a high level by that time.

South Vietnam had more of the form than the substance of democracy, but the latter was not wholly lacking. The political opposition, for example, received representation. In the elections for the Constituent Assembly in 1956, one-third of the winning candidates were anti-Diem, and this proportion would have been higher had some parties not boycotted the election. When the assembly convened, it promptly rejected

Diem's draft for the new constitution and rewrote the document itself. But American-style democracy always evoked skepticism in Diem, for he knew meaningful elections consisted of more than ballots and voting stations. As he once asked a reporter, "What can parliamentary democracy mean to a Montagnard when his language does not even have a term to express it?"

Most of Diem's popularity came from the vast array of social programs and reforms that he instituted with American financial and technical assistance. Schools proliferated in the countryside. Land was redistributed to tenant farmers. Pesticides were sprayed to combat malaria. Rice production soared. Roads and bridges were built. Foreign investment increased. Light industry sprang up around Saigon. Two or three days a week, Diem would tour the countryside, scrutinizing the progress of his plans on the local level and inundating officials with advice. Although his programs often taxed his government's meager administrative capabilities, their effect was overwhelmingly beneficial.

When the two leaders are compared side-by-side, the suggestion that Ho would have outpolled Diem head-to-head seems ridiculous. Yet during the war, many critics of the American effort to save South Vietnam argued this very point. They said that the Geneva Declaration of 1954 legally bound Diem's government and the United States to unify the two halves of Vietnam through elections and that Ho would have inevitably come out the winner. They were wrong on both counts.

The text of the Geneva Declaration about elections was not legally binding on the United States or South Vietnam. Nine countries gathered at the conference and produced six unilateral declarations, three bilateral cease-fire agreements, and one unsigned declaration. The cease-fire agreements alone were binding for their signatories; the provision concerning reunification elections appeared in the separate final declaration. Only four of the nine states attending committed themselves to the declaration's terms. The United States did not join in it. South Vietnam, which was not even present in Geneva, retained its freedom of action by issuing a formal statement disavowing the declaration. North Vietnam also did not associate itself with the declaration. Very simply, it had no legal force.

Nor did any of the participants expect elections to occur. The Geneva Conference was intended not to establish peace for all time through the ballot box but rather to create a partition of Vietnam similar to that of Korea. Partition was formally treated as a temporary expedient, but all major participants expected it to be permanent. Whatever their words about elections, their actions revealed their intent: They established two governments, allowed for two separate military forces, and arranged for the movement of refugees between the zones. It would have been senseless to go through all this trouble in 1954 only to turn around and undo it after elections in 1956.

The whole idea was wildly unrealistic in any case. Reunification was supposedly to be decided by free elections. Because elections would not be free in North Vietnam, South Vietnam could legitimately object to holding them. A stalemate was inevitable. North Vietnam understood this. After the conference, its delegate, Pham Van Dong, told a reporter, "You know as well as I do that there won't be elections."

When the time came to discuss elections in 1956, Diem refused to participate, and the United States supported him. We were not afraid of holding elections in Vietnam, provided they were held under the conditions of genuine freedom that the Geneva Declaration called for. But we knew that those conditions would exist only in South Vietnam, and this sentiment was bipartisan. Senator Kennedy said that neither the United States nor South Vietnam should be a party to an election "obviously subverted and stacked in advance." After spending two years crushing every vestige of freedom in North Vietnam, Hanoi's leaders would never have allowed internationally supervised free elections to decide their fate. Following later consultations, even the Soviet Union agreed that a plebiscite was unfeasible.

North Vietnam, with a cynicism appalling even for Ho, briefly pressed the issue. But balloting conducted in Viet Minh territory in 1946 revealed just what they had in mind for 1956. Ho never permitted any suspense about the outcome. In order to secure the participation of other political parties, he openly guaranteed the leaders of one party that they would win twenty parliamentary seats and those of another that they would take fifty. The returns themselves made Diem's elections look like a model of good government. Ho received 169,222 votes in Hanoi, a city with a population of only 119,000. That amounted to 140 percent of the vote, if every person regardless of age cast a ballot.

Ho's distaste for uncontrolled free elections had not abated by 1956. Pham Van Dong told a reporter how Ho expected the election to be run. There would have to be a multiparty contest in South Vietnam, but the ballot in North Vietnam, where the people had been "united," would have only the Communist party on it. This would have made the election a sure thing for Hanoi, because North Vietnam contained 55 percent of the total Vietnamese population. An election that guaranteed victory was the only kind Ho ever would have accepted.

Many in the American antiwar movement claimed that Ho would have defeated Diem in a fair contest. They argued that even President Eisenhower conceded this point in his memoirs. The passage they always cited reads: "I have never talked or corresponded with a person knowledgeable in Indochinese affairs who did not agree that had elections been held as of the time of the fighting, possibly 80 percent of the population would have voted for the Communist Ho Chi Minh as their leader rather than Bao Dai." Those who conclude from this quotation that Ho would have won *any* elections overlook two facts. The Geneva-sponsored election was to be held not *at the time of the fighting*, by which Eisenhower meant 1954, but rather in 1956. And Ho's opponent would have been not a hapless French puppet, Bao Dai, but a popular anti-French nationalist, President Diem.

Ho would not have fared well in a fair election. In 1954, one out of every thirteen North Vietnamese fled the country rather than live under his rule. His so-called land-reform program had convulsed the country, produced severe food shortages, and sparked major peasant revolts that began in Ho's home province and spread into at least two others. General Giap later admitted that in putting down the unrest, his government killed 50,000 people. By 1956, Ho was hardly the man to head up a ticket. Diem, whose popularity was then peaking, would have won decisively. There was only one reason why North Vietnam's leaders, like those of any other Communist country, never would have dared to hold genuinely free elections: They knew that they would lose.

For the United States to have forced South Vietnam to hold elections blatantly stacked to guarantee a Communist victory would have been legally absurd, strategically senseless, and morally ludicrous.

Ho never wavered in his determination to unite all of Vietnam under Communist rule. It was never a question of *whether* he would try to conquer South Vietnam, but only of *when* and *by what means* he would try to do it.

According to captured documents and the testimony of high-ranking Communist defectors, North Vietnam's decision to conquer South Vietnam came shortly after the Geneva Conference. Ho waited several years before launching the assault. He needed to consolidate his power in North Vietnam, and he expected Diem's government to succumb to the chaotic conditions immediately after the partition and fall of its own accord. His Communist network in southern Vietnam, though substantial, had never been as powerful as the one in the North, and Diem's attacks on it had severely reduced its strength.

But his preparations for the offensive against the South began before the ink of his delegate's signature dried on the cease-fire agreements in Geneva. He had pledged to freeze the size of his army, but within four months North Vietnam's forces expanded from seven divisions to twenty. Meanwhile, South Vietnam demobilized 20,000 troops. In May 1959, at its Fifteenth Plenum, the North Vietnamese Communist party gave the order to begin the offensive. It resolved that "the basic path of development of the revolution in the South is to use violence, and that according to the specific situation and present requirements of the revolution the line of using violence is using the strength of the masses and relying principally on the political forces of the masses, in combination with armed forces to a greater or lesser degree, depending on the situation, in order to overthrow the rule of the imperialists and colonialists and set up a revolutionary regime of the people."

By September, large-scale infiltration of Communist guerrillas into South Vietnam had started, the total topping 4,000 in less than two years. Most of these troops were southerners who had moved north in 1954. But the identity of the prime mover was never in doubt. As North Vietnamese General Vo Nguyen Giap declared in January 1960, "The North has become a large rear echelon for our army." With the North serving as the rear, where else could the front be but in the South?

Thus, if wars begin in the minds of men, the Vietnam War began in the mind of Ho Chi Minh. For thirty years he had relentlessly pursued his goal of uniting Vietnam under his totalitarian rule. His undying dream was an unending nightmare for millions of Vietnamese. He had expected the French to turn Vietnam over to him through the March 6, 1946, agreement. He had expected the Soviet Union and Communist China to deliver it to him over the conference table in Geneva in 1954. He had expected South Vietnam to fall into his hands after a brief interval under President Diem. He probably even hoped to win South Vietnam through an election on reunification that would have been a patent sham.

In 1959, after all these had failed, Hanoi went to war.

WHY AND HOW WE WENT INTO VIETNAM

Never in history has so much power been used so ineffectively as in the war in Vietnam.

Seldom has one country enjoyed a superiority in arms greater than the United States held over North Vietnam in 1959. The war pitted a nuclear superpower with a gross national product of $500 billion, armed forces numbering over 1 million, and a population of 180 million against a minor military power with a GNP of less than $2 billion, an army of 250,000, and a population of less than 16 million. On paper it looked like a hopeless mismatch. But wars—and particularly guerrilla wars—are not fought on paper.

North Vietnam held one decisive advantage over the United States: Its leaders had a limitless capacity for barbarity and tenacity. They resorted to any tactics, no matter how cruel or immoral, and were willing to fight indefinitely, no matter how much suffering resulted. American leaders, quite properly, were constrained by morality, and the American people eventually would tire of the burdens of war. Our enemy could never defeat us; he could only make us quit.

Those who opposed our involvement in the war relentlessly pressed one question onto the national debate: Why are we in

Vietnam? Of all the questions asked during those years, none had an answer more simple or apparent. The United States intervened in the Vietnam War to prevent North Vietnam from imposing its totalitarian government on South Vietnam through military conquest, both because a Communist victory would lead to massive human suffering for the people of Vietnam and because it would damage American strategic interests and pose a threat to our allies and friends in other non-Communist nations.

To understand what went wrong in Vietnam, the critical question is not why we were in Vietnam but how we got into Vietnam. In 1950, President Truman gave France $10 million in financial aid to support its war against the Communist Viet Minh. By 1960, President Eisenhower had stationed 685 noncombat advisers in South Vietnam and had given its government $2 billion in aid. But our commitment remained clearly limited, contingent on whether the South Vietnamese government undertook needed reforms and represented the true nationalist aspirations of its people.

President Kennedy made the first major escalation in our commitment. He raised the number of American military personnel in Vietnam to over 16,000 and permitted them to go into combat. In 1965, President Johnson ordered air strikes against North Vietnam and sent additional American combat troops to fight in South Vietnam. After four years of steadily deepening involvement, the number of American servicemen in Vietnam reached nearly 550,000. By the end of 1968, the war had cost the United States over 31,000 lives, and Americans were being killed at a rate of 300 a week. Yet we were no closer to victory than we had been a decade before.

Our critical error was to ignore one of the iron laws of war: Never go in without knowing how you are going to get out. Successive American administrations upped our commitment by increments—first in aid, then in noncombat advisers, and finally in combat soldiers—without having clearly in mind how these increases would achieve our goals. Policymakers based their decisions on what was needed to prevent defeat rather than what it would take to reach victory.

Several fatal flaws plagued American policy in Vietnam from 1960 through 1968. We failed to understand that the war was an invasion from North Vietnam, not an insurgency in South Vietnam. We failed to prevent North Vietnam from establishing a key supply route, the Ho Chi Minh Trail, through Laos and Cambodia. We failed to foresee the consequences of our backing the military coup that overthrew South Vietnam's most capable leader, President Diem, and that ushered in years of debilitating political instability. We failed to tailor our military tactics to the political circumstances of the war. We failed to understand the determination of our enemy and what it would take to defeat him. We failed to explain the war to the American people and mobilize them behind it.

Our goals were noble in Vietnam. But a just cause is not a substitute for strategy. We were morally right in trying to help South Vietnam defend itself, but we made crucial errors in how we went about it.

The first rule of war is that one must know the enemy and understand his strategy and tactics. The second is that one must adopt strategy and tactics suited to the circumstances of the war. In the early years of the Vietnam War, North Vietnam conducted an invasion of South Vietnam that was cloaked as an indigenous insurgency. The United States mistook the nature of the war, choosing to fight against the insurgency instead of the invasion, and in the early 1960s compounded this error with three others. By the mid-1960s, American forces found themselves fighting the wrong kind of war with the wrong kinds of tactics.

The North Vietnamese invasion that began in late 1959 proved Hanoi's leaders had learned a lesson from the Korean War. North Korea's blatant invasion across the border had given the United States clear justification to intervene and had enabled President Truman to rally the American people and our United Nations allies to the defense of South Korea. North Vietnam therefore shrewdly camouflaged its invasion to look like a civil war. But in fact the Vietnam War was the Korean War with jungles.

Hanoi's invasion came under and around the border instead of over it. By 1963, North Vietnam had infiltrated more than 15,000 troops or advisers into the South, most of them southerners trained by the Communists in the North. Subsequently, the infiltration became predominantly northern. North Vietnam sensed that victory might be at hand and consequently stepped up the attack. It sent 12,000 troops in 1964, 36,000 in 1965, 92,000 in 1966, and 101,000 in 1967. After the Tet Offensive in early 1968, the fighting was conducted almost exclusively by the North Vietnamese Army.

Hanoi also had a fifth column in South Vietnam. Ho had ordered thousands of Communist Viet Minh to stay in the South after the 1954 partition in anticipation of his push to conquer the whole of Vietnam. They organized the National Liberation Front, a coalition of political groups opposing the South Vietnamese government. These included idealistic youths, peasants in areas where land reform had failed, Saigon intellectuals, and victims of Diem's anti-Communist campaign. It was a classic example of the Communist tactic of the united front. Though some non-Communist groups gathered under this umbrella organization, the Communists always dominated it. As distinguished from the Cuban and Nicaraguan revolutions, in which the Communists captured what were at the outset primarily non-Communist movements, the guerrilla insurgency in South Vietnam was started, controlled, and dominated by the Communists from the beginning. When the non-Communists were no longer useful to the Communist cause, they were eliminated.

The nature of the National Liberation Front became a central issue in the debate over the propriety of the American intervention in the Vietnam War. There were two critical questions: Was the front an indigenous political movement independent of North Vietnam? Did it represent the legitimate aspirations of the South Vietnamese? The answer to both questions was unequivocally no.

It was vitally important for North Vietnam to create the appearance that the National Liberation Front was an independent movement. Communist leaders went to elaborate lengths to maintain this illusion. But Hanoi's hand was hidden only from those who chose not to see it.

North Vietnam decided to use armed force to unite Vietnam in January 1959 and sent out orders to that effect in May. By July, Communist infiltration into South Vietnam markedly increased. These agents organized a political and military revolt against the Saigon government. A few months later, the number of guerrilla attacks escalated dramatically. In September 1960, North Vietnam's Communist party publicly called for "our people" in South Vietnam to "bring into being a broad National United Front against the United States and Diem." In January 1961, the creation of the National Liberation Front was announced in Saigon. North Vietnam called for the formation of separate military and political organizations for South Vietnam's Communists. By December 1962, both the People's Liberation Army and the People's Revolutionary party had appeared.

One Communist defector explained that North Vietnam could hardly permit the International Control Commission, which supervised compliance with the 1954 Geneva cease-fire agreements, to say that there was an invasion from the North, "so it was necessary to have some name . . . to clothe these forces with some political organization." When two other defectors were shown American publications arguing that the National Liberation Front was independent of Hanoi, they remarked with amusement that North Vietnam had been more successful than expected in concealing its role.

There was direct evidence of North Vietnam's role as well. In April 1960, North Vietnamese Communist Party First Secretary Le Duan said, "The liberation of the South is not only a task for the southern people, but also of the entire people, of the South as well as of the North. The northern people will never neglect their task with regard to one half of their country, which is not yet liberated." At the Geneva Conference on Laos in July 1962, a leading member of the North Vietnamese delegation divulged to journalists that the names of some members of the Central Committee of his country's Communist party were being kept secret because "they are directing military operations in South Vietnam."

A few simple calculations proved that the guerrillas in the South could not hold out for long without material support from North Vietnam. Until mid-1964, the National Liberation Front conducted low-level military assaults while it recruited members and organized and strengthened its structure. Then it was ready to step up the size of its attacks. In 1964, its main forces grew from 10,000 troops to 30,000, and its paramilitary forces increased from 30,000 to 80,000. These men needed weapons. Caches left behind before the 1954 partition contained 10,000 weapons. The National Liberation Front had captured 39,000 weapons and lost 25,000, producing a net gain of 14,000. But this would have left 86,000 troops unarmed. AK-47s did not grow on trees and could not be carved from bamboo shoots. The weapons had to come from North Vietnam.

If there was any doubt during the war that the National Liberation Front was merely a front, it was quickly dispelled after the war ended. North Vietnamese General Van Tien Dung, in his account of the final victory of his armies in 1975, barely mentions the role of South Vietnam's Communists. In southern Vietnam, all key government positions were given to northerners, and the forces of the People's Liberation Army were immediately absorbed into the North Vietnamese Army. In May 1975, Le Duan said, "Our Party is the unique and single leader that organized, controlled, and governed the entire struggle of the Vietnamese people from the first day of the revolution."

Those who had been members of the front organization came forward after the war to testify that Hanoi had from the start

156

planned and orchestrated a war of conquest against the South. In December 1975, Nguyen Huu Tho, a former president of the National Liberation Front, remarked in a speech that his organization had been "wholly obedient to the party line." After he escaped from Vietnam, Truong Nhu Tang, a founder of the front, wrote that "we discovered that the North Vietnamese Communists had engaged in a deliberate deception to achieve what had been their true goal from the start, the destruction of South Vietnam as a political or social entity in any way separate from the North."

North Vietnam's war might have been justified if it advanced the wishes of the people of South Vietnam. Many critics of American policy argued that the National Liberation Front could operate as freely as it did in the countryside because Communist ideology was in tune with Vietnamese culture and because the humanitarian policies of the guerrillas had won the support—the "hearts and minds," in the fashionable phrase—of the villagers. The Communist revolution in South Vietnam, they said, was as legitimate as the American Revolution.

To compare the two in any respect is a ludicrous libel of America's Founding Fathers.

Love of communism did not dwell in the "hearts and minds" of the Vietnamese. Hatred of it ran in their veins. In Vietnamese tradition, a leader should win power by his virtue, but the Communists sought to control by virtue of their power. In Vietnamese culture, the individual does not exist merely to serve the community; instead, society should maximize the freedom of each individual. A tenacious belief in private property, a deep desire for individual freedom, and a resentment of power not based in moral authority are all part of the Vietnamese character. Communism, on the other hand, completely subordinates the individual to the state. It destroys freedom of expression, abolishes private property, and demands blind obedience. The Communists were well aware that their ideology was antithetical to Vietnamese culture. One of the main reasons they set up the National Liberation Front was to keep the people from learning that the Communists were behind the revolution.

The Communists won converts by cultivating not hope but hatred. Even a prominent antiwar writer observed that one key to the success of the National Liberation Front was its "systematic encouragement of hatred." Like almost all developing nations, South Vietnam had problems in providing social justice and avoiding governmental abuses. The Communists made it their mission to exacerbate the problems in order to help them whip the Vietnamese people into a frenzy of hatred. "Promotion of hatred," stated one National Liberation Front directive, "must be permanent, continuous, and directly related to the struggle movement as closely as a man is to his shadow." To Communist leaders, positive reforms were a danger. Where these were instituted, they warned, Communist agents "have tended to be self-satisfied with their records and less eager to continue promoting hatred among the masses, and thus . . . the Revolution does not boil and remain violent."

Violence was the other key to the successes of the National Liberation Front. Communist forces systematically attacked not only the government and its army but also South Vietnamese civilians. Their purpose was to promote instability and insecurity, to destabilize the government by killing its most able officials, and to intimidate the people by demonstrating that they could not be protected.

For the National Liberation Front, terror and atrocities were calculated policies.

In Long An, after failing to persuade a man to ask his sons to desert the South Vietnamese army, the Communists coldly shot him in the back as he turned to go back to his home. When they captured the village of Cai Be in 1967, the Communists murdered forty wives and children of the members of the local militia. In Dak Son in 1967, they killed 252 civilians, two-thirds of whom were women and children, by incinerating the hamlet's straw huts one by one with flamethrowers. They buried mines on roads used only by villagers taking goods to market; threw grenades into crowded public squares, pagodas, and schools; shelled crowded refugee camps; and fired 122mm rockets indiscriminately into Saigon, Danang, and other major cities. This continual terrorism killed thousands of South Vietnamese civilians every year.

Isolated atrocities committed by American soldiers produced torrents of outrage from antiwar critics and the news media. When it was revealed in December 1969 that United States troops killed 175 civilians at My Lai during the Tet Offensive of 1968, it dominated the front pages and the television news for weeks. Communist atrocities, on the other hand, were so common that they received hardly any attention at all. Certainly we should not have ignored the war crimes on our side. But it also is vitally important that we keep one distinction in mind. The United States sought to minimize and prevent attacks on civilians. North Vietnam made attacks on civilians a centerpiece of its strategy. Americans who deliberately killed civilians received prison sentences. Communists who did so received commendations.

The National Liberation Front also had a systematic policy of assassination or abduction of anyone likely to stand up to it and provide anti-Communist forces with leadership. Its secret service, operating out of North Vietnam's Ministry of Public Security, was present throughout South Vietnam. The Communists drew up lists of victims and then deployed specially trained teams to kidnap or kill the targets. From 1957 to 1973, they assassinated 36,725 South Vietnamese and abducted another 58,499. The real figures are much higher; accurate statistics could not be kept during the Tet Offensive in 1968. Some of those kidnapped were returned after indoctrination, but many were never seen again. They were either forced to fight with the guerrillas or executed as enemies.

The death squads of the National Liberation Front focused on leaders at the village level. The guerrillas cynically differentiated between honest and corrupt hamlet chiefs. One National Liberation Front defector explained that when faced with dishonest leaders "the Communists will publicly denounce the government and demand that it be overthrown, but actually they will support and encourage the corrupt hamlet chiefs. On the other hand the honest hamlet chief who has done much for the people and who has a clear understanding of the party is classified by the party as a 'traitor of major importance.' He is eliminated.''

The target lists also included anyone who improved the lives of the peasants, such as medical personnel, social workers, and schoolteachers, whether he had any links with the government or not. When asked why teachers were assassinated, one Communist defector said, ''Because they were people with a profound understanding about politics, people who were pure nationalists, who might be able to assume anti-Communist leadership in their area. Such people are very dangerous and hence are classed as traitors.''

Those labeled ''traitors'' faced a grim fate. Once, the Communists occupied a village whose chief had cooperated with the Saigon government. Guerrillas assembled all the villagers outside, including the chief and his family. While everyone watched, they disemboweled the chief's wife and dismembered his children one by one, cutting off their arms and legs despite their screams. Then they castrated the village chief. After witnessing these grisly executions, no one in the village dared cooperate with the central government.

That was not an isolated incident. In February 1966, United States forces were ordered to liberate a coastal village in Binh Dinh Province. A young woman who was working for the South Vietnamese government urged the peasants not to resist. The Communists captured her, tied her to a coconut tree, and gathered the villagers. First, the leader of the Communists screamed accusations against her. Then, as she struggled against the ropes, he raised a broad, long-handled knife with a curved point that peasants used to open coconuts. While two other men restrained her, he twice plunged the knife into her, leaving her lower body in tatters. Her entrails seeped out and dripped onto the ground. ''Death to traitors of the people,'' he read from a piece of yellow paper. "The same will happen to all who betray the just cause of our liberation struggle." He stuck a small bamboo stick through the paper and shoved it into her gaping wound. The Communists left her there to die as an example for the others.

That we became preoccupied with the insurgency in South Vietnam, which was instigated and controlled by the real aggressors in North Vietnam, showed that Ho Chi Minh was a master of the art of political magic. A magician depends on sleight of hand, and the essence of sleight of hand is diversion. At the moment he switches the ball from the first shell to the second, he must be sure that the attention of the audience is focused on the third. That North Vietnam was engaging in aggression against South Vietnam was clearly evident to anyone who bothered to look carefully. The United States was aware of the facts, but failed to draw the logical conclusions. We focused on Ho's diversion—the insurgency in South Vietnam—and like a master magician, he played us for suckers.

American military and political leaders fell for Ho's diversion because they were wearing strategic blinkers. In the early 1960s, the Communist tactic of "revolutionary war" obsessed our strategists. Mao had used it to win power in China; Fidel Castro used it in Cuba. In January 1961, Soviet Premier Nikita Krushchev announced that he intended to support "wars of national liberation." The Soviets now would seek to take over countries from within by sending military supplies to Communist movements in the target countries rather than by attacking across a border.

President Kennedy believed the Communists saw revolutionary war as the wave of the future. He remarked to an aide that he would wager with nine-to-one odds that the next war would be a revolutionary war and considered the Vietnam War a classic example. His aides urged him, and later Johnson, not to attack North Vietnam until we had defeated the revolutionary war in South Vietnam. Their advice was based on the naïve premise that if we could counter the causes of insurgency in the target country, it would not be necessary to attack those outside the country who were directly responsible for it.

Kennedy's advisers displayed not only appalling naïveté but also fundamentally poor judgment. They failed to understand the vitally important distinction between revolutionary war and guerrilla war. Guerrilla warfare is a military operation; revolutionary warfare is a political operation. Guerrilla warfare supplements normal conventional military operations by in-filtrating small units behind enemy lines to disrupt his communications, interrupt his supplies, and harass his forces; revolutionary war aims to subvert the enemy's control by leading the people to rise up against him. Guerrilla war helps regular armies achieve victory by weakening the enemy; revolutionary war achieves victory on its own through a popular uprising.

In Vietnam the insurgency was not primarily a revolutionary war, because the people as a whole were not rising up against the government. The real war in Vietnam was an invasion from North Vietnam that came in the guise of a guerrilla insurgency. While we treated the symptom, the disease went unchecked.

Because we failed to understand the nature of the war, the chances were small that we would choose the correct strategy to fight it. Our first error probably doomed us to follow the wrong path, but we sealed our fate by committing three more.

The first resulted from events half a world away from Vietnam. In April 1961, 1,400 anti-Communist Cubans, who were organized, trained, armed, and directed by the United States Central Intelligence Agency, landed in the Zapata Swamp of Cuba's Bay of Pigs with the mission of leading an anti-Castro revolution. Within three days, they capitulated after a valiant effort against vastly greater and better-supplied enemy forces. It was a debacle for the United States. The freedom fighters had been promised American air cover, and never would have gone forward with the plan without such a commitment. When we did not deliver it, their attack stalled quickly. Without air support, they could neither advance nor even be resupplied. As a result, they literally ran out of ammunition on the beaches.

After this disastrous failure, President Kennedy ordered Robert Kennedy and General Maxwell Taylor to undertake an investigation. They concluded that the CIA was not equipped to handle large-scale paramilitary operations and that the Pentagon should be put in charge of them. Our involvement in Vietnam fell into this category, even though at the time we were only training and advising South Vietnam's army.

This decision had enormous consequences. The CIA's political sophistication and on-the-spot feel for local conditions went out the window as people who saw the world through bureaucratic and technological lenses took over the main operational responsibility for the war. Our armed forces were experts at mobilizing huge resources, orchestrating logistic support, and deploying enormous firepower. In Vietnam, these skills led them to fight the war *their* way, rather than developing the new skills required to defeat the new kind of enemy they faced. They made the mistake of fighting an unconventional war with conventional tactics.

The second critical mistake took place in Laos. For years the Laotian people had been fighting a three-cornered civil war. The Communist Pathet Lao controlled two northeastern provinces bordering on North Vietnam. Neutralists held the central plain. Rightists ruled the areas bordering on Thailand along the Mekong River in southern Laos. The fighting had never been intense—until North Vietnam began to intervene.

Running through Laos were the best routes around the demilitarized zone between the two Vietnams for infiltrating men and arms into South Vietnam and Cambodia. Hanoi therefore set up Group 559 in May 1959 and Group 959 in September 1959. According to the North Vietnamese history of the war, the task of Group 559 was "creating the first foot travel route connecting the North and South, and organizing the sending of people, weapons, and supplies to the revolution in the South." Group 959 was set up for providing military specialists

163

for the Pathet Lao, organizing "the supplying of Vietnamese material to the Laotian revolution and directly commanding the Vietnamese volunteer units" operating in Laos.

With these actions, Hanoi had set out to crush the Pathet Lao's two non-Communist rivals and take total control of the country in order to facilitate their invasion of South Vietnam. By December 1960, the North Vietnamese had stationed 7,000 troops in Laos.

President Eisenhower believed that Laos was the key domino in Southeast Asia. Defending Laos was the major specific action Eisenhower urged on President-elect Kennedy when they met in January 1961. Eisenhower told Kennedy that if Laos were to fall into Communist hands, we would have to write off all of Indochina. But in the event that efforts to reach a political solution failed, he advised, the United States should intervene militarily with its allies if possible, or alone if necessary.

Kennedy's initial moves in Laos were promising. On March 23, 1961, he said forcefully that unless Communist attacks on its neutral government were stopped, "those who support a truly neutral Laos will have to consider their response." He warned that no one should doubt his resolution on this point. "The security of all Southeast Asia will be endangered if Laos loses its neutral independence," he said. "I know that every American will want his country to honor its obligations to the point that freedom and security of the free world and ourselves may be achieved."

He instructed the CIA to supply arms to the neutralists and rightists who were fighting against the expansion of Pathet Lao and North Vietnamese control. It was a limited commitment, involving fewer than 700 American advisers, but it was enough to stalemate the war and keep North Vietnam's larger forces off-balance.

One month later, however, Kennedy backed away from his commitment to keep Laos independent. He decided that Laos was beyond our security perimeter in Southeast Asia and that it was the wrong place to draw the line against North Vietnamese aggression. If he had to engage American forces in the area, he preferred to do so in South Vietnam.

His advisers provided him with persuasive arguments to support his reversal on Laos. Laos enjoyed little national unity. Its armed forces were small and poorly trained. Its terrain was forbidding. Its geography made it difficult to apply American air and naval power. Its common border with Communist China stirred fears that any American action might provoke Mao to intervene as he had in Korea.

The Bay of Pigs disaster on April 19, 1961, reinforced Kennedy's reluctance to act. When I saw him at the White House on April 20, I pledged bipartisan support for any action he decided was necessary to prevent a Communist conquest of Laos. His response was that he did not see how we could make any move in Laos, which was thousands of miles away, if we did not make a move in Cuba, which was only ninety miles away. Kennedy also told an aide that one of the lessons he had learned from his defeat in Cuba was that the United States should pursue a political solution in Southeast Asia rather than a military one.

Accordingly, he instructed Averell Harriman to negotiate an agreement in Geneva that would neutralize Laos. The talks began in May 1961 and soon ran up against implacable North Vietnamese intransigence. Ho stalled because he sensed the United States would abandon Laos even without an agreement. After ten months of Communist delays, Kennedy sent 5,000 marines to Thailand and put American forces at Okinawa on standby. Ho appeared to back down, and within two months there was an agreement in Geneva. Fifteen countries signed a treaty in which they pledged to recognize a new neutralist coalition government in Laos, to withdraw any military forces they had in the country, and to stop any paramilitary assistance to the rival political factions. The agreement was hailed by foreign-policy pundits in the media as a significant contribution to peace in Southeast Asia.

All countries complied except one: North Vietnam.

The agreement had stated that all foreign troops would leave

Laos through internationally supervised checkpoints. Ho never took any serious steps to remove his 7,000-man contingent from Laos. The total number of North Vietnamese soldiers recorded as leaving was forty.

Unlike the American administration, Ho viewed all of Indochina not as four separate countries but as one strategic theater. His motive in signing the Geneva agreement was simple and cynical: He hoped it would enable him to restrict our zone of operation while his armies continued to operate freely throughout Indochina.

When the plan worked, the North Vietnamese wasted no time in exploiting their advantage. Through the work of their Group 559, they virtually annexed southern Laos and constructed an elaborate system of infiltration routes—dubbed the "Ho Chi Minh Trail"—into South Vietnam and Cambodia.

Those who argued that the war in Vietnam was an internal South Vietnamese conflict minimized the importance of the Ho Chi Minh Trail or even questioned its existence. The official North Vietnamese history of the war does not. It reads: "During the sixteen years of operation, Group 559, which at first had only a few hundred people who primarily used cargo bicycles on narrow trails, became a force with many components: transportation troops, military engineers, infantry, antiaircraft artillery, [fuel supply] troops, communications units, etc., totalling tens of thousands of people and thousands of cargo trucks organized into many divisions, regiments, troop encampments, workshops, stations, etc. There was created a strategic route bearing the name of the great Uncle Ho which crossed the Troung Son mountains [in Laos], connected the battlefields, and amounted to a relatively complete land route, pipeline, and river route network."

The Ho Chi Minh Trail became a lifeline for the Communist aggressors in Indochina and, in the end, a noose for their victims. By 1970, North Vietnam had stationed almost 70,000 troops in Laos and had transported over 500,000 troops along their network of roads. The Geneva agreement on Laos in 1962 paved the way for the Communist victory in South Vietnam in 1975.

The United States' response to North Vietnam's massive violations was tepid. Our friends in Laos were begging for help as the renewed Communist offensive drained their stocks of ammunition, but for months Harriman refused to allow the CIA to send any military or paramilitary assistance. He later reluctantly permitted covert shipments of ammunition, provided that he had approved the cargo manifest of each supply flight and that the arms be used for defensive purposes only. With North Vietnam's offensive in high gear, it was not difficult to satisfy the second condition.

The Kennedy and Johnson administrations steadily stepped up our covert operations in Laos, which later became known as "the secret war." But our actions were sharply circumscribed and never matched those of North Vietnam. Neither administration wished to abandon the Geneva agreement entirely. Both sought to observe the spirit, if not the letter, of the agreement by enforcing two critical limitations on our involvement: They refused to give enough aid to our Laotian allies to enable them to expel the North Vietnamese, and they rejected plans to intervene directly in Laos with American ground forces. Our anti-Communist friends in Laos fought a valiant guerrilla war that exacted a high toll on North Vietnamese forces. But because of our sharp limits on aid, they never succeeded in denying Hanoi effective control of Laos.

Our policy was a sad combination of wishful thinking and willful ignorance. In 1964, when I spoke with Ambassador Henry Cabot Lodge in Saigon, I sensed that he was uncomfortable as he tried to explain the reason for the administration's opposition to sending forces into Laos and Cambodia in hot pursuit of Communist units and to cutting off the Ho Chi Minh Trail. The administration contended that this would violate the neutrality of these countries, undermine the Geneva agreement, and widen the war. But it was obvious that North Vietnam had already widened the war by taking over southern

Laos and eastern Cambodia. By failing to defend Laos, the Kennedy and Johnson administrations made it easier for North Vietnam to wage their war against South Vietnam by sending tons of weapons and thousands of men down the Ho Chi Minh Trail.

In conversations I had with President Diem and with the leaders of Thailand in 1956, they expressed deep distress at the lack of safeguards in the 1954 Geneva treaty and the ease with which North Vietnam flouted the treaty's terms in Laos. They understood, as Eisenhower had, that Laos was vital to the security of all Indochina. Years later it would be fashionable in academia to deride the domino theory. But whatever academics would say about it, the dominoes certainly believed it.

Our failure to prevent North Vietnam from establishing the Ho Chi Minh Trail had fatal consequences. Hanoi could not have waged the kind of a war it did in the South without a free run down the Laos panhandle. If the Communists had been unable to use Laos and Cambodia as staging grounds for their invasion, they would have had to strike across the forty-mile-long border of the demilitarized zone. On this narrow front, South Vietnam would have been able to defend itself without the assistance of American forces.

Our acquiescence in Hanoi's violations of the 1962 Geneva agreement lengthened the front that Saigon had to defend from 40 to 640 miles. Our unilateral restraint gave North Vietnam privileged sanctuaries from which to attack American and South Vietnamese forces.

At first, when the Communists fought in small guerrilla units, they could pick and choose their targets, execute hit-and-run raids, and slip back across the border before reinforcements could arrive. Later, when they used division-size conventional units, they could concentrate overwhelmingly superior offensive power against overextended defensive forces. Our failure in Laos turned over the strategic and tactical initiative to Hanoi.

Had the Geneva agreement turned Laos into a genuine neutral buffer state, our problems in Vietnam would have been reduced to manageable proportions. It did not, but we acted as if it did. We treated the fate of Laos as if it were of secondary importance to that of South Vietnam. But the two were inextricably linked. Guerrilla attacks were breaking out across South Vietnam. North Vietnam was the driving force behind them, and its troops and armaments arrived via Laos.

By allowing the Ho Chi Minh Trail to become a freeway for Hanoi's invasion, we put Ho Chi Minh in the driver's seat in the Vietnam War.

We made our third critical mistake in South Vietnam in 1963. The Kennedy administration, increasingly frustrated with President Diem, encouraged and supported a military coup against his government. This shameful episode ended with Diem's murder and began a period of political chaos in South Vietnam that forced us to send our own troops into the war.

Being a ruler of a Third World country usually means making enemies. Diem was no exception. He was a bold decision-maker, initiating vast programs for the betterment of his country. Often, he alienated those who supported a different plan or who saw his reforms as a threat to their interests in preserving the status quo.

Like all leaders, Diem made some poor decisions. He replaced the old custom of village self-government with a centralized system of appointed leaders, thereby undermining the local initiative on which democracy depends. He alienated many important civilian and military leaders in the aftermath of an attempted coup against him in 1960. He started to rely too heavily for his rule on members of his own family. As his strong political base began to erode, he became more authoritarian.

Diem jealously guarded his independence, often rejecting or ignoring the advice of his American advisers. After all, he was a proud Vietnamese nationalist who would not take orders from Americans any more than he had from the French. "America has a magnificent economy and many good points," he once told a reporter. "But does your strength at home automatically mean that the United States is entitled to dictate everything here in Vietnam, which is undergoing a type of war that your country has never experienced?"

Diem assumed that despite his occasional difference of opinion with American policymakers, the United States was an ally he could depend on in the end. He also assumed that the United States saw no alternative to his leadership. He was wrong on both counts.

As Kennedy and his advisers grew increasingly unhappy with their strong-willed ally, they began to lose sight of the fact that the issue was not whether South Vietnam would develop a perfect constitutional democracy but whether it would have a government capable of resisting an expansion of Communist control that would destroy all democracy. In the early 1960s, South Vietnam was already under military attack. While assassinations, abductions, and terrorist and guerrilla raids proliferated, our officials acted as if the real problem were gerrymandered electoral districts and stuffed ballot boxes.

The crisis that convinced the Kennedy administration to abandon Diem began in May 1963. After Catholics flew dozens of Vatican flags during public celebrations in Danang, Diem, himself a Catholic, enacted a law to prevent the subordination of the national flag to religious ones. It prohibited any group from flying its flag above the national flag in public demonstrations; the display of flags within a house of worship was not affected. Buddha's birthday fell two days later, with major celebrations scheduled across the country. Diem was aware that many Buddhists would fly their banner without knowing about the new law, so he suspended enforcement of it.

Word of Diem's action arrived too late in Hue, and what became known as the "Buddhist crisis" resulted. Local police took down several Buddhist flags that were flying above the South Vietnamese banner. Thich Tri Quang, a Buddhist priest who practiced his politics more devoutly than his religion and who was eager to find fault with the Catholic President, delivered a bristling antigovernment tirade in his pagoda during religious ceremonies.

Hue's Buddhists were primed for dissent. Mayor Ngo Dinh Thuc, who was one of Diem's brothers, was a notorious religious bigot. Tri Quang took a recording of his anti-Diem speech to a radio station and demanded that it be broadcast. Outside the station, a bomb exploded in the crowd of protesters who had followed him, killing eight people. Buddhist leaders accused government soldiers of detonating an American-made concussion grenade. Diem denied the charge, and a United Nations commission eventually determined that the blast resulted not from a grenade but from plastic explosives, a favorite weapon of the National Liberation Front. But the Buddhists escalated their political attacks and demanded that Diem personally accept responsibility for the tragedy.

Then, on June 11, a Buddhist monk doused himself with gasoline and set himself on fire in protest against Diem's government. The next day, the grisly picture of the scene—the monk with his hands clasped in prayer as the flames consumed him—ran on the front page of almost every American newspaper.

The monk's self-immolation was a carefully contrived ritual staged for the American news media. Buddhist leaders had tipped off the press beforehand and afterward quickly distributed mimeographed copies of antigovernment letters purportedly written by the monk. None of that was reported. The picture stood alone and seared a single word into the minds of many Americans: repression.

Here a small group of influential American reporters in Saigon, all of whom opposed Diem, had a decisive impact on events. Some of them worked for the United States' most influential newspapers. They accepted almost any anti-Diem accusation as gospel, and met frequently to compare stories with one another so that their line would be consistent. Tri Quang rightly considered them allies, so much so that he distributed copies of their stories as propaganda to win converts. That the South Vietnamese President was a devout Catholic made him an ideal candidate to be painted as a repressor of Buddhists. During the crisis, the reporters obligingly portrayed Diem as an enemy of all the people and a holdover from the French colonialist who practiced ruthless repression against nationalist and Buddhist South Vietnamese. They wrote that 70 percent of the South Vietnamese were Buddhist. The true figure was at most 30 percent.

Facts, however, were not important to these correspondents. Undercutting Diem, perhaps even destroying him, was all that mattered. This was one of the few times during the Vietnam War when the United States government and the American press would find themselves working toward the same goal.

The issue of religious repression was a complete fabrication. Diem appointed his top officials without regard to their faith. Of his eighteen cabinet ministers, five were Catholic, five Confucianist, and eight Buddhist, including the vice president and the foreign minister. Of his thirty-eight provincial governors, twelve were Catholic and twenty-six were either Confucianist or Buddhist. Of his nineteen top generals, three were Catholic and sixteen were Taoist, Confucianist, or Buddhist. He permitted Buddhists to exempt themselves from mandatory military service on religious grounds, while Catholics and others were required to serve. No Buddhist was ever arrested for practicing his religion, and not a single piece of credible evidence has ever been produced to show that Diem repressed Buddhists on the basis of religion.

Politics, not religion, was on the minds of those behind the crisis. A few ambitious Vietnamese had shaved their heads, donned Buddhist monk's clothing, and contrived the crisis to advance their own political agenda. Their leader was Tri Quang, and they operated out of the Xa Loi pagoda in Saigon. It was hardly a place of reverence. Mimeograph copiers churned out propaganda sheets. Organizers barked out instructions on where to hold the day's demonstrations. Messengers hurried about with newly painted banners. Journalists and photographers milled around hoping to get the inside word on the location of the next burning. Anyone who glanced in the door could see that the Xa Loi pagoda was not a house of worship but the political headquarters of a movement intent on bringing down Diem's government.

During a United Nations investigation of the charges against Diem, two young Buddhists who had been prevented from burning themselves to death testified about how Tri Quang's General Buddhist Association had recruited them. Both were told horror stories about how Diem's government was burning pagodas and beating, torturing, and disemboweling Buddhists. One said a recruiter told him that "the Buddhist Association worked for the Communists" and that ten volunteers were needed for death by fire. After he volunteered, he was told that the "suicide-promotion group would make all the arrangements." This included providing him with a gasoline-soaked robe, driving him to a location that would maximize publicity, and writing letters of protest for him that would be handed out to the waiting press.

The other, who came from a remote province, said he was horrified when a recruiter told him Diem had burned Saigon's pagodas. He volunteered to die when he was informed that by doing so he might be reincarnated as a Buddha. He was brought to the capital and given a carefully prescribed route, designed to avoid the city's thoroughly intact pagodas, to reach the location for his suicide. When he changed course because a street was blocked off, he came upon a pagoda where Buddhists were peacefully worshiping. He then voluntarily surrendered to a policeman.

Just as he sought to deceive the world, Tri Quang deceived his victims in order to achieve his political ends. After Diem had yielded to all reasonable demands, Tri Quang injected unreasonable ones to keep the crisis alive. He was interested not in compromise but in conflict. As one monk at Xa Loi asked a reporter, "How many suicides will it take to get rid of Diem?"

Tri Quang made no secret of his real goals. He had been arrested twice by the French for working with the Viet Minh. He admitted that after 1945 he had served with Buddhist

groups that were nothing more than Communist front organizations to help Ho's army. He was a disciple of Thich Tri
Do, the leader of the Communist-dominated Buddhist church
in North Vietnam, and had once said that Buddhism was entirely compatible with communism. On one occasion, a reporter asked Tri Quang whether it was ethical to induce young
monks to commit suicide in so painful a manner just to be
able to fly the Buddhist flag a notch or two higher. Tri Quang
shrugged his shoulders and said with perfect candor that "in
a revolution many things must be done."

Storms of outrage broke out in the United States and Europe
when the Buddhist suicides began. Sensationalized news
media reports made matters even worse. The suicides were
political ploys by a few fanatic extremists, but the media said
they represented the mainstream opinion of South Vietnamese
Buddhists. The press played up the Buddhists as oppressed
holy people, and the world blamed their political target, Diem.

Most critics attributed the suicides to Diem's repression.
Nobody seemed to notice when the number of suicides increased after he was overthrown. The radical Buddhists had
sought to get rid of Diem not because of religious repression
but because he blocked the road to a revolutionary overthrow
of South Vietnam's non-Communist government.

News-media reports of Buddhist repression had the desired
effect: They turned American public opinion against Diem.
One of the three reasons Secretary of State Dean Rusk listened
when the Kennedy administration first considered abandoning
Diem in August 1963 was the pressure of American public
opinion.

The Buddhist crisis escalated dramatically on August 21
when Diem sent units of his special forces to raid the pagodas
at the center of the Buddhist rebellion. Diem had not singled
out the Buddhists; he would have cracked down on any group
that openly sought to overturn the government. His forces did
not rampage through holy places. No one was killed. They
seized only pagodas, like Xa Loi, that were political command
posts. Diem's raids affected just twelve of South Vietnam's

4,776 pagodas. His troops seized spears, daggers, guns, and plastic molds for making bombs, together with documents linking the radical Buddhists to the National Liberation Front.

Kennedy's advisers now lost all perspective. They accused Diem of outright repression. Even recently, a top official from that era displayed his lack of understanding by characterizing the crisis as one in which "a Frenchified Catholic Vietnamese President began to beat up the pagodas and kill Buddhist priests and Buddhist nuns." This view was typical and totally at odds with the facts. Kennedy's anti-Diem advisers had refused to believe the balanced reports on the crisis sent previously by Ambassador Frederick Nolting and instead came to rely on the news accounts of stridently anti-Diem reporters. Roger Hilsman, the assistant secretary of state for Far Eastern affairs, summed up the Kennedy administration's attitude when he commented, "After the closing of the pagodas on August 21, the facts became irrelevant."

With the facts deemed irrelevant to policymaking, the Kennedy administration proceeded to make disastrous policy. Support for the anti-Diem policy was not unanimous. Vice President Johnson, CIA Director John McCone, and General Maxwell Taylor were opposed to abandoning Diem. But three days after the pagoda raids, a powerful coalition of top officials set in motion events that resulted in a military coup against Diem's government, acting with at best cursory consideration of the consequences. A sober examination of Diem's likely successors was never undertaken. No attention was paid to the abysmally low caliber of the men with whom they were plotting. None of the generals even approached Diem in leadership qualities.

On August 24, Harriman, Hilsman, Rusk, and Undersecretary of State George Ball collaborated on a telegram to Henry Cabot Lodge, the new American ambassador in Saigon. Kennedy approved it over the phone from his vacation home in Hyannisport. It stated that the current situation was intolerable and that Diem's brother and closest adviser, Ngo Dinh Nhu, whom Kennedy's men held responsible for the raids, had to be replaced. "We wish [to] give Diem reasonable opportunity to remove Nhu," the cable read, "but if he remains obdurate, then we are prepared to accept the obvious implication that we can no longer support Diem. You may tell appropriate military commanders we will give them direct support in any interim period of breakdown [of the] central government mechanism." It added that Lodge should "urgently examine all possible alternative leadership and make detailed plans as to how we might bring about Diem's replacement if this should become necessary."

The cable's message was unequivocal. Since everyone knew Diem would never dismiss his brother Nhu, Lodge interpreted it as a direct order from the highest authority to prepare a coup against Diem. Another cable somewhat qualifying the first was sent to Lodge a few days later, but it was too late to slow the momentum of events in Saigon. The gun aimed at Diem's head had already been fired; the bullet could not be recalled. Lodge was an efficient ambassador, and he carried out his orders. He instructed the CIA in Saigon to make the rounds of their contacts in the military. Several South Vietnamese generals later testified that they had been sounded out by United States officials that summer on the possibility of leading a coup.

On August 29, Kennedy told his National Security Council staff that he supported the idea of a coup if its success was guaranteed. Lodge was already reporting progress. In a cable to Rusk, Lodge said, "We are launched on a course from which there is no respectable turning back: the overthrow of the Diem government." He added, "The chance of bringing off a Generals' coup depends on them to some extent; but it depends at least as much on us." Rusk authorized Lodge to suspend aid to Diem at a time of his choosing and instructed him to do whatever was necessary to "enhance the chances of a successful coup." Rusk also ordered the head of the American military mission in Saigon to establish a liaison with the coup leaders and to review their plans. One plot misfired in late August, but the generals soon regrouped.

Meanwhile, direct, relentless pressure was leveled on Diem.

United States delegations toured South Vietnam without calling on him. Lodge granted Tri Quang political asylum in the American embassy. The CIA cut off support for South Vietnam's special forces. The White House publicly suspended United States aid for financing commercial imports. Kennedy stated in a televised interview that South Vietnam's government needed changes in policy and "perhaps" in personnel. The administration sought to do everything possible to show its disapproval of Diem and to do nothing to undermine the impression that it would welcome a change in government.

On November 1, 1963, the troops of General Tran Van Don and General Duong Van Minh besieged the Presidential Palace. Four days earlier, Lodge had asked those plotting the coup if they needed any help and assured them of American support afterward. Throughout the fighting, a CIA agent in constant contact with the United States Embassy was present at the military's headquarters. Diem and Nhu temporarily eluded the generals and surrendered only when Lodge and the generals gave them guaranties of safe conduct. But after they turned themselves in, the generals murdered them in cold blood with American weapons in the back of an American-made armored personnel carrier.

The Kennedy administration had concluded that Diem should be overthrown because he had completely lost touch with his people. But in fact Kennedy and his advisers were the ones who were out of touch. Kennedy was shocked when he heard that Diem had been murdered by the generals, but he should not have been surprised. Diem's assassination was no accident. Those who overthrow popular leaders frequently must kill them in order to remove the possibility of their return to power. General Minh later explained, "Diem could not be allowed to live, because he was too much respected among simple, gullible people in the countryside, especially the Catholics and the refugees."

Prime Minister Tran Van Huong, whose government lasted only three months amid the political chaos in late 1964, concurred with Minh, saying, "The generals knew very well that having no talent, nor moral virtues, and no popular support whatsoever, they could not prevent a spectacular comeback of the President and Mr. Nhu if they were alive."

President Diem stabilized South Vietnam as a keystone holds up a dome. Political forces converged on him from all directions, but by balancing one against another, he locked all of them into place. And just as a keystone's importance is not apparent unless it is removed, Diem's vital role became clear only after his demise, when the entire South Vietnamese political system came crashing down.

What the coup supporters in the Kennedy administration should have known all along now became painfully clear: The choice in South Vietnam had been not between Diem and somebody better but between Diem and somebody worse.

Whatever his faults, Diem possessed a significant measure of legitimacy. He was a strong leader of a nation that desperately needed strong leadership. With him gone, power in South Vietnam was up for grabs. The administration officials who had so eagerly hatched the plots against Diem soon discovered that their South Vietnamese collaborators were hopelessly bad leaders. Skills needed to overthrow a government are not useful for running one. Leading a coup and leading a country are two entirely different jobs. The chaotic leadership crisis that followed in South Vietnam was a direct consequence of the overthrow of President Ngo Dinh Diem.

For two years, the gates of the Presidential Palace were a revolving door. South Vietnam endured ten changes of government, and even more in the military high command. Intrigue became Saigon's form of government. During one chaotic week, a new government took power, one faction attempted a coup against the commander in chief, another faction suppressed the attempt, and then the suppressors of the coup ousted the commander in chief. Every time I visited South Vietnam in that period, I found a new President or Prime Minister in power. I have never met more pitiful incompetents.

South Vietnam's military had thrown out not only Diem but

also the country's constitution. The Military Revolutionary Council was now responsible for appointing the government. Politics among its members were a free-for-all. Loyalties ran not to the country but to personal careers. Unity of purpose or policy did not exist. Opportunism was the only common ideal. Never were the generals sufficiently united to appoint effective government leaders and back them up with complete support.

Journalists, who thought only they knew what was best, had always characterized American policy with the ditty "Sink or swim with Ngo Dinh Diem." South Vietnam foundered at times under Diem. Now it was going down for the third time, sinking toward political collapse. It would take two years for power to come into the hands of another strong leader, General Nguyen Van Thieu.

As government-by-intrigue became business as usual, the business of fighting the war ground to a halt. Hanoi was elated. Diem, who had personified stubborn resistance to communism, had been eliminated without their having to lift a finger. Nguyen Huu Tho, the head of the National Liberation Front, said, "The Americans have managed to do what we couldn't do for nine years." He added in disbelief that the coup was "a gift from heaven."

Ho seized the opportunity the United States and the generals had given him. Captured documents and the testimony of defectors indicated that Ho now believed North Vietnam could win quickly. Within months, he injected regular units of the North Vietnamese Army into the South. At the beginning of each year, Radio Hanoi customarily proclaimed that it would be a "year of victories." But in 1965, after political chaos overtook South Vietnam, Hanoi declared that this would be *the* year of victory.

South Vietnam's survival all along had depended on whether it developed stable institutions and the ability to defend itself before North Vietnam acquired the power to deal it a death blow. Diem at least had his country moving in the right direction. Now, while Saigon's government and army were sliding downward by every index, Communist strength on the battlefield skyrocketed. Guerrillas inundated the countryside. Communist forces began to form larger units and engage in set-piece battles. Outside Saigon, Danang, and other major cities, Communist forces crushed South Vietnam's mobile reserve battalions one by one, and soon there would be no reserves at all left.

Time was running short. The United States would have to act soon. President Kennedy's assassination had followed Diem's by three weeks. As Vice President, Lyndon Johnson had strongly opposed the steps we took against Diem. He later told aides that our complicity in the coup was the greatest mistake we made in Vietnam. Now, as President, he had to try to pick up the pieces.

When we arrogated to ourselves the right to choose South Vietnam's government, we also assumed responsibility for its fate. Johnson wanted neither an American war nor a Communist victory. With the unraveling of South Vietnam, those choices were rapidly becoming our only choices. We could let the Communists conquer South Vietnam or send in our own troops to prevent it. The Kennedy administration sowed the seeds of intrigue that led to the overthrow and murder of Diem. Now we would reap a bitter harvest.

Most Americans believe that the Tonkin Gulf incident triggered our entry into the Vietnam War. Although it was an important turning point, it was not our opening volley.

President Kennedy had increased the number of United States military advisers in Vietnam to over 16,000 in 1963. They did much more than simply give advice; Kennedy had authorized them to accompany South Vietnamese forces into battle and to return fire if fired upon. Whether we called them "training personnel" or "combat advisers" was a matter of semantics; by the end of 1963, our forces had sustained 612 casualties. President Johnson stepped up our involvement in 1964. He ordered limited air strikes against the Ho Chi Minh

Trail in Laos and increased the number of our advisers by 7,000.

The first direct American attack on North Vietnam was a reprisal for two North Vietnamese attacks on our ships in August 1964. On August 2, while patrolling in the Tonkin Gulf to gather intelligence and spot Communist infiltration of men and supplies into South Vietnam by sea, the destroyer USS *Maddox* was attacked by three North Vietnamese torpedo boats. Our ship sustained no serious damage, and President Johnson ordered no retaliation. At the time, South Vietnam had been making a series of small-scale strikes on North Vietnamese shore facilities from which Communist infiltration operations were launched. Johnson believed that the North Vietnamese might have mistakenly thought the *Maddox* was involved in one such attack, though the ship was 120 miles away at the time. He therefore ordered that our ships stay even farther away from South Vietnamese coastal forays. But on August 4 North Vietnamese patrol boats attacked the *Maddox* and the USS *C. Turner Joy* with torpedos and gunfire. The Johnson administration retaliated with our first air strikes on targets in North Vietnam.

Years later, antiwar journalists asserted that the August 4 incident never occurred and accused Johnson and the military of fabricating it as a pretext to intervene in the war. While some respected military observers have questioned whether the attack took place, I have concluded that it did and there is no credible evidence that we provoked it. Even official North Vietnamese histories of the war include it in their narratives. And when Admiral Thomas Moorer, who was in charge of the ships on patrol, was later asked whether the attack really happened, he said the North Vietnamese bullets that were dug out of the *Maddox* looked real enough to him.

On August 7, President Johnson, who had wanted for some time to "get Congress on board" before taking strong actions in Vietnam, sent Congress the Southeast Asia Resolution or, as it became known, the Tonkin Gulf Resolution. It was not,

181

as some would later say, a cynical ploy to obtain broad powers to fight the war. It was an honest effort to get congressional support for the deepening involvement that had been forced upon us.

The Tonkin Gulf incidents were not the reason we went into Vietnam, just as the sinking of the *Lusitania* was not why we entered World War I. Johnson's resolution stated that the attacks were "part of a deliberate and systematic campaign of aggression that the Communist regime in North Vietnam has been waging against its neighbors and the nations joined with them in the collective defense of their freedom." It resolved "that the Congress approves and supports the determination of the President, as Commander-in-Chief, to take all necessary measures to repel any armed aggression against the forces of the United States and to prevent further aggression."

We did not go to war because of two brief naval skirmishes but because North Vietnam was trying to take over Indochina.

Many have faulted Johnson for not asking Congress for a declaration of war. He almost certainly could have gotten one after the Tonkin Gulf incidents. But he had several reasons to stop short of a declared state of war.

Neither Congress nor the Pentagon was demanding a declaration of war, because nobody expected the conflict to last very long. Johnson believed that tactical bombing in South Vietnam and limited strategic bombing in North Vietnam would soon cause the Communists to cease their aggression. He feared that China might intervene in Vietnam as it had in Korea and that a formal declaration of war would enable North Vietnam to cash in on both Chinese and Soviet security guaranties. And finally, Johnson, understandably, did not want to go to war in an election year.

Congress approved the Tonkin Gulf Resolution overwhelmingly. The House voted 416 to 0 in favor of it after only forty minutes of debate. The Senate debated the resolution for eight hours and passed it 88 to 2. These votes showed that Johnson had a solid consensus behind his policy. Congressional sentiment was best summarized by one legislator who later became a vehement opponent of the war. "There is a time to question the route of the flag," said Senator Frank Church, "and there is a time to rally around it, lest it be routed. This is the time for the latter course, and in our pursuit of it, a time for all of us to unify."

Those who supported the resolution but later turned against the war tried to absolve themselves by accusing Johnson of duping the Congress about the extent of the powers it was delegating or of acting beyond his authority. Neither was the case. The record of the Senate debate shows that Congress went into the war with its eyes open. Senator John Sherman Cooper asked, "[I]f the President decided that it was necessary to use such force as could lead us into war, we would give that authorization by this resolution?" Senator J. William Fulbright, who steered the measure through the Senate, answered, "That is the way I would interpret it." Senator Daniel Brewster asked whether "the resolution authorized the landing of large American armies in Vietnam or in China." Fulbright answered that this was the last thing the administration wanted but that "the language of the resolution would not prevent it. It would authorize whatever the Commander-in-Chief feels is necessary." And one of two senators who voted against the resolution, Ernest Gruening, warned that it was "an authorization which would be the equivalent of a declaration of war by Congress."

The Tonkin Gulf Resolution was not the President's sole legal basis for conducting the war. Johnson was acting in accordance with the security provisions of the Southeast Asia Treaty Organization (SEATO). And Congress exercised its war powers every year when it authorized spending for our forces in Vietnam.

Congress reaffirmed its support for the war in March 1966, long after our troops had become deeply involved in the ground war. Senator Wayne Morse introduced a measure that denounced the way the President used the powers granted by the Tonkin Gulf Resolution. Johnson made it a test of congressional support for his policy. He urged that "senators who want to reverse the Tonkin resolution because of a change of heart should vote for the Morse amendment." The Senate rejected the amendment—and therefore supported the war—by a vote of 92 to 5.

In July 1965, eleven months after the approval of the Tonkin Gulf Resolution, we took our most fateful step into the quicksand of the Vietnam War. President Johnson simultaneously faced two sets of critical decisions: He had to maneuver the legislation for his Great Society programs through Congress, and he had to decide what to do to prevent the imminent collapse of South Vietnam. How he resolved these two problems set the pattern for his handling of the war and had a great deal to do with what went wrong in it.

Until 1965, Johnson hoped words, not deeds, would be enough to deter North Vietnam's aggression. "We will remain as long as is necessary," he said in April 1964, "with the might that is required, whatever the risk and whatever the cost." But like Kennedy on Laos in 1961, Johnson, however expansive his rhetoric, was reluctant to take the military action necessary to back it up. For about a year he had made little use of his war powers under the Tonkin Gulf Resolution. At first he ordered limited bombing in Laos and North Vietnam and then deployed additional ground troops in South Vietnam, but only to protect our air bases. Johnson made the fatal mistake of committing American prestige without committing adequate American forces to back it up.

He hoped that these limited actions would not only lead North Vietnam to seek peace but also increase the combat effectiveness of South Vietnam's army by bolstering its morale. His hopes were disappointed. With South Vietnam tottering on the edge of defeat, morale alone could not turn the tide, and Ho Chi Minh's mind was set on military conquest, not compromise.

In the summer of 1965, North Vietnam began a concerted drive for total victory. Now, to fulfill his pledge to keep South Vietnam free, Johnson decided he had to undertake a huge military buildup in Vietnam and order our troops to take over the war against the guerrillas. This decision made it America's war rather than South Vietnam's.

The most critical week of the Johnson presidency began on July 21, 1965. The President had long been torn between the conflicting demands of the war in Vietnam and the war on poverty. Now he had to assign priorities.

On July 21, Secretary of Defense McNamara reported to the National Security Council that the military picture was rapidly deteriorating. He recommended that the President send another 100,000 men to Vietnam by October and said that an additional 100,000 might be needed in early 1966. McNamara also suggested that the administration ask Congress for authority to call up 235,000 troops from the reserves.

The cost for these steps would add up to $8 billion. The President could get the money either by seeking a supplemental appropriation from Congress or by juggling the accounts in the Pentagon budget. As Johnson contemplated such a major escalation of our role in Vietnam, he also had to decide whether to mobilize the country behind the war. Meanwhile, the Great Society hung in the balance in Congress. During the week of July 21, two centerpieces of Johnson's domestic program—the civil rights bill and Medicare—had reached crucial stages in Conference Committee. Another twenty-six major bills were moving through the House and Senate, while eleven more awaited scheduling.

Johnson knew that the Great Society and the Vietnam War were on a collision course. He was convinced that any action which focused attention on the war undermined the prospects for his domestic program. He later exploded in exasperation, "If I left the woman I really loved—the Great Society—in order to get involved with that bitch of a war on the other side of the world, then I would lose everything at home." On the one hand, if he let North Vietnam win the war, the acrimonious debate about who lost South Vietnam would wreck his plans for the Great Society. On the other hand, if he went all out to win the war, conservatives would use it as an excuse to gut his domestic programs. "History provided too many cases where the sound of a bugle put an immediate end to the hopes and dreams of the best reformers," Johnson later told a biographer. He added that once the Vietnam War had begun, "all those conservatives in the Congress would use it as a weapon against the Great Society."

It was a terrible dilemma for Johnson. He could not afford to lose the war, and he could not afford to do what was necessary to win it. Either way he would lose the Great Society. He made the worst possible choice: He would fight—not to win, but only not to lose.

Johnson decided to pursue a policy of guns *and* butter. He gave his Great Society programs priority over Vietnam and tried to prosecute the war out of the public spotlight. As he approved additional military actions in Vietnam, he told his National Security Council that he did not want to be "overly dramatic and cause tensions." His fear was not that bellicose rhetoric would lead to a superpower confrontation but that a public debate on the war would kill his domestic plans.

He deliberately downplayed the importance of the actions he was taking in Vietnam. He announced that he was sending our armed forces into war in a short opening statement during an afternoon press conference. He did not seek authority from Congress to call up the reserves. He did not ask for a resolution of national emergency or even a supplemental appropriations bill. He did not present his plan for the war in a prime-time address to the nation. He did not publicly disclose the size of the anticipated call-up through the draft or explain that our troops would now engage in direct combat. He did not cut back social programs or increase taxes to put the economy on a wartime footing.

Making the point that Vietnam was a just war would have been easy, but Johnson deliberately chose to avoid the question. While he sporadically made strong statements on the war, he never marshaled a concerted public campaign to explain why we were in Vietnam. It was the greatest political error this master politician ever made. American leaders cannot wage war without the solid support of public opinion, and the

American people will go to war only if they are convinced that it is in a just cause. An American President therefore must never commit his troops to battle without getting the people to commit themselves to the war.

When Johnson intervened in Vietnam, he had to deal with the war as he found it. It was being fought in South Vietnam with guerrilla tactics, and the government in Saigon was near collapse. Our first priority was to stop our ally's slide toward defeat at the hands of Communist guerrillas. But that alone could not ensure South Vietnam's survival. Our second priority should have been to blunt North Vietnam's invasion through Laos and Cambodia. And because our forces eventually would be withdrawn, our third priority should have been to prepare South Vietnam to defend itself against both the internal and external threats it faced.

From 1964 through 1968, our strategy primarily addressed our first priority—and by virtually ignoring the other two, guaranteed its own failure. Had we addressed all three problems from the outset of our involvement, President Johnson could have ended the Vietnam War before he left office. Instead, it became our longest war.

Democracies are not well equipped to fight prolonged or limited wars. A totalitarian power can coerce its population into fighting indefinitely, but a democracy fights well only as long as its public opinion supports the war, and public opinion will not continue to support a war that is fought indecisively or that drags on without tangible signs of progress. This is doubly true when the war is being fought half a world away.

Some say that our mistake was in failing to follow Douglas MacArthur's dictum that in war there is no substitute for victory. According to them, we should have either stayed out of the war entirely or sought unconditional victory over the enemy as we had in World War II. But few wars have been all-or-nothing propositions. Unlimited or total wars have been a rarity. Except for World War II, none of our foreign conflicts has been a total war. We did not demand the surrender of

Madrid in the Spanish-American War or march on Berlin in the First World War, and we accepted an armistice to end the Korean War.

The goal of victory is essential for a democracy at war. But seeking victory does not just mean waging an unlimited war with the sole goal being the total defeat and surrender of the enemy. There can be victory in a limited war like the one in Vietnam. Victory must be defined in terms of concrete political goals that are to be reached using military means. In Vietnam, victory meant preventing the imposition of a Communist government on South Vietnam. But when we intervened in the war, we failed to tailor our means to this end.

A sound strategy in Vietnam would have begun with the recognition of five facts.

First, the theater of conflict included all of Indochina. Cambodia and Laos were involved in the war just as much as South Vietnam was. This was true not only because Ho Chi Minh's ultimate goal was to rule all of what once was French Indochina, but also because the North Vietnamese Army occupied and operated from territory in all of these countries.

Second, North Vietnam's external aggression was the *central* cause of the war. Forming our strategy required us to determine the origin of the war. Could the enemy have waged the war without major support from North Vietnam? Or was North Vietnam's participation indispensable to the enemy's conduct of the war? In the first case, it would have been in essence a civil war. In the second, it would have to have been classified as foreign aggression. If it had been a civil war, we probably should not have intervened in the first place. But all the evidence pointed to North Vietnamese aggression. The Johnson administration was well aware of the facts and even released documentary evidence to prove them in its "White Papers." Our problem was not a failure to realize the facts but an unwillingness to *act* on them. Had we acted on the facts, we would have taken whatever steps were necessary to cut off the Ho Chi Minh Trail.

Third, while we dealt with North Vietnam's invasion

through Laos and Cambodia, South Vietnam ideally should have taken responsibility for defeating the guerrillas within its borders. But circumstances in Vietnam were not ideal. Guerrilla warfare was North Vietnam's principal tactic at the time of our intervention. There was no way that we could have avoided a direct role in fighting the guerrillas, especially with South Vietnam as enfeebled as it was. But had we kept the proper division of labor in mind, our priorities would have been different. Even as we battled the guerrillas in South Vietnam, we would have focused our attention on cutting North Vietnam's invasion routes and on training our ally to take over the fight against the insurgents.

Fourth, the war against the Communist guerrillas in South Vietnam could not be won with conventional military tactics. Traditionally, the military object in war is to destroy the armed forces of the enemy. But the war in South Vietnam was as much a political struggle as a military one. The political battle was not over votes or popularity but over whose government would control the countryside. We did not have to convince the South Vietnamese that communism was bad. Apart from the members of the National Liberation Front, the great majority of the people were against Hanoi. But they could not oppose the guerrillas unless we could offer protection from Communist reprisals. For this, we did not need a strategy designed to wear down the enemy with search-and-destroy missions that won only temporary control of an area. We needed one aimed at permanently extending the reach of South Vietnam's government and securing it through local defenses.

Fifth, as Eisenhower had emphasized to Kennedy in 1961, Laos was the key to a winning strategy. North Vietnam's invasion passed through it, and the insurgents in South Vietnam depended on their sanctuaries in both Laos and Cambodia. We should have landed a large contingent of troops just below or above the demilitarized zone with orders to push its way across Laos to the Mekong River and take up positions along this route that would have quarantined North Vietnam. This maneuver would have extended the demilitarized zone 100 miles

189

to the west. More important, it would have created a defensible border and cut off North Vietnam's routes for sending men and matériel to its guerrillas in the South. Without this barrier, North Vietnam would endlessly replace its casualties and re-supply its fighters. With it, South Vietnam's forces could mop up the indigenous insurgents once and for all.

But that is not the way we fought the war. A blind belief in esoteric counterinsurgency doctrine, an unwarranted faith in the Geneva agreement on Laos, an unjustified fear of Communist Chinese intervention, and an unwillingness to mobilize the American people to win the war led the Johnson administration to adopt a strategy of gradual escalation and to limit the ground war to South Vietnamese territory. Johnson said that "we seek no wider war" and pledged not to invade North Vietnam or to overthrow Ho Chi Minh. But by dispelling North Vietnam's fears that we might make use of our enormous military superiority, he eliminated any incentive for its leaders to cease their war against South Vietnam.

From 1964 through 1968, we became caught between our desire to limit the war and our talent for waging unlimited war. As a result our armed forces ended up fighting a war for which we were not suited, with tactics that were not suited to it.

During the first years of our intervention, we pursued two totally inadequate strategies. In South Vietnam, we tried to fight a war of attrition with American forces. But we failed to see that we could never succeed as long as we did not seal off the infiltration routes through Laos and Cambodia and provide the rural population with protection from guerrilla attacks. In North Vietnam, we kept our military pressure sharply limited and increased it only in gradual increments in the hope of inducing North Vietnam to seek a negotiated peace. We should have known that we never could coax Ho Chi Minh into abandoning a war he had chosen to start. We should have *forced* him to abandon it.

Defeating a well-organized guerrilla insurgency is a difficult task. There were those who said it was impossible. But revolutionaries using guerrilla tactics have failed far more often than they have succeeded. Greece defeated Communist guerrillas immediately after World War II. So did Thailand, the Philippines, and Malaysia. Guerrilla warfare is a tactic of the weak. Its chances for success are therefore rarely strong.

One expert on guerrilla war observed that the success of an insurgency depends on whether the revolutionaries have a popular cause and an effective organization. If they have both, the insurgents will almost certainly win. If they have neither, even an ineffective government will prevail. If their cause is popular but their organization is weak, an effective government will snuff out the insurgency. But if their cause is not popular while their organization is strong and effective, the war will become a long-drawn-out battle. That is what happened in Vietnam.

There were two sides—one political and the other military— to the war in South Vietnam.

The Communists waged their political struggle in the villages and hamlets. It was not a matter of passing out leaflets to win the hearts and minds of prospective supporters but a ruthless attempt to replace the current government with one of their own. First, they sought to destroy the Saigon government's presence in the countryside by assassinating or abducting its local officials. Second, they tried to turn the South Vietnamese people against the central government. The insurgents sought either to incite the peasants to hate the government by championing and distorting popular grievances or, if that failed, to terrorize the people with violence in order to cow them into submission.

Outside the villages, the Communists waged the military struggle with the tactics of guerrilla war. Platoon-size units were dispersed in the hills. These were deployed individually for hit-and-run attacks and consolidated only for a major assault.

One side of the war was intimately intertwined with the other: The political war helped create the base for the military war. Some South Vietnamese freely supported the Communists. But most submitted to them only because they were the ones who had the guns.

Those who voluntarily served the Communist cause were integrated into a highly organized secret network, or infrastructure, at the village level. It kept track of who was cooperating with the government. It provided the guerrillas with supplies, intelligence, and recruits. It helped them find food and shelter, conceal caches of weapons, and escape from patrolling government troops. Without an infrastructure involving perhaps 10 percent of the local population, the guerrilla war would have become unsustainable.

But Communist control of the countryside depended on the creation of an atmosphere of fear. Saigon's armed patrols could move freely through most of the countryside during the day. But after nightfall, when they withdrew to their outposts, Communists troops had free run of virtually every village. It was impossible for twenty government soldiers to protect all the peasants from an outpost at the corner of an area of twenty square miles. When Communist officers appeared at the door, no one in his right mind would have refused to comply with whatever they demanded, whether it was to hand over a tax of ten pounds of rice or hand over a son to serve with the guerrillas.

We had three possible strategies to deal with the enemy's tactics. We could try to grind down the guerrilla forces in a war of attrition. We could try to uproot their infrastructure in the villages through pacification. Or we could seek to do both.

Waging a military and a political battle simultaneously was the key to victory. There was a lot of talk about counterinsurgency doctrine in the Kennedy and Johnson administrations. But neither had a strategy to defeat both sides of the insurgency as the British had done in Malaysia. Our efforts to foster democracy and economic growth neither deterred the North Vietnamese who were directing the guerrilla war nor bolstered Saigon's control at the village level.

Our counterinsurgency doctrine ended up meaning only that

we would fight the war on South Vietnamese territory. Specialized units, like the Green Berets and the Combined Action Platoons, which focused on providing security at the village level and on uprooting the Communist infrastructure, were never more than a low-priority sideshow. Our military advisers trained South Vietnam's army to wage a large-unit conventional war, and our own forces acted as if they were fighting a conventional war in Europe or Korea.

General Earle Wheeler, army chief of staff, said in 1962, "It is fashionable in some quarters to say that the problems in Southeast Asia are primarily political and economic rather than military. I do not agree. The essence of the problem is military." The Pentagon, which had been put in charge of managing day-to-day operations in Vietnam following the Bay of Pigs disaster, proceeded to devise a purely military solution. It was the strategy of attrition. Our forces were to "seek out and destroy" major Communist military units, bases, and other facilities. This, combined with efforts to cut off the infiltration of additional men and matériel from North Vietnam, would lead to the "progressive destruction" of Communist military forces.

Search-and-destroy missions became our principal tactic. In theory, American forces would use their vastly superior firepower and mobility to liberate enemy-occupied territory and would then turn over the area to South Vietnamese forces, who were to root out the Communist infrastructure and provide permanent security. In reality, South Vietnam's army was unable to follow up our victories because it did not have enough well-trained troops. We tallied up hundreds of victories in these battles—often retaking the same hill over and over—but they did not add up to victory in the war. Many areas we liberated reverted to Communist control almost as soon as we left.

By virtually ignoring the political aspect of the war, we stepped onto a treadmill. While our troops spent their time finding, engaging, and destroying the enemy's larger units, the Communists ruled the villages. Their presence was constantly felt. Their infrastructure remained intact. Their troops returned a few days after ours left, and their war effort resumed almost without a hitch.

When the British army advocated a purely military solution in Malaysia, Britain's counterinsurgency expert, Sir Robert Thompson, disagreed, saying, "It's all very well having bombers, masses of helicopters, tremendous firepower, but none of these will eliminate a Communist cell in a high school which is producing 50 recruits a year for the insurgent movement." In Vietnam, while we were fighting in the hills, the Communists had free run of the hamlets.

Attrition was a fatally flawed strategy. We underestimated the enemy's ability to control his losses and to bring in reinforcements from North Vietnam. No matter how hard we tried to engage him in decisive battles, he could avoid them by either evading our troops or withdrawing to sanctuaries in Cambodia and Laos. Guerrilla units in the field received excellent intelligence about our troop movements from the Communist infrastructure in cities and villages. If the guerrillas did not want to fight, they simply let our forces pass through the areas they occupied. Because the guerrillas controlled the tempo of the fighting, the Communists were able to control their own casualty rates and thereby prevent the attrition of their ranks.

Our strategy ultimately failed because we did not stop the steady stream of reinforcements coming down the Ho Chi Minh Trail from North Vietnam. The success of a strategy of attrition depended on whether we would pass the point where enemy losses exceeded new recruits in the South and reinforcements from the North. That point was never reached. From January 1965 through December 1967, Communist losses totaled 344,000, including 179,000 troops killed in action. Despite these staggering figures, Communist forces in South Vietnam increased from 181,000 in December 1964 to 262,000 in December 1967. Over those three years, North Vietnam and recruitment in South Vietnam had supplied over 400,000 reinforcements. Population statistics indicated that this rate could be sustained: Another 120,000 North Vietnamese boys reached military age each year.

We should have realized that it was impossible to win a war of attrition against the guerrillas in South Vietnam as long as the Ho Chi Minh Trail remained open for business. But during the years of our deepening involvement, we never formulated a strategy to put North Vietnam's invasion out of business.

From 1965 through 1968, the United States carried out an aerial bombing campaign against North Vietnam. President Johnson's objective was not military but political. He was not trying to stop North Vietnam's invasion but rather to raise South Vietnamese morale and to increase steadily the cost to Hanoi's leaders of their infiltration of men and matériel into the South. Civilian advisers had convinced him that we should pursue a strategy of gradual escalation coupled with repeated offers to negotiate settlement. Our bombing would begin at a low level and increase in gradual increments. It was naïvely assumed that when Hanoi recognized the pattern of our mounting pressure, it would come to the negotiating table and call off its war against South Vietnam in order to avoid the destruction of North Vietnam.

Our bombing was always sharply restricted in practice. President Johnson once boasted that the military "can't even bomb an outhouse without my approval." Both Johnson and Secretary of Defense McNamara, who personally chose the targets for the bombing program, were afraid of provoking the intervention of China or the Soviet Union and therefore limited the intensity and frequency of our attacks. No strategic bombers such as B-52s were used. No targets apart from roads, railroads, bridges, power plants, barracks, and supply dumps were attacked. No bombing was permitted within a twenty-five to thirty-mile-deep buffer zone along the Chinese border, a thirty-mile radius around Hanoi, and a ten-mile radius around the port of Haiphong.

In accordance with its strategy of gradual escalation, the administration unilaterally declared sixteen pauses in the bombing, ranging from twenty-four hours to thirty-six days, and sent out seventy-two diplomatic peace initiatives in the hope that North Vietnam would take reciprocal steps toward ending the war.

Our attempt to fine-tune our bombing in order to send precise political messages to Hanoi wasted our military advantage. Eisenhower saw that it was folly. While he supported Johnson's war effort in public, he was bluntly critical of the policy of gradualism in private. He told me in 1966, "If an enemy holds a position with a battalion, give me two battalions and I'll take it, but at a great cost in casualties. Give me a division and I'll take it without a fight."

Our gradual escalation gave North Vietnam time to adapt to the additional pressure by dispersing its people, military supplies, and industry. Also, our restraint put many important military targets off limits. Johnson forbade air strikes against Haiphong, the port through which 85 percent of North Vietnam's supplies arrived, because Soviet and Chinese ships docked there. When Soviet antiaircraft missile sites began to appear, he prohibited attacks on them while they were under construction to avoid the possibility of killing any Soviet personnel.

Hanoi exploited our restraint. When it was clear that we would not bomb a small airfield outside Hanoi because it was used by couriers from Moscow and Peking, the Communists put their best airplanes there. And whenever we declared a bombing pause, the Communists immediately accelerated their shipments of troops and supplies into South Vietnam.

Our policy sent the wrong political message to Hanoi. Johnson's advisers stated publicly that we faced a long and difficult war in Vietnam; that we feared Soviet and Chinese intervention; and that we would not "widen" the conflict into North Vietnam. Meanwhile, the administration carried out a limited bombing campaign in fits and starts and sent out a cascade of peace feelers almost begging Hanoi to come to the negotiating table. Ho Chi Minh, who had deliberately begun the Vietnam War and who had never indicated a willingness to settle on any terms other than his own, could only have interpreted our gradual escalation as a sign not of restraint but of weakness.

When a President sends American troops to war, a hidden timer starts to run. He has a finite period of time to win the war before the people grow weary of it. In February 1968, President Johnson ran out of time.

A single event brought to a halt the steady deepening of American involvement in the Vietnam War. A concerted, nationwide Communist assault—the Tet Offensive—caught the United States and South Vietnam off-guard and shocked the American people. Our forces quickly crushed the enemy. It turned out to be a major military defeat for the Communists in South Vietnam, but grotesquely inaccurate news-media reporting turned it into a major political and psychological victory for them in the United States.

North Vietnam's leaders launched the Tet Offensive because they thought victory was at hand. In late 1967, the North's Communist party stated that the political situation in South Vietnam was right for a "general offensive and general uprising in order to achieve a decisive victory for the revolution." Ho Chi Minh knew he did not have the military power to rout the armies of South Vietnam and the United States. But he believed he could win anyway.

His plan came straight out of a handbook on revolutionary war: Communist forces would strike South Vietnam's cities, and these attacks would trigger the South Vietnamese people to revolt and to join the Communists in bringing down the government in Saigon. The plan's critical assumption was that in their hearts and minds the people supported the Communists.

On January 31, 1968, the Communists began their offensive. It was timed to coincide with the start of a truce they had pledged to observe during the celebrations of Tet, the Vietnamese new year. General Westmoreland had warned that a major enemy offensive was in the works. But nobody expected it to come during the Tet truce, when half of South Vietnam's army would be on holiday leave. Nor did anyone anticipate the size or scope of the attack. Over 70,000 Communist troops attacked more than 100 cities and towns and scores of military bases throughout South Vietnam. Four thousand Communist troops surged into Saigon itself. Ugly urban warfare ensued. Because they achieved total surprise, the Communists won early gains. Within a day, we reversed the tide. Within a week, we cleared out all but their strongholds. Within a month, we routed them. It is particularly significant to note that Ho's plan failed because none of his attacks was followed by a popular uprising.

Years later, a CBS News documentary claimed that the enemy's successes during the Tet Offensive resulted in part from a conspiracy led by General Westmoreland to suppress intelligence estimates that Communist troop levels were twice as high as the figures in our official order of battle. The documentary's vicious attack on the personal integrity of one of America's most distinguished military leaders was yellow journalism at its worst. Westmoreland is a straight-arrow, almost painfully by-the-book military professional. I cannot think of a military man who would have been less likely to deceive American political leaders or the public by giving a falsely optimistic appraisal of the military situation in Vietnam. On the contrary, I found him more realistic and at times even more pessimistic in his assessments than other military and civilian leaders I met on my trips to Vietnam.

In Vietnam, order-of-battle figures were difficult to fix with precision because so much depended on how we defined an enemy *combatant*. No one questioned the inclusion of the troops in Communist mobile battalions. But some, including those who produced the allegedly suppressed estimates, wanted to count members of the Communist infrastructure and unarmed self-defense forces. Westmoreland decided that only those who contributed directly to the enemy's military strength in the field would be tallied in his order of battle. All of this was explained to President Johnson and his national security adviser. Westmoreland acted rightly and honorably. Throughout this whole controversy, the only deceptions have been those of CBS in its documentary.

The Tet Offensive was a military disaster for North Vietnam. Ho had staked everything on the roll of the dice and lost. American and South Vietnamese forces mauled his best military units. Thousands of his most dedicated and experienced troops and combat leaders were killed or seriously wounded. Official North Vietnamese reports soon expressed alarm at plummeting morale as troops "lost confidence" in their leaders, became "doubtful of victory," and displayed "shirking attitudes." It would take two years for the North Vietnamese Army to recover.

Also, the National Liberation Front was broken as a military force. Expecting victory, Ho had ordered all secret Communist operatives and terrorists in South Vietnam to abandon their covers. When his offensive failed, those agents not killed in combat were identified and captured. South Vietnam's police were able to uproot almost the entire Communist network.

Finally, the Tet Offensive was a political disaster for the Communist cause in South Vietnam. Ho Chi Minh lost the "people's war." The Communists never had the support of more than a small minority of the South Vietnamese, but that did not mean the majority supported the government in Saigon. The Communist threat had seemed distant to many, especially those living in the cities, and the anti-Communist cause was weak and disorganized. The Tet Offensive radically altered the political landscape. It galvanized the South Vietnamese through the shock of the urban fighting and the horror of widespread Communist atrocities. Far from producing the uprisings Ho expected, it created a strong counterreaction that led to the full mobilization of the South Vietnamese people against the Communist aggressors.

Although it was an overwhelming victory for South Vietnam and the United States, the almost universal theme of media coverage was that we had suffered a disastrous defeat. This was true not only in the first chaotic hours of the offensive but also weeks later after the fog of war had lifted. One network reporter flatly said we were "losing" the war. Another stated that it was increasingly clear that "the only rational way" out of the war "will be to negotiate, not as victors, but as an honorable people." The steady drumbeat of inaccurate stories convinced millions of Americans that we had lost a major battle.

Reporters, most of whom knew nothing about military affairs, missed the big picture. Instead, they focused on isolated, dramatic incidents, often getting their stories dramatically wrong. At first the media played an attack on the American Embassy in Saigon as an enemy triumph. One television anchorman reported that "twenty suicide commandos" were "holding the first floor of the embassy." That was not what happened. A platoon of insurgents had blown a hole in the embassy wall, and a few entered the grounds of the compound before all of them were gunned down by our guards.

Later the news media fixed their attention on the nine-week battle of Khesanh. They described the siege of the 6,000-man American base as if it were a reenactment of Dien Bien Phu, with one network reporter intoning that "the parallels are there for all to see." In fact, we were never in danger of losing Khesanh. North Vietnam threw 40,000 men into the battle and lost over 10,000 of them. It was the most costly single battle for the enemy in the entire Vietnam War.

Even more glaring was the news media's failure to report on the massacre at Hue.

When the Communists overran the city, they came prepared with "blood-debt lists" drawn up five months before. These contained the names of all policemen, government personnel, and political enemies of the National Liberation Front who could be killed on the spot without consulting a higher authority. Once inside Hue, Communist death squads quickly killed the 200 targets on their lists. But they did not stop there. They began murdering anyone who, in their eyes, had any link to the Saigon government. These included a part-time janitor at a government office who was executed in his front yard along with his two young children, and a cigarette vendor who was assassinated simply because her sister was a government worker. Eyewitnesses later reported seeing victims forced to dig their own graves before being gunned down by firing squads.

It should have made a big story. After all, the fate of Hue, the only provincial capital to fall to the Communists during the Tet Offensive, certainly indicated what the Communists had in mind for the rest of South Vietnam. But the total news coverage of the massacre amounted to six stories on the wire services and seven in the major dailies. Nothing appeared on network television. These stories described the discovery of the first mass grave and estimated the death toll to be between 200 and 400. No reports came out when another eighteen mass graves were found in the following days. Nor did reporters flock to the area as more burial sites were found in nearby mountains, jungle clearings, and coastal-sand flats. The death toll would climb to 2,810 by mid-1970, while another 1,946 remained missing.

During their twenty-five days in power in Hue, the Communists had killed between 5 and 10 percent of the city's population, but the news media did not find it newsworthy.

The stark contrast between the extensive media coverage of the American massacre at My Lai and the minimal reports on the massive Communist atrocities at Hue illustrated one of the most striking differences between democratic and Communist regimes: We advertise our faults; they bury theirs.

News media accounts of the Tet Offensive disillusioned the American people with the Vietnam War and thereby turned the offensive into a major political and psychological victory for North Vietnam. The Johnson administration had always exuded optimism about our progress in the war. Now the people heard that we were losing the war as they watched street fighting in Saigon on their television sets. That this could even happen caused them to question the validity and credibility of the administration's policy.

In November 1967 and February 1968, Gallup polls surveyed public opinion on how the war was going. The proportion who said the United States was losing the war rose from 8 percent before the Tet Offensive to 23 percent afterward. The second poll also indicated that 61 percent believed we were either losing ground or standing still in Vietnam. Public opinion was not caught up in antiwar sentiments. Unlike many in the antiwar movement, the American people did not want to see their country humiliated. But after almost three years of fighting, they were frustrated because no quick end to the war was in sight.

The Tet Offensive shook the Johnson White House to its foundations. Serious doubts arose in the minds of many of his advisers about whether we could win in Vietnam. When Johnson consulted a group of former high officials he called the "wise men," all of whom had been strong supporters of our commitment in Vietnam, he found that six favored disengagement in some form, four advocated standing firm, and one straddled the fence. "If they had been so deeply influenced by the reports of the Tet Offensive," Johnson later wrote, "what must the average citizen in the country be thinking?" On March 31, President Johnson answered his own question by announcing that he would not seek reelection.

After the Tet Offensive, Johnson's growing pessimism about the war led him to engage in the most wishful exercise of diplomacy in American postwar history: the talks leading to the complete halt in the bombing of North Vietnam on November 1, 1968.

Johnson passionately wanted peace and was shaken by the sharp increase in antiwar sentiment after the Tet Offensive. His advisers told him that North Vietnam was eager to reach a negotiated resolution of the war and that American public opinion would soon no longer support our military efforts in Vietnam. On March 31, in accordance with their advice, Johnson declared a unilateral halt to all bombing of North Vietnamese territory above the twentieth parallel, and later the nineteenth, in the hope that Hanoi would take reciprocal steps toward peace.

But reciprocity was not in character for Ho Chi Minh.

Months before, he had decided to adopt a strategy of "talking and fighting." He knew that peace negotiations would create high hopes in the United States that would restrict our conduct of the war. It would be harder to escalate our pressure on North Vietnam, because public opinion would perceive it as detrimental to the peace talks. When Johnson announced his partial bombing halt in March, the North Vietnamese responded by saying, "The government of the Democratic Republic of Vietnam declares its readiness to appoint its representative to contact a United States representative with a view to arranging, with the American side, the unconditional cessation of United States bombing raids and all other acts of war against the Democratic Republic of Vietnam so that talks may start." Ho was not offering to talk about peace, or even to talk about starting peace talks. He was offering to talk about his preconditions for sitting down to talk about starting peace talks.

The Johnson administration treated this as if it were a breakthrough. Hanoi was demanding in effect that we lay down our arms before preliminary procedural negotiations could even begin. Johnson appointed Averell Harriman and Cyrus Vance as our representatives. Over the five months of negotiations, our side put forward four conditions for a complete halt to the bombing of North Vietnam: (1) Serious peace talks, which would include representatives of South Vietnam, must begin a few days after the bombing halt; (2) North Vietnam must not violate the demilitarized zone, either by infiltrating troops through it or by firing artillery or rockets over it; (3) Communist forces must not launch large-scale attacks on or fire rockets or artillery into major South Vietnamese cities; (4) North Vietnam must permit unarmed American reconnaissance planes to fly over its territory.

North Vietnam categorically rejected our conditions. But Harriman and Vance convinced Johnson that Hanoi's leaders were serious about wanting peace. Harriman argued that the only obstacle to progress was our demand that the conditions for a bombing halt be part of a formal agreement. Johnson therefore authorized them to accept an implied agreement to honor our conditions. When Hanoi continued to be obstinate, they gradually reduced our demands as to how firm North Vietnam's pledges had to be.

Finally, on October 11, Harriman and Vance told the North Vietnamese, "It is very important to understand that we are not talking about reciprocity or conditions but simply a fact that after cessation of all bombardment the President's ability to maintain that situation would be affected by certain elemental considerations." The art of diplomacy has seldom produced such gobbledygook. What we had previously treated as conditions were now, in the words of our negotiators, "a description of the situation which would permit serious negotiations and thus the cessations to continue."

On October 31, five days before the 1968 presidential election, Johnson announced that all bombing of North Vietnam would stop and that negotiations would begin. Within weeks, Hanoi had violated all the conditions we had originally insisted upon. We did nothing. Ho had called us and found us bluffing. We had traded away our most important negotiating asset—the bombing of North Vietnam—for a set of fuzzy "understandings" that Hanoi had never agreed to and had no intention of honoring. In the end, the bombing halt accomplished nothing except to make a cliff-hanger out of the 1968 presidential election.

Ho, who had made a career of exploiting the weaknesses of his adversaries, did not miss this opportunity. We had limited our intervention to South Vietnam's territory. We allowed North Vietnam to send men and matériel freely down the Ho Chi Minh Trail. We let Ho Chi Minh fight the war at his leisure, on our turf, and on his terms. We ignored the fact that war—particularly guerrilla war—is a question of willpower as much as military power. While we fought a war of attrition against his forces in South Vietnam, he was waging a war of attrition against our will to resist. At the end of 1968, it appeared that time was on his side.

The debate over whether we should expand our intervention in the Vietnam War ended with the Tet Offensive and the

November 1 bombing halt. These foreclosed the option of committing ourselves even deeper. Whatever the merits of our cause and whatever our chances of winning the war, it was no longer a question of whether the next President would withdraw our troops but of how they would leave and what they would leave behind.

How We Won
the War

On January 27, 1973, when Secretary of State William Rogers signed the Paris peace agreements, we had won the war in Vietnam. We had attained the one political goal for which we had fought the war: The South Vietnamese people would have the right to determine their own political future.

Ironically, though it had led President Johnson to withdraw from the election campaign, the enemy's Tet Offensive in 1968 was one of the war's most important turning points in our favor. As a result of our decisive military victory, we had a window of opportunity in Vietnam. North Vietnam, whose guerrilla forces and infrastructure in South Vietnam were largely destroyed, was forced to turn increasingly to the use of conventional military tactics. South Vietnam began to build up its military strength. The South Vietnamese people united behind the war effort.

But in the United States, the American people were tiring of the burdens of the war, and congressional opposition soon began to build. We had a limited period of time to prevail in Vietnam before the political support we needed to fight the war evaporated in Congress.

South Vietnam's freedom depended on whether our short-term military and political advantages in Vietnam could be converted into victory before the long-term erosion of American support for the war undermined our ability to wage it. Our window of opportunity was closing quickly.

On January 20, 1969, I became the fifth American President in twenty-three years to deal with the problem of Vietnam. For Harry Truman, Dwight Eisenhower, and John F. Kennedy, Vietnam had been a relatively minor irritant. For Lyndon Johnson, the war in Vietnam became the issue that destroyed his presidency.

When I came into office, I had two major long-term foreign-policy goals: to open a new relationship with the People's Republic of China and to develop a new relationship of negotiation rather than confrontation with the Soviet Union. But I recognized that my first priority had to be to end the Vietnam War in a way that would achieve the goal for which we had fought for so long. The war was tearing American society apart. It had been the major foreign-policy issue in the 1968 election. And the way in which the United States met its responsibilities in Vietnam could also be crucial to the Soviet and Chinese assessments of American will, and thus to the success of any new relationships with those two powers.

As I reviewed the record of the previous twenty-three years, I found that each of my predecessors had been motivated by different considerations in formulating his Vietnam policy.

Throughout his presidency, Harry Truman demonstrated that he would take strong action to stop Communist aggression. But he faced a dilemma in Vietnam. While he saw the danger of Communist conquest in Vietnam, he also opposed French colonialism. He believed that unless the French committed themselves to giving independence to the Vietnamese people, France might not be able to defeat the Communists. But Vietnam was a secondary issue for Truman. His primary concern immediately after World War II was to block Communist expansion in Europe. He needed French support to achieve that goal. Consequently, he continued to provide aid to France for its fight against the Communists in Indochina without insisting that the French give their colonies independence.

Dwight Eisenhower believed that Vietnam was of great strategic importance and that a loss there would lead to the loss of other Southeast Asian countries. But as a military man, he was instinctively opposed to committing ground troops to a land war in Asia. After ending the war in Korea, he did not want to become involved in another war. He was adamant that we not intervene militarily in Vietnam without the participation of our major European allies or without the assurance of bipartisan support in Congress. He seriously doubted that he could obtain either. Consequently, he did not take actions to prevent the French defeat at Dien Bien Phu, and while he provided technical advisers and financial assistance to the government of South Vietnam from 1954 through 1961, he refused to commit any United States combat personnel to the war.

In his inaugural address in 1961, John F. Kennedy declared: "Let every nation know, whether it wishes us well or ill, that we shall pay any price, bear any burden, meet any hardship, support any friend, oppose any foe to assure the survival and the success of liberty." He followed this up with another strong statement at his March 1961 press conference when he unequivocally indicated that the United States had a vital strategic interest in preventing Communist domination of Laos.

But he backed away from taking strong action to match his strong words. The Bay of Pigs disaster, where we used military power and yet failed to eliminate a Communist beachhead in Cuba, cooled his ardor for taking military action to prevent the Communist conquest of Laos. He agreed to "neutralize" Laos and committed 16,000 combat "advisers" to South Vietnam. Kennedy's advisers convinced him that President Diem's repressive policies and alleged persecution of the Buddhists made the South Vietnamese leader a liability. Kennedy concluded that the problem in South Vietnam was primarily political rather than military and could be solved only by the removal of Diem. He approved the coup that resulted in Diem's assassination and did not himself live to see the tragic consequences.

Lyndon Johnson inherited the chaos that followed Diem's fall. South Vietnam was swept up in political instability. Communist attacks increased. Johnson was a strong man who believed in strong actions, but like his predecessors, he was torn by conflicting concerns. Throughout his public career, his primary interest had been domestic rather than foreign policy. He wanted his legacy to be the Great Society. He was determined to avoid any actions in Vietnam that would jeopardize public or congressional support for his Great Society programs.

But Johnson was also a dedicated anti-Communist, and he hated to lose. In order to forestall defeat, he increased American combat forces from 16,000 to 550,000 troops over five years. Against his better instincts, however, he refused to give his military commanders the authority to conduct the war in a way that would have won it. He desperately wanted to end the war by negotiations. To demonstrate his desire for peace, he repeatedly ordered pauses in the bombing of North Vietnam—all of which, he ruefully told me in 1969, had been mistakes. Johnson could not bring himself to do enough to win the war against the Communists in Vietnam because he feared it might cause him to lose the war on poverty in the United States.

Truman, Eisenhower, Kennedy, and Johnson each saw the war differently. But these four Presidents, coming from different political parties and different backgrounds, were in total agreement on three fundamental points: A Communist victory would be a human tragedy for the people of Vietnam. It would imperil the survival of other free nations in Southeast Asia and would strike a damaging blow to the strategic interests of the United States. It would lead to further Communist aggression, not only in Southeast Asia but in other parts of the free world as well.

I strongly agreed with those conclusions. But I knew that the challenge I faced in seeking to prevent a Communist victory was formidable. Over a half-million American combat troops were stationed in Vietnam. Three hundred twenty-eight American POWs were held in North Vietnam's prison camps. Over fourteen hundred Americans had been killed or wounded in action during the week before I was inaugurated. No strategy existed either for winning the war or for ending it.

This was not the worst of the legacy I inherited. Johnson had pledged in the bombing-halt agreement of November 1, 1968, that the United States would stop all air strikes against North Vietnam in exchange for the start of negotiations and some vague understandings from Hanoi's leaders that they would not step up the fighting in South Vietnam. In two months the peace talks in Paris had produced no progress except for an agreement on the shape of the negotiating table.

The nation was bitterly divided. Lyndon Johnson had literally been driven from office by antiwar activists. I had been harassed by thousands of antiwar demonstrators, many of them violent, throughout the 1968 campaign. Hubert Humphrey had had the same problem until he came out in support of a bombing halt in mid-October. On Inauguration Day, the Secret Service refused to allow Mrs. Nixon and me to ride in an open car in the parade because hundreds of demonstrators waving Viet Cong flags were lining the motorcade route and scores of threats against us had been received. Even in the closed limousine, we could hear the protesters' chant: "Ho, Ho, Ho Chi Minh. The NLF is going to win."

I had begun a reappraisal of our Vietnam policy before I was inaugurated. During the transition, Henry Kissinger, whom I had chosen to be my national security adviser, began reviewing all the possible policies toward Vietnam and distilled them into a full spectrum of specific options, with massive military escalation at one extreme and immediate unilateral withdrawal at the other.

At one end of the spectrum, some hawks argued that we should go all out in pursuing military victory. Because I could not allow my heart to rule my head, I ruled out this option very early. Opinion polls showed that a significant percentage of the public favored a military victory in Vietnam—but only a victory won by delivering a knockout blow that would end the war quickly. Only two strategies existed that might have won the war in a single stroke. We could have bombed the elaborate system of irrigation dikes in North Vietnam, though this would have resulted in floods that would have killed hundreds of thousands of civilians. Or we could have used tactical nuclear weapons against enemy forces. Like Eisenhower in 1954, I gave no serious consideration to the nuclear option. I also categorically rejected the bombing of the dikes.

By the time I took office in 1969, the only strategy for pursuing a military victory that deserved serious consideration would have been to order a major escalation of the conventional war. We could have resumed the bombing of North Vietnam that Johnson had suspended in November 1968. We could have threatened to invade North Vietnam and thereby tied down North Vietnamese forces along the demilitarized zone. We could have crippled Hanoi's supply lines by mining Haiphong Harbor. We could have authorized the hot pursuit of Communist forces into their sanctuaries in Cambodia and Laos.

While we had the resources to pursue these tactics and while they might have brought victory, I knew it would probably require as much as six months and maybe more of highly intensified fighting and significantly increased casualties before the Communists would finally be forced to give up and accept a peace settlement.

None of these options was compatible with political reality.

If we had chosen to go for a knockout blow by bombing the dikes or using tactical nuclear weapons, the resulting domestic and international uproar would have damaged our foreign policy on all fronts.

I decided against an escalation of conventional fighting for three reasons. First, I doubted whether I could have held the country together for the period of time needed to win in view of the numbers of casualties we would be sustaining. As the close election results demonstrated, Johnson's bombing halt had been enormously popular, and though the Paris peace talks were stymied by North Vietnamese intransigence, the American people still had high hopes for their success. Second, having seen Vietnam paralyze American foreign policy for years, I was determined not to take actions in the war that would destroy our chances of developing a new relationship with the Soviet Union and the People's Republic of China. Third, I knew a military victory alone would not solve our problem. Assuming that we committed the forces and adopted the tactics needed to win militarily, what would happen after we had won? Unless the South Vietnamese were prepared to defend themselves, they would be overrun by the Communists as soon as we left.

For all these reasons, I decided against pursuing a purely military solution to the war.

Other hawks suggested a different approach. They conceded to the doves that we should not have gone into Vietnam in the first place, but contended that now that we were there, we had no choice but to see it through. Our goal, they argued, should not be to defeat the enemy but to stay long enough so that after we withdrew there would be a "decent interval" before South Vietnam fell to the Communists. I believed that this was the most immoral option of all. If our cause was unjust or if the war was unwinnable, we should have cut our losses and gotten out of Vietnam immediately. As President, I could not ask any young American to risk his life for an unjust or unwinnable cause.

Some doves urged that we simply continue the policy we had inherited. They believed that if we vigorously pressed the peace negotiations in Paris and presented our adversaries with "reasonable" proposals, the North Vietnamese would eventually agree to a cease-fire and a negotiated settlement of the war on terms we could accept. In dealing with the North Vietnamese, I had very little faith in a policy that relied on the negotiating process alone. To seek peace at any price was no answer to an enemy who sought victory at any price. I was convinced that unless we backed up our diplomatic efforts with strong military pressure, the North Vietnamese would continue their strategy of talking and fighting until we tired of the struggle and caved in to their bottom-line demand: that the United States withdraw unilaterally and acquiesce in the overthrow of the South Vietnamese government in exchange for the return of American prisoners of war. I considered it unthinkable that we would fight a bitter war for four years, lose 30,000 men, and spend tens of billions of dollars for the goal of getting our POWs back.

Finally, other doves urged that we end the war quickly by announcing the immediate withdrawal of all American forces. A compelling case for this option could be made in political terms. Several of my political allies advised me to blame the war on Kennedy, who had sent 16,000 Americans to Vietnam, and Johnson, who had increased their number to nearly 550,000. If I brought our troops home, they argued, I would be a hero regardless of what happened to South Vietnam and its people.

I rejected this option, too. Had I chosen it, the conquest of South Vietnam by North Vietnam would have been inevitable. That was a result I would not accept. As Vice President, I had been a strong advocate of measures that might have prevented this tragedy. As a private citizen, I had emphatically supported the decision to intervene in the war, though I had disagreed just as strongly with the way my predecessors had handled it. As President, I continued to believe that the moral and geopolitical reasons behind our intervention remained valid. Neither my head nor my heart would permit me to sacrifice our South Vietnamese allies to the enemy, regardless of the political costs I undoubtedly would incur by not withdrawing from the war immediately.

As I studied the option papers before my inauguration, I realized that I had no good choices. But Presidents are not elected to make easy decisions.

213

. . .

When Johnson administration officials briefed me about Vietnam before I took office, they presented no plan for how we should end the war. No progress had been made in the negotiations in Paris. No comprehensive American peace proposal had been announced. No plans existed to bring home any of our 550,000 troops in Vietnam. On the contrary, sending more troops had been under consideration.

In the first months of my administration, we put together a five-point strategy to win the war—or, more precisely, to end the war and win the peace. Our goal was not to conquer North Vietnam but to prevent North Vietnam from conquering South Vietnam.

VIETNAMIZATION. Since 1965, the United States had furnished most of the money, most of the arms, and a substantial proportion of the men to help the South Vietnamese defend their freedom. In the chaos following Diem's assassination, we had no choice but to take the lead role in the prosecution of the war. But as a result of this policy, the South Vietnamese military had developed an unhealthy, and unsustainable, dependence on the United States. Now we decided to train and equip South Vietnam's army so that it would have the capability of defending the country itself. This involved more than handing over our automatic rifles and the ignition keys of our tanks. The most optimistic estimates were that it would take at least three years to create a fighting force that could stand up to the North Vietnamese Army. Secretary of Defense Melvin Laird carried out this plan and dubbed it, appropriately, "Vietnamization." Our whole strategy depended on whether this program succeeded.

PACIFICATION. Our defeat of the Tet Offensive had produced a political vacuum in the countryside. Areas that the National Liberation Front had controlled for years were now up for grabs. We knew that whichever side won the race to take control of the hamlets would have won half the battle. We therefore abandoned the strategy of attrition, which had produced many casualties and few results, and replaced it with one of pacification. Our principal objectives shifted to protecting the South Vietnamese at the village level, reestablishing the local political process, and winning the loyalty of the peasants by involving them in the government and providing them with economic opportunity. General Creighton Abrams had initiated this shift in strategy when he took command of our forces in Vietnam in 1968. I reemphasized the critical importance of our pacification programs and channeled additional resources toward them.

DIPLOMATIC ISOLATION. All of North Vietnam's war matériel came from the Soviet Union or Communist China. I had long believed that an indispensable element of any successful peace initiative in Vietnam was to enlist, if possible, the help of the Soviets and the Chinese. Though rapprochement with China and detente with the Soviet Union were ends in themselves, I also considered them possible means to hasten the end of the war. At worst, Hanoi was bound to feel less confident if Washington was dealing with Moscow and Peking. At best, if the two major Communist powers decided that they had bigger fish to fry, Hanoi would be pressured into negotiating a settlement we could accept.

PEACE NEGOTIATIONS. Our decision to forgo a quick military victory increased the importance of the negotiating process in Paris. I was far less optimistic than some of my advisers about the possibility of quick progress in the negotiations unless we coupled our diplomatic efforts with irresistible military pressure. Ho Chi Minh and his battle-hardened colleagues had not fought and sacrificed for twenty-five years in order to negotiate a compromise peace. They were fighting for total victory. But in the hope that I was wrong, I vigorously pursued the negotiating process. I had another compelling reason for doing so. I knew it would not be possible to sustain public and congressional support for our military efforts unless we could demonstrate that we were exploring every avenue for ending the war through negotiations. I insisted on only two conditions: I made it clear I would reject any settlement that did not include the return of all our POWs and that did not protect the right of the South Vietnamese people to determine their own future.

GRADUAL WITHDRAWAL. The key new element in our strategy was a plan for the complete withdrawal of all American combat troops from Vietnam. Americans needed tangible evidence that we were winding down the war, and the South Vietnamese needed to be given more responsibility for their defense. We were not recklessly pulling out according to a fixed schedule. We linked the pace of our withdrawal to the progress of Vietnamization, the level of enemy activity, and developments at the negotiating table. Our withdrawal was to be made from strength, not from weakness. As South Vietnamese forces became stronger, the rate of American withdrawal could become greater. The announcement of the withdrawal program made another subtle but profoundly important point: While the French had fought to stay in Vietnam, the United States was fighting to get out.

Our new strategy in Vietnam sought to achieve the goal for which we had fought for four years. While the United States was going to end its involvement in the war, it would keep its commitments to South Vietnam. We would continue to fight until the Communists agreed to negotiate a fair and honorable peace or until the South Vietnamese were able to defend themselves on their own—whichever came first.

All five elements of our strategy needed time to take hold. I knew that we would have enough time only if the level of the fighting remained low. If the war heated up, American casualty rates and, in turn, domestic pressure to get out of Vietnam would increase dramatically. I also knew that the North Vietnamese would negotiate at the conference table only if we convinced them that they could not win on the battlefield.

In February 1969, while we were negotiating in Paris and

preparing a new peace initiative to probe Hanoi's intentions, the North Vietnamese launched a savage offensive in South Vietnam. Communist forces killed 453 Americans in the first week, 336 in the second, 351 in the third. South Vietnamese troops were being killed at a rate of over 500 per week. North Vietnamese forces launched a direct attack across the demilitarized zone and indiscriminately fired rockets into Saigon.

These moves were a deliberate test. If there were any truly binding understandings given in exchange for the bombing halt in November 1968, the North Vietnamese were blatantly violating them. I believed that if we let the Communists manipulate us at this early stage, we might never be able to negotiate with them from a position of strength, or even equality. The only way we could get things moving on the negotiating front was to do something on the military front. I therefore concluded that retaliation was necessary.

Our first option was to resume the bombing of North Vietnam. Ideally, we should have dealt a swift blow that would have made Hanoi's leaders think twice before they launched another attack in the South. But I was stuck with Johnson's bombing halt. I knew that even though we could show that North Vietnam clearly had violated the "understandings," bombing North Vietnam would produce a violent outburst of domestic protest. This, in turn, would have destroyed our efforts to bring the country together in support of our plan for peace. I decided that the importance of our domestic unity outweighed the need to retaliate directly against North Vietnam.

Our second option was to bomb North Vietnam's military sanctuaries just inside Cambodia along the border with South Vietnam. Cambodia was formally neutral. But its neutrality was a formality. We honored Cambodia's neutrality; North Vietnam trampled it. Since 1965, the Communists had established a string of bases on Cambodian territory because they knew that their forces in these areas would be immune to attack. North Vietnam in effect annexed these territories, expelling virtually all Cambodian civilians who lived in or near them. Once secured, the bases were stocked with thousands of tons of supplies shipped in through the Cambodian port at Sihanoukville. For four years Communist troops had struck across the border at American and South Vietnamese forces and then escaped back to the safety of their jungle sanctuaries. A classic example of this tactic was their offensive in February 1969. In March we decided to bomb one of these bases in retaliation.

We also decided to keep the bombing secret. We did this for two reasons: We wanted to avoid the domestic uproar that might result from a publicized air strike, and we wanted to avoid putting Prince Norodom Sihanouk, Cambodia's head of state, in a perilous political position.

I had first met Sihanouk sixteen years before. From the long talks I had with him when I visited Phnom Penh in 1953, I knew he was a clever, opportunistic survivor. His actions did not govern events; events governed his actions. What he did or could do depended largely on what happened in Vietnam. For years he had maneuvered to appease the North Vietnamese because he believed that they represented the side with the best chance of winning. In 1965, when South Vietnam was tottering on the brink of collapse, he severed diplomatic relations with Washington and acquiesced in the establishment of Communist sanctuaries and supply lines in Cambodia.

By the late 1960s, when the tide of the war had turned, Sihanouk began to grow deeply concerned about the Communist military presence in his country. He looked to the United States for help. "We don't want any Vietnamese in Cambodia," he told an emissary from President Johnson in January 1968. "We will be very glad if you solve our problem. We are not opposed to hot pursuit in uninhabited areas. You will liberate us from the Viet Cong. For me only Cambodia counts. I want you to force the Viet Cong to leave Cambodia." Also, in a press interview in December 1967, Sihanouk said that he would grant American and South Vietnamese forces the right to go into his country in "hot pursuit" of North Vietnamese and National Liberation Front troops, as long as no Cambodians were harmed.

As we considered the bombing of the sanctuaries in March 1969, we made these calculations. We knew Sihanouk would approve of the air strikes. But we also knew that he could not afford to endorse our bombing publicly, both because it would violate his formal neutrality and because it would risk provoking a North Vietnamese reprisal. If we bombed the sanctuaries secretly, we believed Sihanouk would probably remain silent. If we announced our bombing publicly, we believed he probably would feel compelled to protest our actions. Cambodian protests, in turn, would create pressure on us to stop the bombing. We therefore proceeded in secrecy.

On March 18, our first bombing run in Cambodia took place. It was a great success. We received reports that our bombs touched off multiple secondary explosions, which meant that they had hit ammunition dumps or fuel depots. Crew members observed a total of seventy-three such explosions in the target area, ranging up to five times the normal intensity of a typical secondary explosion. Politically, Hanoi's diplomatic foot-dragging ended as its delegate in Paris quickly took up our proposal to convene a session of private talks.

Originally we had contemplated only this one attack. We were prepared to defend our action publicly if we received a formal protest. But none was made. Hanoi's leaders had no grounds for complaint, because they had for years denied that they had any troops in Cambodia. And Sihanouk, as we expected, assented to our bombing through his silence.

In April and May, I ordered air strikes against a string of enemy-occupied areas within five miles of the border. White House approval was required for each attack through August 1969; thereafter, I turned over general authority to conduct the bombing campaign to our commanders in the field. Our sorties, now conducted regularly against the sanctuaries, wreaked havoc with the enemy's logistics and forced the Communists to abort planned offensives. By curtailing the enemy's ability to attack within South Vietnam, the secret bombing saved the lives of many of our fighting men and bought us valuable time to press forward with Vietnamization.

In May 1969, leaks to the news media revealed our operations. Sihanouk's response to the stories showed that he was in favor of what we were doing. "Here it is," he said at a press conference, "the first report about several B-52 bombings. Yet I have not been informed about that at all, because I have not lost any houses, any countrymen, nothing, nothing. Nobody was caught in those barrages—nobody, no Cambodians." He added, "If there is a buffalo or any Cambodian killed, I will be informed immediately. But this is an affair between the Americans and the Viet Cong—Viet Minh without any Khmer witnesses. There have been no Khmer witnesses, so how can I protest?"

Some critics later contended that the secret bombing was an illegal abuse of presidential power. There was no substance to this charge. No reasonable interpretation of the Constitution could conclude that the President, as commander in chief, was forbidden from attacking areas occupied by enemy forces and used by them as bases from which to strike at American and allied troops. Congress was consulted within the limits imposed by the necessary secrecy of the operation. Richard Russell and John Stennis, the chairman and ranking member of the Senate Armed Services Committee, were informed and approved of our plans.

Former President Eisenhower was the only one outside of government that I informed about the bombing. When I briefed him on the operation at Walter Reed Hospital, he strongly endorsed the decision.

The charge that our bombing was illegal under the standards of international law also was without foundation. It is illegal to bomb a neutral country. But neutrality is more than pacifism. As the Hague Convention of 1907 stated, "A neutral country has the obligation not to allow its territory to be used by a belligerent. If the neutral country is unwilling or unable to prevent this, the other belligerent has the right to take appropriate counteraction." North Vietnam was using Cambodian territory as a staging bound for its aggression. South Vietnam and the United States therefore had the right to strike back at the North Vietnamese forces inside Cambodia.

By mid-1969, Sihanouk made it plain that he understood it was North Vietnam's actions, not those of the United States, that were endangering his people and threatening to pull his country into the war. In June he complained at a press conference that Hanoi had crowded so many Communist troops into one of Cambodia's northeast provinces that it was "practically North Vietnamese territory." A month later he invited me to visit Cambodia to mark the improving relations between our two countries.

While we applied pressure on the military front, we continued to push forward on the diplomatic front. On December 20, 1968, I had sent a message to Hanoi indicating our interest in a fair negotiated settlement. The message was sent through Jean Sainteny, a personal friend whom I had met at the home of Paul Louis Weiller in the south of France in 1965 and who had good relations with the North Vietnamese leaders. On February 1, 1969, in one of my first directives to the National Security Council staff, I had ordered a preliminary exploration of the possibility of a rapprochement with Communist China. We had also taken the first steps toward a detente with the Soviet Union. On April 14, Kissinger met with Soviet Ambassador Anatoly Dobrynin and presented a proposal for setting up a private negotiating channel with North Vietnam.

On May 14, in a nationally televised address, I put forward a new peace proposal. Its terms went beyond any proposal made by Johnson. I proposed that we arrange for a mutual withdrawal of American and North Vietnamese forces and for internationally supervised, free elections to decide the future of South Vietnam. I instructed our delegate to the peace talks, Henry Cabot Lodge, to be as forthcoming as possible to North Vietnamese counterproposals. On June 8, I met with President Thieu on Midway Island. He expressed his support for our peace proposal. We also announced that the United States was withdrawing 25,000 military personnel from Vietnam—the first reduction since combat forces arrived in 1961. On July 16, I sent another appeal for peace to Ho Chi Minh in a letter delivered through Jean Sainteny. On August 2, I met with Romanian President Nicolae Ceausescu, and he agreed to use his influence with the North Vietnamese to get the peace talks off dead center.

All our conciliatory moves proved useless. On August 25, Ho Chi Minh's reply to my personal letter arrived. He coldly rebuffed our peace proposals and insisted that we withdraw unilaterally from Vietnam and overthrow President Thieu's government as we left.

On September 3, Ho Chi Minh died. Some observers speculated that his successors might be more amenable to ending the war through negotiations. They proved to be wrong. North Vietnam's leader had changed, but its policies remained the same.

Meanwhile, public support for our war effort was eroding. Our peace initiatives, the start of our withdrawal program, and our conciliatory speeches slowed the erosion, but they also whetted the appetites of the antiwar activists. As we approached the first anniversary of the bombing halt on November 1, 1969, I knew the time had come for a bold move to mobilize American support for our military efforts so that we could secure a diplomatic settlement that would achieve the goal for which American soldiers had fought and died for over five years: a South Vietnam free from Communist domination and capable of defending itself against both its internal and external enemies.

What we needed most was time. No President has a limitless amount of time to invest in any policy. Because my predecessors had exhausted the patience of the American people with the Vietnam War, I was acutely aware that I was living on borrowed time. If I was to have enough time for my policies to succeed, my first priority had to be to gather as much political support as possible for the war from the American people.

In late October 1969, I began preparing a national address on the war in Vietnam to be delivered on November 3, 1969. When I went to Camp David to make a final review of the speech, I took with me a memorandum from Senate Majority Leader Mike Mansfield, who had been a personal friend for over twenty years and whose views on foreign policy I greatly respected.

He opened by stating, "The continuance of the war in Vietnam, in my judgment, endangers the future of this nation." He said that his concern went beyond the loss of lives or the waste of money and resources. "Most serious," he wrote, "are the deep divisions within our society to which this conflict of dubious origin and purpose is contributing." He said that he would give articulate support to "any or all of the following decisions" if I found them necessary to end the war rapidly. He then listed actions that amounted to a unilateral cease-fire and withdrawal. "I know that a settlement arrived at in this fashion is not pleasant to contemplate," he concluded, "especially in view of the dug-in diplomatic and military positions which, unfortunately, were assumed over the past few years."

I realized that with this memorandum Mansfield was offering what would be the last chance for me to end the war I had inherited. I interpreted his references to it as a "conflict of dubious origin" and to the positions "unfortunately" assumed over the years as signals that he would even allow me to claim that I was making the best possible end of a bad war my Democratic predecessors had begun. When I decided not to take up Mansfield's offer, I knew that from a political standpoint what had been Kennedy's and Johnson's war would become Nixon's war. But as President I believed that I had no choice but to end the war on terms consistent with our national honor. My task then became to persuade the American people to commit themselves to this goal as well.

My speech on November 3 addressed the questions of what a defeat in Vietnam would mean for South Vietnam, the world as a whole, and the United States. It summarized the reasons why we were in Vietnam.

I began by making the moral case for our intervention. Our original decision to intervene was justified because we were trying to stop foreign aggression: "Fifteen years ago North Vietnam, with the logistic support of Communist China and the Soviet Union, launched a campaign to impose a Communist government on South Vietnam by instigating and supporting a revolution." Our continued involvement was just because it prevented massive human suffering: A precipitate withdrawal of American forces would "inevitably allow the Communists to repeat the massacres which followed their takeover in the North."

I then explained that a unilateral withdrawal from Vietnam would be a disaster for the cause of peace in the world. Our acquiescence in aggression would encourage further aggression: "Our defeat and humiliation in South Vietnam without question would promote recklessness in the councils of those great powers who have not yet abandoned their goals of world conquest. This would spark violence wherever our commitments help maintain the peace—in the Middle East, in Berlin, eventually even in the Western Hemisphere." Peace could not be won through a withdrawal bordering on surrender. "It would not bring peace," I said. "It would bring more war."

After outlining my plan to end the war and the steps I had already taken to do so, I concluded by speaking about the consequences of a precipitate withdrawal for the United States. "The immediate reaction would be a sense of relief that our men were coming home," I said. "But as we saw the consequences of what we had done, inevitable remorse and divisive recrimination would scar our spirit as a people." I observed that while it was not fashionable to speak of patriotism or national destiny in these troubled times, it was clear that "any hope the world has for the survival of peace and freedom will be determined by whether the American people have the moral stamina and the courage to meet the challenge of free world leadership."

I had spent hours writing the conclusion, in which I sought to go over the heads of the antiwar opinion makers in the media and to appeal directly to the American people for unity: "And so tonight—to you, the great silent majority of my fellow Americans—I ask for your support." I said that I had initiated policies that would enable me to keep my campaign pledge to end the war. "The more support I can have from the American people," I stated, "the sooner that pledge can be redeemed; for the more divided we are at home, the less likely the enemy is to negotiate in Paris. Let us be united for peace. Let us also be united against defeat. Because let us understand: North Vietnam cannot defeat or humiliate the United States. Only Americans can do that."

The speech was the most effective of my presidency. I had told the American people that our cause in Vietnam was just and that our policies would end the war in a way that would not betray our cause. Ours was not the easy way out, but it was the right way out. And the American people showed that they concurred.

The minute I left the air after delivering what came to be known as the "Silent Majority speech," the White House switchboard lit up, and the calls continued for hours. It soon became the biggest response ever to a presidential speech. More than 50,000 telegrams and 30,000 letters poured in, few of them critical. A Gallup telephone poll taken immediately after the speech indicated that 77 percent of the public approved of it. Congressional opinion soon showed the impact of this outpouring of popular support. By November 12, 300 members of the House of Representatives—119 Democrats and 181 Republicans—had cosponsored a resolution of support for my Vietnam policies. Fifty-eight senators—twenty-one Democrats and thirty-seven Republicans—had signed letters expressing similar sentiments.

With this response, the American people demonstrated that

deep down they understood what was happening in Vietnam better than those who reported on the war in the news media. The American news media had come to dominate domestic debate about the purpose and conduct of the war in Vietnam and about the nature of the enemy. The North Vietnamese were a cruel and ruthless enemy, but news media coverage continued to concentrate primarily on the failings and frailties of the South Vietnamese and of our own forces. Each night's television news reported the fighting battle by battle and, more than in any previous conflict, showed the terrible human suffering and sacrifice of war. But it conveyed little or no sense of the underlying purpose of the fighting. News-media coverage fostered the impression that we were fighting in military and moral quicksand, rather than toward an important and worthwhile objective.

Public-opinion surveys showed that the American people were weary of the war but wanted peace with honor. In March 1965, the proportion who said that we had *not* made a mistake by going into Vietnam was 61 percent. By May 1971, when the pollsters stopped asking the question regularly, the same percentage believed that it *had* been a mistake to enter the war. But this did not mean the American people wanted to cut and run. In the New Hampshire primary in 1968, a large proportion of those who voted for the antiwar candidate, Senator Eugene McCarthy, actually favored military victory in Vietnam. When Johnson failed to provide a plan to win or end the war, the proportion of those who disapproved of his handling of the situation increased steadily, hitting 63 percent in March 1968. I came into office having promised to end the war and win the peace—to wind down the war without abandoning our allies. Over the four years it took to do so, the proportion of those who approved of my handling of the war averaged 52 percent.

The November 3 speech was a turning point in the war. The approval rating for our Vietnam policy shot up to 64 percent. Now, for a time at least, North Vietnam's leaders could no longer count on dissent in America to give them the victory they could not win on the battlefield. I had the public support I needed to continue a policy of waging war in Vietnam and negotiating for peace in Paris until we could bring the war to an honorable and successful conclusion.

On April 20, 1970, I announced the withdrawal of another 60,000 troops from Vietnam in 1970 and another 90,000 in 1971. Ten days later I told the American people that our forces and those of our ally had launched a ground offensive against the North Vietnamese sanctuaries in Cambodia. To the public, it seemed like an inexplicable reversal of policy. But events beyond our control had forced our hand.

In 1969, during the secret bombing of the Communist sanctuaries in Cambodia, Sihanouk had begun to tilt his policy toward the United States. But this maneuvering was not enough to satisfy some of his opponents within the Cambodian government. Along with most of the country's deeply nationalistic people, they strongly objected to Sihanouk's acquiescence in North Vietnamese violations of Cambodian sovereignty. Cambodians, whose lands had been confiscated and colonized by the Vietnamese over many centuries, harbored traditional enmities toward their neighbors to the east. North Vietnam's sanctuaries in Cambodia aroused those ancient hatreds. Sihanouk seemed oblivious to the risks he was running by appeasing the Vietnamese Communists. His failure to expel North Vietnam's forces was rapidly eroding his political base.

In March 1970, while he was vacationing in France, Sihanouk lost control of events. Demonstrations broke out to protest the North Vietnamese occupation of Cambodian territory. Twenty thousand youths sacked the North Vietnamese and National Liberation Front embassies in Phnom Penh. Meeting in special session, both houses of the Cambodian Parliament demanded that the government defend its national territory and urged that the army be expanded. Cambodia's Foreign Ministry announced that it had informed the North Vietnamese and the National Liberation Front that they were to with-

227

draw their armed forces from the country within forty-eight hours.

On March 18, while Sihanouk was in Moscow asking the Soviets to press North Vietnam to remove its troops, the Cambodian National Assembly and Council of the Kingdom voted 92 to 0 to depose him. Marshal Lon Nol, who had played a role in fomenting the protests against North Vietnam, headed the new government. Two days later in Peking, Sihanouk threw in his lot with the Communists, vowing to fight "until victory or death" against the "stooges of American imperialism" who now ruled Cambodia. He did not explain why Lon Nol, presumably the leading "stooge" in Phnom Penh, had served Sihanouk for years as both Defense and Prime Minister.

Lon Nol's coup came as a complete surprise to us. We neither encouraged it nor knew about it in advance. Those who have insinuated that the CIA instigated the coup have managed to overlook the fact that we did not have even one intelligence agent in the country at the time. In fact, our first notice that the *possibility* of a coup existed, which came through a third party, arrived on the very day of Sihanouk's ouster.

My initial reaction was that we should do everything possible to help the new government. Lon Nol made it clear that he wanted to align Cambodia with the United States. He closed the port at Sihanoukville to shipments of supplies from North Vietnam and soon asked us to equip his army with modern weapons so that it could evict the Communist troops from their sanctuaries. These were acts of courage. I thought we should act immediately on his requests. But we held back to avoid giving North Vietnam a pretext to unleash a full-scale invasion of Cambodia. Instead, we undertook initiatives to explore the possibility of restoring the neutrality of Cambodia, all of which were rebuffed instantly by North Vietnam. We should have known better than to hesitate as we did. If there was one lesson that our experience in Vietnam should have taught us, it was that North Vietnam did not require a pretext before invading another country. Through the end of March, while we showed restraint, North Vietnam geared up for an attack on Cambodia.

In early April the North Vietnamese assault began. After two weeks, Lon Nol's Cambodian forces had been attacked in Svay Rieng, Takeo, Kampot, Prey Veng, Mondolkiri, and Kampong Cham provinces. In the following weeks, the North Vietnamese troops pressed forward with their attacks. A siege of Phnom Penh was becoming an imminent possibility as Communist forces struck within twenty miles to the south of it. They also interdicted key highways linking the capital to the provinces and began harassing shipping on the Mekong River, the city's lifeline. By the end of April, North Vietnam's forces had occupied a quarter of Cambodia's territory and were tightening their noose around Phnom Penh.

Our response was pathetic. Cambodia was in desperate straits. On April 14, Lon Nol declared that "because of the gravity of the situation, it is deemed necessary to accept from this moment all unconditional foreign aid from all sources." Five days before, he had made his first request for American assistance. He intended to expand his armed forces dramatically and asked for an immediate shipment of 100,000 to 150,000 weapons with ammuniuon and a later delivery of another 50,000 to 150,000. Kissinger and I pushed for action. But our foreign-policy and military bureaucracies delayed and temporized. By the end of April, our total military aid to Cambodia consisted of 3,000 rifles provided covertly.

North Vietnam was threatening to convert all of eastern Cambodia into one huge base area, with convenient supply lines and favorable geography, that would enable its forces to strike at both Phnom Penh and South Vietnam at will. This would have been a disaster. If we had acquiesced in this development, we would have been signing a death warrant not only for Cambodia but for South Vietnam as well. A Communist-dominated Cambodia would have placed South Vietnam in an untenable military situation and would have endangered the lives of thousands of United States troops. I therefore decided the time had come to take action against the Communist sanctuaries in Cambodia, both to relieve the pressure on Phnom Penh and to reduce the threat these North Vietnamese bases posed to South Vietnam.

The Joint Chiefs of Staff worked out the plan of attack. The Communist sanctuaries were centered in two main areas—the Parrot's Beak and the Fishhook. The Parrot's Beak was a sliver of land that pushed into South Vietnam and reached to within thirty-eight miles of Saigon. One of South Vietnam's strongest divisions was stationed on the border in this area. The Fishhook was a thin, curving piece of Cambodian territory that jutted into the heart of South Vietnam about fifty miles northwest of Saigon. Intelligence reports indicated that North Vietnam's heaviest concentrations were in the Fishhook and that this area was the primary area of operation for the Central Office of South Vietnam (COSVN). COSVN was the Communists' floating command post of military headquarters, supplies, food, and medical facilities. The Fishhook was the nerve center of the Communist forces in the sanctuaries. It would be heavily fortified and strongly defended.

On April 26, acting on the recommendations of the Joint Chiefs of Staff, I decided that South Vietnamese units would go into the Parrot's Beak and that a joint United States–South Vietnamese force would go into the Fishhook. Three days later the attack on the Parrot's Beak began. On April 30, I delivered a nationally televised address about the Cambodian incursions at the same time as our troops began the joint assault on the Fishhook. I described the Communist offensive against Cambodia, explained the grave dangers we would face if it succeeded, and emphasized the fact that our forces would stay in Cambodia only sixty days and would go no deeper than twenty-one miles.

On May 1, I went to the Pentagon for a firsthand briefing. Colored pins on a map indicated the positions and movements of the various forces. As the briefers described the initial success of the operation, I noticed the map showed that four other areas besides the Parrot's Beak and Fishhook were occupied by Communist forces. I began wondering whether between South Vietnam's forces and our own we could mount offensives against the other sanctuaries as well.

"Could we take out all the sanctuaries?" I asked. The Pentagon officials answered that although this was feasible, it had not been offered as an option because of the negative reaction that attacking more than two areas would have produced in the media and Congress. "Let me be the judge as far as the political reactions are concerned," I said. "The fact is that we have already taken the political heat for this particular operation. If we can substantially reduce the threat to our forces by wiping out the rest of the sanctuaries, now is the time to do it." I knew we would take just as much political heat for taking out two sanctuaries as we would for taking out six. I then made an on-the-spot decision: "I want to take out all of those sanctuaries. Make whatever plans are necessary, and then just do it. Knock them all out so that they can't be used against us again, ever."

This was a textbook case of one of the most frustrating problems I had to deal with in conducting the war: the tendency of our armed forces to confuse *military* analysis with *political* analysis. Given the political restrictions imposed on the military during the early years of the war, and given the abuse heaped on them by the antiwar movement and the media, I could understand why they were so tentative by the time I came into office. I could sense that they were surprised and pleased when I directed them to take out all the sanctuaries. More than anyone else, they knew that taking half measures in war is the surest way to lose. The fashionable idea that all military leaders are superhawks who will generally take bold and even rash action has no basis in fact. It has been my experience that professional military leaders are by training and instinct cautious and seldom advise bold action. The Pattons and LeMays are not the rule but the exceptions.

Our troops went into Cambodia on schedule and came out on schedule. Yet some critics contended that the United States and South Vietnam had "invaded" neutral Cambodia. That was fatuous nonsense. We stayed in Cambodia for only two months and advanced to a depth of only twenty-one miles. North Vietnam occupied parts of eastern Cambodia for over five years and reoccupied them after we left. As a British newspaper put it, condemning the United States for invading neutral Cambodia—in the sense of committing an aggressive act—was as absurd as condemning Britain for invading neutral Holland in 1944.

On June 30, the last American troops left Cambodia. Our troops had captured 22,892 individual weapons, enough to equip seventy-four full-strength North Vietnamese battalions; 2,509 big crew-served weapons, enough to equip twenty-five full-strength North Vietnamese infantry battalions; 15 million rounds of ammunition—about what the enemy had fired in South Vietnam during the past year; 14 million pounds of rice, enough to feed for four months all the Communist combat battalions estimated to be in South Vietnam; 143,000 rockets, mortars, and recoilless-rifle rounds, enough for fourteen months of fighting; 199,552 antiaircraft rounds; 5,482 mines; 62,022 grenades; and 83,000 pounds of explosives. And according to an intercepted radio transmission from the COSVN, our forces were at times close to overrunning it.

Our Cambodian operation dealt a crushing blow to North Vietnam's military campaign in the Mekong Delta region. We saved Lon Nol's government and thereby ensured that the port at Sihanoukville would remain closed to Communist arms shipments. We destroyed or captured an estimated 40 percent of North Vietnam's supplies in Cambodia and thereby eliminated the chance of a major Communist offensive in the region for the next two years. Our casualties dropped from ninety-three per week in the six months before the operation to fifty-two per week in the six months afterward. We sapped Hanoi's strength so severely that when the North Vietnamese launched their spring offensive in 1972, their attacks in the delta region were easily repulsed.

Most important, we achieved the operation's two main goals: We prevented the fall of Cambodia and relieved the pressure

on Phnom Penh. We undercut North Vietnam's offensive striking power and thereby bought time to press forward with Vietnamization. Our Cambodian incursion was the most successful
military operation of the entire Vietnam War.

Of all the myths about the Vietnam War, the most vicious
one is the idea that the United States was morally responsible
for the atrocities committed after the fall of Cambodia in 1975.
The critics charged that the actions we took against North
Vietnam's Cambodian sanctuaries, starting with the bombing
of Communist bases in 1969, began a series of events that
brought the murderous Khmer Rouge to power. This is a total
distortion of history and complete perversion of moral judgment.

The myth runs like this: Our secret bombing in 1969 not
only slaughtered countless civilians but also pushed the Vietnamese Communist forces deeper into Cambodia and thereby
destabilized Sihanouk's neutral government. Our incursions
against the sanctuaries in 1970 swept peaceful Cambodia into
the war and led the North Vietnamese to give massive aid to
their Communist Khmer Rouge allies. Therefore, because
American actions set in motion the events that brought the
Khmer Rouge to power, the United States was to blame for the
ensuing holocaust, in which over 2 million Cambodians were
killed.

These arguments are wrong on every point. Our bombing
caused minimal civilian casualties because the Communists
had long before cleared all Cambodians out of their base areas.
A Joint Chiefs of Staff memorandum written in April 1969
pointed out that "Cambodians rarely go into areas under de
facto control of the [National Liberation Front and North Vietnamese Army]." It added, "Cambodian villages and populated
areas are readily identified and can be essentially avoided in
conducting preplanned operations into the base areas."

Nor did our bombing destabilize Sihanouk's government.
No evidence exists to show that our 1969 air strikes pushed
the Vietnamese Communist forces deeper into Cambodia.

These forces grew at the time of the bombing, both because a steady stream of new troops was coming down the Ho Chi Minh Trail and because United States and South Vietnamese military sweeps in South Vietnam were pushing more Communist troops into Cambodia. But none of these forces went deeper into Cambodia as a result of the bombing. Communist forces simply dispersed themselves and their supplies more widely along the border with South Vietnam.

Sihanouk was overthrown because of discontent, both among the people and within the government, over his unwillingness to take vigorous steps to expel the Vietnamese Communist forces from the country. Years later Sihanouk admitted as much, saying, "If I lost my *Fauteuil présidentiel* and my Chamcar Mon Palace in Phnom Penh to Marshal Lon Nol who occupied them for five years, it was because I tremendously helped the Viet Cong and the North Vietnamese."

Our incursions into Cambodia in 1970 did not widen the war. Since 1965, North Vietnam's forces had occupied the border areas of Cambodia. In March 1970, Hanoi infiltrated into Cambodia over 20,000 Khmer Rouge guerrillas who had been trained in North Vietnam. In April, after Cambodia's government tried to reassert its authority over its own territory—hardly an unreasonable demand—North Vietnam launched an invasion of the country. Hanoi's delegate to the private peace talks in Paris freely admitted to us that North Vietnam intended to bring down the government in Phnom Penh. In May and June, when American and South Vietnamese forces cleared out the Communist sanctuaries, Cambodia was already swept up in the war. If we had not acted, we would have guaranteed the victory of the Communist forces both in Cambodia and South Vietnam. Thus, the charge that our incursion drove the North Vietnamese out of the border areas and toward Phnom Penh is false on its face. The Vietnamese Communists moved deeper into Cambodia two weeks after the fall of Sihanouk and a month *before* our incursion occurred.

During the war in Vietnam, those who now concoct apologias for Indochina's totalitarians opposed American policies that sought to prevent a Communist victory and the human tragedy that would follow inevitably in its wake. No doubt these apologists are now at least subconsciously motivated by feelings of guilt. Simple ethics holds those who took an action responsible for its consequences. To assign blame for the genocide in Cambodia to those in the United States who sought to prevent a Communist victory, rather than to the Communists who committed the atrocities, is an immoral act in and of itself.

Our critics claimed that our operations in Cambodia deepened our involvement in the war. But the opposite was true: Our attacks on the Communist sanctuaries were the single most important move that enabled us to continue our policy of steadily withdrawing American forces from Vietnam. We reduced the pressure on our forces in South Vietnam, allowing them to devote more time and resources to training the South Vietnamese to defend themselves.

In January 1969, the United States had 542,000 troops in Vietnam. By July 1970, as our operations in Cambodia came to an end, our troop level was down to 404,000. With the breathing room we gained through our actions and progress in Vietnamization, we accelerated our withdrawals. We pulled out an additional 179,000 troops in the next twelve months. By July 1972, we would have only 45,600 troops stationed in South Vietnam.

Many of my congressional supporters had urged me to announce a complete withdrawal schedule in 1969 so the American people would know our involvement in Vietnam was coming to an end. I discussed this idea in a conversation with Dean Acheson, who despite our bitter differences in the past had become one of my most astute unofficial foreign-policy advisers. In his usual blunt and incisive manner, he said, "That would be a stupid move, both on the battlefront and on the home front. If you tell the North Vietnamese in advance that you are going to withdraw all our forces on a certain date in the future regardless of what they do, you lose all negotiating leverage. They will just continue the war until we get out and take over when we leave." He added that, because the American people were tired of the war, we had to buy time until South Vietnam was able to defend itself. If I revealed a complete withdrawal schedule now, he warned, I would have nothing to announce later to show that the war was winding down. "Parcel out the good news," he advised. "Don't put it all out now and have nothing left later, when you may need it to sustain public support."

A few months after our incursion into Cambodia, one prominent politician who was against our involvement said that our best young men had gone to Canada. In his view, those who evaded the draft represented the best of American youth because they were acting on their belief that the Vietnam War was immoral.

Draft dodgers acted out of a whole range of motivations. Some were conscious pro-Communists who wanted North Vietnam to win; others were sincere pacifists who believed no war could be just. But most were not acting out of moral convictions. Many, drawn into the moral vacuum of the 1960s, saw no moral issue at stake in the war. Some of them felt that we had nothing worth fighting *for* because they had lost faith in what the United States stood for in the world. Others felt that we had nothing worth fighting *against* because they believed that life in North Vietnam was as good as or better than life in South Vietnam. One of the great tragedies of the Vietnam years was that for the first time many draft evaders either wanted the enemy to win or did not care which side won. But most who fled the country or feigned illness to evade the draft acted out of expediency: Like most draft dodgers in our previous wars, including the two world wars, they were understandably afraid of risking their lives.

Antiwar protesters were another matter. Some were pacifists who opposed all wars, or idealists who believed our values were being corrupted by the Vietnam War. Others were pragmatists who did not believe that this war could be won. Still others were isolationists who did not want to see the United

States play a world role But many key leaders of the antiwar movement were hard-core militants of the New Left who hated the United States and wanted to see our country humiliated in Vietnam. They did not hide their allegiance. They openly flew the Viet Cong flag at their rallies. Destroying the American system was their goal, and they did not shrink from using violence to try to achieve it.

Today, many Americans remember the demonstrations against the war as flocks of flower children marching in orderly candlelight processions. But what we saw from the White House at the time was quite different. Until 1968, antiwar demonstrators were basically peaceful, seldom doing more than holding "teach-ins" and symbolically burning their draft cards. But that had changed by 1969. Students shot at firemen and policemen, held college administrators hostage at knife-point, stormed university buildings with shotguns in hand, burned buildings, smashed windows, trashed offices, and bombed classrooms. In the academic year 1969-70, there were 1,800 demonstrations, 7,500 arrests, 247 arsons, 462 injuries—two-thirds of them to police—and 8 deaths. The violence was not limited to college campuses; it was a national epidemic. From January 1969 through February 1970, there were over 40,000 bombings, attempted bombings, or bomb threats, most of which were war related. These caused $21 million of property damage, hundreds of injuries, and 43 deaths.

Violence was becoming the rule, not the exception, in campus protests. Following the announcement of the incursions into Cambodia, a new wave of violent protest swept the country. At the University of Maryland, fifty people were injured when students ransacked the ROTC building and skirmished with police. In Kent, Ohio, a crowd of hundreds of demonstrators watched as two young men threw lighted flares into the army ROTC building on the campus of Kent State University and burned it to the ground. Ohio's governor called in the National Guard. A few days later, a large crowd of students began throwing rocks and chunks of concrete at the guardsmen, forcing them up a small hill. At the top, the soldiers turned, and someone started shooting. Four people—two protesters and two bystanders—were killed. In August a van packed with explosives was blown up next to a building at the University of Wisconsin, killing one graduate student, injuring four others, and doing $6 million in damage. Underground newspapers across the country reported ecstatically that another blow had been struck against the "pig nation." No one could justify the decision of the guardsmen at Kent State to fire on the crowd, but neither should anyone have defended the actions of a confrontational mob or of murderous bombers.

I had mixed emotions about the antiwar protesters. I appreciated their concerns for peace. I was angered by their excesses. But most of all I was frustrated at their moral righteousness and total unwillingness to credit me or my predecessors with a genuine desire for peace. Whatever my view of their motives and whatever their estimate of mine—the practical effect of their actions was to give encouragement to the enemy to fight on or refuse to negotiate a peace. That the brightest and the best in our great educational institutions could not recognize that their peace protests prolonged the war is one of the tragic ironies of the Vietnam era. More than once North Vietnamese negotiators taunted our delegates at the Paris peace talks and Henry Kissinger at our secret negotiations by quoting the statements of the antiwar leaders on our campuses and in the Congress.

The demonstrators wanted to end the war in Vietnam. So did I. But they did not see anything wrong with abandoning the South Vietnamese people in order to end the war immediately. I did. I saw no moral purpose served in letting the totalitarians in Hanoi set up shop in Saigon. It was my duty as President to do what I thought was right for the country. Our policy had to be made in the voting booth, not in the streets.

News reporting tended to portray America's young people as unanimously opposed to the war. That might have been true on a number of college campuses. But it was not the case in the country as a whole. Opinion polls showed that support for the war was always highest among those who were twenty-one to twenty-nine years old. In March 1966, when asked whether our involvement in Vietnam was a mistake, 71 percent answered that it was not. Even after the Tet Offensive, polls indicated that a plurality of young people, averaging about 45 percent, said that we acted rightly in going into the war. And in the presidential election of 1972, I split the youth vote evenly with my antiwar opponent, Senator George McGovern.

Our best young men did not go to Canada. They went to Vietnam. When I visited our servicemen in South Vietnam in July 1969, I found the most idealistic young Americans of an idealistic generation. But they knew better than their contemporaries at home what it took to give life to ideals in a world that was far from ideal. Any war is difficult to fight in. But the war in Vietnam was the most difficult one in which American soldiers had ever fought. Front lines were seldom clearly drawn. Enemy soldiers were often hard to identify. Our men were constantly bombarded by media reports telling them that the war was unwinnable, that our cause was unjust, and that a majority of the American people opposed it. But to their credit, our men did their duty. They honored their country. They served well the cause of freedom and justice.

News media reporting portrayed our troops as divided along racial lines, undisciplined and addicted to drugs, and guilt-ridden over their involvement in the war. None of these problems was unique to the Vietnam War. But all of them were exaggerated in the press.

It was commonly asserted during the war that blacks constituted a disproportionate number of combat casualties and that this injustice, in turn, stirred racial animosities. But in fact casualties among blacks were not out of proportion to their share of the population. By March 1973, when blacks comprised 13.5 percent of all American men of military age, blacks accounted for 12.3 percent of combat deaths.

Our armed forces in Vietnam were not collapsing from a lack of discipline or being overrun by drug addiction. Our troops in Vietnam were more disciplined than those in Korea. During the Korean War, for the years in which statistics were kept, the average AWOL rate was 170 per 1,000. In the Vietnam War, the rate was 115 per 1,000. Drug use was a widespread problem for the generation growing up in the 1960s. It was not appreciably worse among military personnel in Vietnam than among those stationed in other countries or among draft-age civilians in the United States. Among students at Harvard College in 1968, 75 percent had smoked marijuana or used hard drugs. In 1971, a survey showed that 50.9 percent of Army personnel in Vietnam had smoked marijuana and that 28.5 percent had used hard drugs, like heroin or opium. Few were truly addicted, and most had used drugs before being sent to Vietnam.

American soldiers were not haunted by doubts about the morality of the war. Overwhelming majorities still believe our cause was right. An opinion poll conducted in 1980 revealed that 82 percent of those who engaged in heavy combat believed that the United States lost the war because the armed forces were not allowed to win it. And 66 percent indicated that they would be willing to fight again in Vietnam for the same cause.

Many believe the war in Vietnam was a war without heroes. But that was not the case. All our fighting men were heroes in the sense that they were risking their lives in a selfless cause. Heroic acts were as common in Vietnam as in any other war. But our prisoners of war, who had been courageous in action and even more courageous in captivity, were among the most remarkable heroes of the Vietnam War.

Many Americans did not know that our POWs were brutally tortured by the North Vietnamese until we freed them in 1973. During the war, the news media virtually ignored reports that trickled out about the mistreatment of our prisoners and were bamboozled by antiwar activists engaged in a concerted propaganda campaign to portray North Vietnam's treatment of our prisoners as humane. Acting out of naïveté or malice, these critics would go to Hanoi, meet a handful of American POWs, and make rosy statements about their condition. What the

American people were not told was that the prisoners who were presented to these activists often had been tortured minutes before to guarantee that they said nothing out of line.

These antiwar activists knew or should have known what was going on. In August 1969, after going to North Vietnam and securing the release of two prisoners, a group of these opponents of the war praised Hanoi's humane treatment of its captives. In a hospital press conference, one of the newly freed POWs refuted their assertions, saying, "I don't think that solitary confinement, forced statements, living in a cage for three years, being put in straps, not being allowed to sleep or eat, removal of fingernails, being hung from the ceiling, having an infected arm almost lost without medical treatment, being dragged along the ground with a broken leg, and not allowing exchange of mail for prisoners are humane." But after a trip to Hanoi in August 1972, former Attorney General Ramsey Clark testified that the POWs were well treated and well fed and were "good, strong Americans." One of the prisoners later said that the Communists "persuaded" him to meet with Clark by hanging him by his broken arm.

North Vietnam's Communists, who were masters at the art of physical and psychological torture, worked overtime in trying to force their captives to turn against their country. But it did not work. Our POWs would not break. When Captain Jeremiah Denton, the first American prisoner of war to get off the plane that had brought the POWs out of North Vietnam, stepped up to the microphone, he did not complain about his hardship or issue an antiwar manifesto. He said, "We are honored to have had the opportunity to serve our country under difficult circumstances. We are profoundly grateful to our Commander in Chief, and to our nation for this day. God bless America."

In the time we won through our Cambodian operations, our new military strategy in Vietnam took hold. Starting in 1968, with the close cooperation of President Thieu, we had replaced the strategy of attrition with one of pacification. We also had begun making steady progress toward turning the fighting over to South Vietnamese forces. By 1972, South Vietnam's government had consolidated its control of the countryside, and its army conducted virtually all of the day-to-day fighting against the North Vietnamese.

Pacification did not begin in earnest until after the Tet Offensive in 1968. Kennedy and Johnson administration officials regularly turned out policy papers that called for mobilizing the South Vietnamese people behind the war. But very little came of these proposals because the United States preoccupied itself with looking for a quick military fix to the war. Pacification programs were little more than misguided political reforms or start-and-stop economic development programs. These well-intentioned efforts read like a laundry list: Reconstruction, Civic Action, Land Development Centers, Agglomeration Camps, Argovilles, Strategic Hamlets, New Life Hamlets, Rural Construction, Rural Reconstruction, and Revolutionary Development. Some, particularly the Strategic Hamlet program in its early years, met with limited success. But none adequately addressed the problem of providing the South Vietnamese with security at the village level.

The decisive defeat of the 1968 Tet Offensive changed the balance of power in South Vietnam. Communist forces lost 37,000 troops by the end of February and compounded these losses by launching unsuccessful small-scale offensives in May and August. In late 1969, General Giap said that his army's casualties totaled more than a half-million men over the last two years; an equivalent loss for the United States would have been 5 million men. In addition, the Communists had sacrificed their political infrastructure; it was exposed during the Tet Offensive, and United States and South Vietnamese forces uprooted it once the tide of battle had turned. North Vietnam's defeat had destroyed its ability to control the countryside. This victory had created a vacuum of power. Winning the war meant winning the race to fill it.

American and South Vietnamese strategies shifted to exploit

this new opportunity. Immediately after the Tet Offensive, the United States moved tentatively. American forces regrouped to defend the towns and cities. President Thieu ordered a general mobilization and the formation of local militias in rural areas. General Abrams put a higher priority on pacification. A campaign to retake rural areas in late 1968 met with great success. Some officials in the Johnson administration advocated the abandonment of the strategy of attrition. But in the final analysis, the United States made a few marginal adjustments in tactics, but no fundamental changes in strategy.

When I came into office, I recognized that we needed a new strategy. The Johnson administration had sent more than a half-million troops to Vietnam, dropped over a million tons of bombs a year, and killed nearly a quarter-million enemy troops in three years. Yet immediately after the Tet Offensive, the United States and South Vietnam controlled no more territory than before the American intervention in August 1965. All the United States had won through our strategy of attrition was a costly stalemate.

We therefore put new strategic emphasis on pacification in 1969. It required us to separate the enemy from the population, reestablish Saigon's control of the countryside, and help the South Vietnamese government win the loyalty of its people through economic and political reforms. Our first step was military. "The key strategic thrust," our new Strategic Objectives Plan read in 1969, "is to provide meaningful continuing security for the Vietnamese people in expanding areas of increasingly effective civil authority." Our previous goal of destroying North Vietnam's regular forces was subordinated to those of providing security at the local level—during both the day and the night—and eliminating the Communist infrastructure. Our next steps were political and economic. I ordered a step-up in our Civil Operations and Revolutionary Development Support (CORDS) program. By 1970, we had over 6,000 military and 1,000 civilian advisers helping to reconstruct South Vietnam's government and economy. These advisers worked with almost a million South Vietnamese throughout the country. Their efforts were the key to solidifying our military gains in the countryside.

President Thieu supported our plans wholeheartedly. After the Tet Offensive, he mobilized his country behind the war. In June 1968, Thieu had announced the conscription of all men between the ages of sixteen and fifty, with those between eighteen and thirty-eight going into the armed forces and the others forming the new People's Self-Defense Force. Confident that the South Vietnamese people opposed a Communist victory, Thieu decided that the best way to wage the war in the countryside was to give weapons to the people. His self-defense force, a part-time unpaid militia designed to combat small enemy units, was filled with peasants, traders, and local craftsmen. Its ranks soon numbered 1.5 million and later grew to over 3 million.

Thieu devoted most of his new draftees to the task of pacification. South Vietnam's military was divided into regular forces, which were composed of the Army, Air Force, Navy, and Marine Corps; and territorial forces, which were made up of the Regional Forces and the Popular Forces. Recruits for the Regional Forces fought in their own provinces and those for the Popular Forces defended their own villages. Both were tailor-made for pacification. In four years Thieu increased their ranks from 300,000 to 532,000 troops, and by 1971 these forces represented 51 percent of South Vietnam's military strength. Though they consumed only 20 percent of the military budget, the territorial forces accounted for 40 percent of enemy troops killed in action. Combat effectiveness was uneven in both the self-defense force and the territorial forces—which was to be expected for any military force assembled so quickly—but they effectively secured the countryside for Saigon.

Thieu recognized that while protecting the rural population was critical in the short term, it would not be enough in the long term. Defeating the Communist revolution required a counterrevolution—not in the sense of just suppressing the insurgency with force but in the sense of countering their revolution with one of his own. He knew that the South Vietnamese people, like those of most poor Third World countries, would probably not fight indefinitely simply to preserve the status quo. Thieu therefore took steps to give them a stake in the war. He turned local administration over to elected village councils, instituted a massive land-reform program, and overhauled South Vietnam's social programs. From 1970 through 1973, Saigon redistributed 2.5 million acres of land to over 800,000 tenant farmers, reducing the proportion of arable land worked by tenant farmers from 60 percent to 10 percent. American aid helped build schools, hospitals, and public works of all kinds. By 1972, over 80 percent of South Vietnamese children of primary-school age were attending classes, and enrollment in secondary schools was expanding rapidly.

Pacification worked wonders in South Vietnam. In 1969, we set ambitious goals. We sought to bring 90 percent of all hamlets under government control, with 50 percent having a high degree of security and the other 40 percent having a significant but lesser degree of security. We reached our goals by October. From 1968 through 1971, the proportion of the population living in secure areas increased from 47 percent to 84 percent, while that figure for those living in contested areas or under Communist control dropped from 23 percent to less than 4 percent. Over a million refugees were returned to their homes. Enemy ground attacks fell to almost half their previous level and were limited to ten sparsely populated provinces. Over 75 percent of South Vietnam's essential roads and waterways were safe for civilian travel. Life for most of South Vietnam returned to normal.

We had won the political struggle for the allegiance of the South Vietnamese people. For years, Communist propaganda had trumpeted that theirs was the winning side, but now our side appeared to be the wave of the future. We were in control of areas that we had previously not dared to enter. We were resettling thousands of refugees displaced by the fighting. We had produced unprecedented economic prosperity.

Even the Communists took note. During 1969, their troops

defected to our side at a rate of 4,000 a month. In many areas the Popular Forces were composed entirely of former Communist soldiers. Kien Hoa Province had been a stronghold of the Communists since World War II. In October 1970, when the local Communist leader defected to our side, he said that his troops had dwindled from 10,000 to 3,000 and that he was abandoning his comrades because he realized that they were on the losing side.

While our pacification strategy was designed to deal with the political aspect of the war, our Vietnamization program readied our allies to handle the military part of it.

During the mid-1960s, South Vietnam's army was a mediocre fighting force. A commonly heard quip was that while United States forces tried to "seek out and destroy" Communist troops, those of South Vietnam sought to "search out and avoid" them. During nine months of 1966, battle reports indicated that 90 percent of American large-scale operations resulted in direct fighting with the enemy, compared with only 46 percent of South Vietnamese army missions. American commanders rated almost a third of South Vietnam's military units as having a marginal or unsatisfactory combat effectiveness. And during this period more than a fifth of Saigon's troops deserted.

There were two reasons for the ineffectiveness of South Vietnam's armed forces: They had little to fight for, and inadequate weapons to fight with. Soldiers go to war to defend the state. It is hard to imagine risking one's life so that a group of pompous incompetents masquerading as generals could continue to play musical chairs in the cabinet room of the Presidential Palace. From Diem's death in 1963 to Thieu's ascent to power in 1965, South Vietnam's armed forces fell into such a pitiful state that it took years to rebuild them into a fighting force that could match the North Vietnamese Army. When the United States intervened in 1965, we complicated the problem. Our troops did more than just take part in the war—they took it over. The more we Americanized the heavy fighting, the more our ally's military muscle atrophied.

But it was a misconception to say that the South Vietnamese were not shouldering their share of the war's burden. From 1965 through 1968, our ally suffered more killed in action than we did in all but three weeks. Generally, our troops fought better than theirs did. But Americans had more firepower and were backed up with more artillery and air support. Shortages of M-16 rifles, machine guns, mortars, radios, trucks, recoilless rifles, and artillery pieces meant that none of these became available in large numbers for South Vietnamese troops until late 1968. Armed only with semiautomatic M-1 rifles of World War II vintage, they were outgunned by the Communists, who were equipped with automatic Soviet-made AK-47s. It was like sending someone armed with a squirt gun into a water fight against an opponent equipped with a fire hose.

When our Vietnamization program began, we knew it would take several years. We quickly redressed our ally's disadvantage in firepower. We distributed automatic M-16 rifles to all regular South Vietnamese units by April 1969 and to virtually all territorial forces by February 1970. Under Thieu's mobilization, South Vietnam's regular army grew from 343,000 troops in 1967 to 516,000 in 1971. Its combat capability increased in every index of combat effectiveness. The South Vietnamese fought well during the Cambodian operations in 1970. From 1970 through 1971, South Vietnam's armed forces conducted three times as many large operations and recorded twice as many enemy killed in action as they did from 1966 through 1967.

But problems remained. South Vietnam's battlefield leadership was often poor. Thieu, who had witnessed firsthand the paralysis that resulted from political intrigue in the military after Diem's fall, was understandably obsessed with preserving his support within the army. He therefore tended to promote officers who demonstrated not their ability to command but rather their personal loyalty to him. This may have helped maintain stability, but it had a severely detrimental effect on the combat effectiveness of South Vietnam's army.

In early 1971, a critical test of Vietnamization took place:

Operation Lam Son 719. In order to blunt North Vietnam's offensive striking power, South Vietnam's army conducted a ground assault on Communist supply routes in Laos, acting for the first time without the help of American ground combat forces.

From 1966 through 1971, North Vietnam had used the Ho Chi Minh Trail to transport into South Vietnam 630,000 Communist troops, 100,000 tons of food, 400,000 weapons, and 600 million rounds of ammunition. Because Lon Nol had denied North Vietnam access to the port at Sihanoukville, all Communist supplies now had to be shipped overland along the Ho Chi Minh Trail. By December 1970, North Vietnam's 1,500 miles of roads in Laos were clogged with men and supplies en route to Cambodia for an offensive in either the spring of 1971 or 1972. To ensure South Vietnam's survival when the offensive came, we had to do something to disrupt North Vietnam's ominous buildup.

In January 1971, I authorized a military operation to cut the Ho Chi Minh Trail. Congressional restrictions made it illegal for us to use American ground troops in Laos. But after studying the reports of my military advisers, I was confident that South Vietnam's armed forces were ready to take on such a mission alone. Our only role would be to take up defensive positions below the demilitarized zone and along the border with Laos, ferry South Vietnamese troops and supplies in by helicopter, and provide air cover with gunships and bombing raids. Our plan called for South Vietnam's forces to drive about twenty miles into Laos along Route 9 to capture the town of Tchpone—on which almost all of North Vietnam's infiltration routes converged—and then to conduct further strikes in surrounding areas to disrupt the Communist buildup. Other South Vietnamese units were to conduct a simultaneous attack on a Communist base area in Cambodia.

On February 8, the operation began. South Vietnamese troops fought bravely and effectively, but some problems soon developed. Communist forces put up stronger resistance than we had anticipated, and American military commanders in

Saigon failed to respond with a corresponding increase in air cover. When South Vietnamese forces sustained large casualties about ten miles into Laos, they made the mistake of temporarily digging in, which gave the North Vietnamese a sitting target to hit. Thieu became overly cautious and ordered his commanders to stop their offensive as soon as casualties reached 3,000. By the middle of March, soon after the South Vietnamese reached Tchpone, their casualties hit Thieu's arbitrary ceiling, and they began to retreat to the southeast along Route 914.

American news-media reports presented a distorted picture of the operation by focusing almost exclusively on the failings of the South Vietnamese troops. Because of inadequate air support during the withdrawal, a few units took such a severe pounding from enemy artillery that they panicked. It took only a few televised films of soldiers clinging to the skids of our evacuation helicopters to reinforce the widespread misconception that South Vietnam's armed forces were incompetent and cowardly.

Contrary to the news-media's stories, the operation was a military success. South Vietnamese forces killed over 9,000 enemy troops and destroyed 1,123 crew-served weapons, 3,754 individual weapons, 110 tanks, 270 trucks, 13,630 tons of munitions, and 15 tons of ammunition for 122mm rockets. Of the twenty-two South Vietnamese battalions involved in the offensive, eighteen fought extremely well and four did poorly. Their withdrawal, though marred by some panic, was on the whole orderly. South Vietnam's operation did not achieve all our objectives. But the bottom line was decisively positive: Despite the largest influx of matériel in the history of the war, there was no Communist offensive in South Vietnam in 1971.

Operation Lam Son 719 was a milestone in the Vietnam War. It marked the first time South Vietnam's army had taken on the North Vietnamese in a frontal assault without American combat advisers. It also marked the last time United States forces were involved in the ground fighting in even a supporting role.

. . .

As our role in the fighting diminished, the news media's opposition to our involvement in the Vietnam War intensified. Objectivity gave way to hostility. On June 13, 1971, when the *New York Times* began publishing a series of articles based on a classified 7,000-page Defense Department study, their conduct reached the height of irresponsibility.

Officially entitled *The History of U.S. Decision-Making Process on Vietnam*, the study soon received a more dramatic label: "The Pentagon Papers." Written at the direction of Robert McNamara, the study's text described the history of our involvement in Vietnam from 1945 through 1968, and its appendixes contained dozens of verbatim documents from the files of the Defense Department, State Department, Central Intelligence Agency, Joint Chiefs of Staff, and the White House. The documents had been illegally turned over to the *Times*. Now, its editors announced that they planned to publish not only portions of the study but also many of the original documents. Their story did not mention that all these materials were still classified a "Secret" and "Top Secret."

My administration faced the difficult question of what to do about the most massive leak of classified documents in American history. We had only two options: We could either do nothing or move for a court injunction that would prevent the *Times* from continuing publication. Good policy argued for moving against the *Times*; safe politics argued against doing so.

My political advisers believed that it would be in my interest to let the Pentagon Papers come out. First of all, the study focused principally on Kennedy's and Johnson's handling of the war. Because it was written in 1968, it could contain nothing about my administration's actions. Furthermore, the *Times* stories about the Pentagon Papers leveled serious charges against my Democratic predecessors. Most of the accusations were based on grotesque distortions of the historical record. But that did not alter the fact that it would be to my political advantage for them to appear on the front page of virtually every newspaper in the country.

Nevertheless, I decided to try to block the publication of the Pentagon Papers because concrete policy considerations outweighed whatever political benefits I might accrue. It posed a significant threat to some of our national security interests. The National Security Agency feared that the more recent documents would provide code-breaking clues and contain information about our signal and electronic intelligence capabilities that would be spotted by the trained eyes of enemy experts. The State Department was alarmed because the study would reveal SEATO contingency war plans that were still in effect. The Central Intelligence Agency was worried that it would expose past or current informants and would contain specific references to the names and activities of agents still active in Southeast Asia. One secret contact dried up almost immediately, and other governments became reluctant to share their intelligence information with us.

We also were concerned that the release of the Pentagon Papers would damage our delicate negotiations with China and the Soviet Union. Diplomacy, especially with Communist powers, depends on secrecy. If leaders cannot express their views frankly for fear that what they say will appear in the next day's headlines, the chances of making progress in negotiations will be sharply reduced. If, for example, word had leaked out about our China initiative, those who opposed it in both countries would have destroyed any chances for success. When the Pentagon Papers were leaked, Kissinger was about to take his first secret trip to Peking, and the Strategic Arms Limitation Talks with the Soviet Union were just getting started. I knew that before going forward with our rapprochement, the Chinese would watch carefully to see how I handled disclosure of the Pentagon Papers. In their eyes, a failure to act would have meant that we were an unreliable partner with whom it would be risky to share sensitive information.

If the New York Times had acted with any degree of responsibility, we could have avoided the battle in the court. But it had not done so. Its editors admitted having had possession of the documents for more than three months before publishing them. Yet never once had they asked anyone in the government whether publication of any of the classified material might threaten national security or endanger the lives of our men in Vietnam.

The Supreme Court ruled against the government. But I still believe I acted responsibly in challenging the right of the *New York Times* to publish the Pentagon's study. Its release was an illegal action. Its publication was a threat to our ability to conduct foreign policy. If we had done nothing, we would have been setting a dangerous precedent: Every disgruntled bureaucrat in Washington would have read our inaction as a signal that he could leak anything he pleased and that the government would simply stand by helplessly. In the thirteen years since the Supreme Court sanctioned the *Times's* publication of the Pentagon Papers, that is exactly what has happened.

Our pacification and Vietnamization programs completely transformed the war in Vietnam. The military picture we faced in 1972 was almost entirely different from the one we faced even as late as 1970. We had countered the Communists' strategy of guerrilla war so effectively that they abandoned it. Their new strategy was to wage a conventional war. In short, Hanoi had chosen to fight our kind of war.

In early 1972, we expected a major Communist offensive that would decide the outcome of the war. The presence of North Vietnamese tanks in Laos indicated that the assault would not be an urban insurrection like the Tet Offensive but an overt invasion by a conventional army. If it succeeded, South Vietnam would be swept off the map. If it failed, North Vietnam would be forced to negotiate an end to the war. We were prepared for their attack because all five elements of our Vietnam policy had come together.

Our Vietnamization program had turned South Vietnam's

military into a formidable fighting force. Its army had 120 infantry battalions organized into 11 divisions, 58 artillery battalions, and 19 armored units of battalion size. Its navy had 43,000 sailors operating 1,680 naval craft. Its air force had 51,000 servicemen operating more than 1,000 aircraft. South Vietnam, with a population of 19 million, had over 1 million men in its armed forces and another 3 million in its local militias.

Our pacification program had extended Saigon's control throughout the country down to the hamlet level. Our South Vietnamese allies had uprooted the Communist infrastructure, thereby depriving enemy forces of supplies and military intelligence. Our economic aid had produced unprecedented prosperity for the South Vietnamese people.

Our great-power diplomacy had unnerved the North Vietnamese by isolating them from China and the Soviet Union. During my summit meeting in China in February 1972, Mao Zedong and Zhou Enlai mildly criticized American actions in Vietnam, but they spoke more in sorrow than anger. I also had initiated the process of detente with the Soviet Union. A summit meeting with Leonid Brezhnev was scheduled for May in Moscow. We were close to resolving several issues of great importance to the Soviets, including a major grain deal and the first Strategic Arms Limitation Agreement. Brezhnev considered the war in Vietnam an issue of secondary significance by comparison. Neither major Communist power had helped us end the war. But both had taken clear steps to distance themselves from Hanoi. Communist leaders by training and practice are master conspirators. They never trust their adversaries and seldom trust each other. The fact that we were meeting with their major allies in Peking and Moscow had to concern the men in North Vietnam's politburo.

Our staged troop-withdrawal program had sustained support for the war effort in Congress and among the American people for three years. By January 1, 1972, we had withdrawn over 400,000 troops from Vietnam. None of the 133,200 troops who remained were involved in the ground fighting, and most were to be withdrawn within six months. I doubt that we could have continued fighting the war if we had not been gradually withdrawing our troops. Since 1969, we had been faced with the danger of Congress legislating an end to our involvement. Antiwar senators and congressmen had been introducing resolutions to force us to trade a total withdrawal of our troops for the return of our POWs. By 1972, the Senate was regularly passing these measures, and the votes in the House were getting close. We were able to prevent the passage of these bills only because our withdrawal announcements provided those whose support for the war was wavering with tangible evidence that our involvement was winding down.

During this period we were making every possible effort to reach a negotiated settlement. With phenomenal stamina, tenacity, and patience, Henry Kissinger tried again and again to break the logjam in sessions of our secret negotiations in Paris. North Vietnam rejected all of our proposals categorically. In October 1971, Kissinger made our final peace offer: a standstill cease-fire followed within six months by a total American withdrawal, a mutual exchange of POWs, and an internationally supervised election in South Vietnam in which the Communists could participate. Our proposal stretched the limits of our generosity. If the North Vietnamese were sincerely interested in peace, they would have been interested in our offer. But Hanoi again refused to negotiate seriously.

For three years the North Vietnamese had ruthlessly exploited our secret negotiations in order to divide Americans on the home front. On the one hand, they had stalemated the peace talks. Hanoi persistently demanded that we withdraw our forces unilaterally and that we overthrow President Thieu's government as we left. These conditions were unacceptable. We had not fought for ten years and lost over 50,000 lives so that we could install a Communist government in Saigon as we withdrew in disgrace. On the other hand, the North Vietnamese planted stories in the press and circulated rumors among antiwar activists to the effect that the United States was blocking progress in the talks. This took a toll on public support of the war. We found ourselves being criticized for failing to make certain concessions that in fact we had already made in the private talks. But we could refute these criticisms only by disclosing the secret negotiations, which we feared might destroy any chance for them to succeed.

Finally I concluded that Hanoi's refusal to respond to our October offer, coupled with reports of a huge North Vietnamese buildup, probably meant that it had opted for a test of arms on the battlefield. I therefore decided that the time had come to make clear to the American people just who was obstructing the talks. Only in this way could we muster support for whatever actions might become necessary when North Vietnam launched its offensive. On January 25, 1972, in a nationally televised address, I revealed the record of the twelve sessions of Kissinger's secret talks and reiterated the terms of our final proposal. In conclusion I said, "The only thing this plan does not do is to join our enemy to overthrow our ally, which the United States of America will never do. If the enemy wants peace, it will have to recognize the important difference between settlement and surrender."

On March 30, 1972, the North Vietnamese launched a massive invasion of South Vietnam. Striking at our ally's weakest point, three full divisions, along with 200 Soviet T-54 tanks and scores of 130mm guns, trampled across the internationally recognized neutral territory of the demilitarized zone. More forces swept in from Laos along Route 9 toward Hue. Other units were poised to strike into the central highlands toward Kontum and Pleiku and to invade southern South Vietnam from Cambodia. It was as blatant as North Korea's invasion of South Korea in 1950.

I considered North Vietnam's attack a sign of desperation. Hanoi clearly believed Vietnamization was working. If it were not, the North Vietnamese could have waited and let it fail after almost all of our troops were gone. They also had to be concerned about the fact that we were developing a new relationship with their allies in Moscow and Peking. They knew

that time was not on their side. I gave no consideration whatsoever to the suggestion of some of my aides that, particularly
with an election coming up, we should let South Vietnam fend
for itself. I believed that it would be not only immoral but
stupid to stand by quietly while North Vietnam bludgeoned
our South Vietnamese allies. Hanoi had refused to settle the
war at the conference table. Now, after the North Vietnamese
had chosen to fight the kind of war we fought best, we were
in a position to force them to settle on our terms.

During the first weeks of the invasion, the news from Vietnam was discouraging. On April 2, just south of the demilitarized zone, North Vietnam's forces mauled South Vietnam's
Third Division. Fourteen bases were abandoned as South Vietnamese resistance collapsed under the intense onslaught.
Communist troops driving toward Hue threatened to isolate
all of South Vietnam's northern units in a giant pincer movement. On April 5, three North Vietnamese divisions struck
into Binh Long Province, about seventy-five miles north of
Saigon. On April 13, in their push toward the South Vietnamese capital, they surrounded the town of Anloc; supplies could
be dropped only by parachute. On April 23, North Vietnamese
troops rolled into the central highlands toward Kontum. South
Vietnam's Twenty-second Division fell apart under attack, but
its Twenty-third Division held the line. On April 27, the North
Vietnamese launched a new wave of attacks along the northern
front, and four days later the provincial capital of Quang Tri
fell to the Communists.

During their offensive, the Communists once again engaged
in barbaric attacks on civilians. At both Anloc and Quang Tri,
North Vietnamese troops indiscriminately fired artillery shells
into crowds of refugees who were fleeing the fighting. Thousands were killed. In Communist-occupied areas of Binh Dinh
Province, there were public executions of hundreds of individuals suspected of having ties to the Saigon government. In
one hamlet, forty-seven local officials were buried alive. In
Quang Ngai Province, Communist troops strung land mines
around forty victims and then, as their wives and children

watched, detonated the mines, blowing the helpless captives to bits.

Our response to the offensive was quick in coming. Hanoi was now fighting a large-unit conventional war. Its infantry divisions, tank columns, and logistics system all made perfect targets for our air power. On April 1, I ordered the bombing of North Vietnamese territory within twenty-five miles of the demilitarized zone. Within two weeks, I authorized air strikes up to the twentieth parallel. I also ordered the Pentagon to assemble a massive sea and air attack force in Southeast Asia. Initially, to augment those forces already in Southeast Asia, I sent two cruisers and eight destroyers for sea bombardment, and twenty B-52 bombers and four squadrons of F-4 fighter-bombers for battlefield air strikes and a renewed bombing campaign against North Vietnam. More deployments followed later.

On May 2, Kissinger met with Hanoi's delegation for a secret negotiating session in Paris. Over the years he had always had to listen to a litany of verbal abuse from his interlocutors during these sessions. Now, confident of imminent military victory, Hanoi's representatives were even more insolent and unbearable. After putting up with insults and invective for three hours, Kissinger broke off the talks.

That was Hanoi's last chance. I decided that now it was essential to defeat North Vietnam's invasion. If the enemy had one Achilles' heel, it was his supply system. Intelligence reports estimated that to sustain their push into South Vietnam his forces needed several thousands of tons of ammunition and fuel every day. Our best chance of halting the invasion was to take decisive action to stop the shipment of these supplies.

It was a difficult decision. Only two months earlier I had gone to Peking and opened our new relationship with the People's Republic of China, and in only three weeks I was scheduled to go to Moscow for my first summit meeting with Brezhnev. I did not know what reaction to expect from China and the Soviet Union, who had strongly backed North Vietnam, if I attacked their ally. But I believed that if we allowed North Vietnam to conquer South Vietnam, the hardheaded realists in the politburos in Peking and Moscow might think a United States that lacked the will to defend its interests was not worth talking to. Consequently, I ordered the mining of North Vietnam's ports, including Haiphong Harbor, and the bombing of prime military targets throughout North Vietnam, including those in Hanoi.

On May 8, I announced this decision in a nationally televised address. After describing the North Vietnamese invasion, I outlined our three options: an immediate withdrawal, a negotiated peace or a decisive military action to end the war. I said that I had rejected the first option because it would be immoral to abandon our South Vietnamese allies to Communist tyranny and because it would encourage aggression throughout the world. I explained that while I preferred the second option, "it takes two to negotiate" and the North Vietnamese had proven to be unwilling partners. Therefore, I said, the United States really had no choice at all: "There is only one way to stop the killing. That is to keep the weapons of war out of the hands of the international outlaws of North Vietnam." In order to leave the door open for later negotiations, I concluded with a reiteration of our basic terms for a fair peace settlement.

Antiwar critics and the news media competed with each other in denouncing our action. One senator remarked that the decision was "reckless and wrong." Another said that "the President must not have a free hand in Indochina any longer." One newspaper called the decision a "desperate gamble" and urged that Congress should cut off funds for the war to "save the President from himself and the nation from disaster." Another claimed that the President "has lost touch with the real world." One legislator topped them all when he breathlessly intoned that the President "has thrown down the gauntlet of nuclear war to a billion people in the Soviet Union and China . . . Armageddon may be only hours away." There was nearly unanimous agreement that, as one network reporter put it, our action "practically kills prospects of a summit" with the Soviet leadership. Most of the members of Congress, my cabinet, and my staff shared the view that the summit would probably be off.

Hanoi claimed our actions were an "insolent challenge" and asked for increased support from its Communist allies. But Moscow and Peking did not man the battle stations. Both went through the motions of protesting our actions, but otherwise did nothing. China expressed its support for North Vietnam and criticized our actions in public and private, but the Chinese did not back up their words with any actions. In fact, Peking reprinted my May 8 speech, complete with my denunciations of North Vietnam's intransigence and aggression, in the official state newspaper.

Kissinger and I agreed there was a good chance the Soviets would cancel or postpone our summit meeting. But signals soon came in indicating that they wanted to go forward with it. Their public criticism was, by Communist standards, muted. Their private protests were limited to the damage caused by our bombing of their ships in port. Their arms-control and trade negotiators affected an attitude of business as usual. In spite of the dire predictions of our critics, our first Soviet-American summit came off on schedule on May 22.

Brezhnev went forward with the summit for two reasons. First, he wanted and needed better relations with the United States, particularly in view of our China initiative. Second, he knew we were worth talking to, because our actions in Vietnam had demonstrated that we had not only the power to defend our interests but also the will to use it. If we had not acted, we might have had to go to Moscow while Soviet-made tanks were rumbling through the streets of Hue and Saigon. We would have been in an intolerable position of weakness. Brezhnev would have assumed that if I could be pushed around in Vietnam, I could also be pushed around in Moscow.

Our diplomacy with Moscow and Peking had turned the tables on Hanoi. It had been an article of faith within the Kennedy and Johnson administrations that making a decisive military move against North Vietnam risked the intervention of China and the Soviet Union. That now changed: Hanoi was fearful that its allies might use their leverage to intervene on the side of its enemy. A North Vietnamese official later complained in an interview, "Nixon is capitalizing on the disunity among the socialist countries in one way or another to be free to act. This affects our war and, thus, our fighting has become very difficult."

During May, South Vietnam's army turned the tide in the ground war. By May 4, after times when it seemed all might be lost, the South Vietnamese had pulled themselves together and reestablished the northern front twenty-five miles north of Hue. Once the initial crisis passed, South Vietnam's army fought better than it had in any previous battle. The failure of the North Vietnamese to launch their three attacks simultaneously was skillfully exploited by the South Vietnamese, who shifted their airborne divisions from front to front, depending on where the fighting was heaviest. When South Vietnam's forces established a defensive perimeter, North Vietnam's troops had to assume fixed positions. This enabled us virtually to destroy them with B-52 strikes.

When I received the first proposals for bombing North Vietnam from the Pentagon during the first week of May, I hit the ceiling. Their proposals were a timid replay of the Johnson bombing campaign from 1965 through 1968. In a long memorandum to Kissinger, I wrote, "I cannot emphasize too strongly that I have determined that we should go for broke." I went on to say that we were in danger of doing too little too late and that it was better to err on the side of doing too much while we had maximum public support. "I think we have had too much of a tendency to talk big and act little," I wrote. "This was certainly the weakness of the Johnson administration. To an extent it may have been our weakness where we have warned the enemy time and time again and then have acted in a rather mild way when the enemy has tested us. He has now gone over the brink *and so have we*. We have the power to destroy his war-making capacity. The only question is whether we have the *will* to use that power." I made it clear that I had the will to take strong actions and was prepared to risk the consequences.

Once I had clarified what I wanted done, our armed forces brought our tremendous firepower to bear on the enemy with stunning results. We mobilized every available ship in the Seventh Fleet. Over 400 B-52 bombers and F-4 fighter-bombers struck at targets both on the front in South Vietnam and in the rear in North Vietnam.

Like Johnson, I restricted our bombing to military targets. Charges that we were systematically bombing North Vietnam's dikes were enemy propaganda. No credible evidence was ever produced to substantiate them. But unlike Johnson, I did not retain personal control over target selection. Since a bombing campaign was a military operation, I put Admiral Moorer, chairman of the Joint Chiefs of Staff, and our military commanders in Vietnam in charge of conducting it. There were bombing restrictions within a twenty-five- to thirty-mile-deep buffer zone and within ten miles of Hanoi and five miles of Haiphong. But even within these areas, field commanders could hit certain types of targets—such as power plants, munitions dumps, and air bases—without approval from Washington.

By November we had pounded North Vietnamese positions near the demilitarized zone with over 16,000 tons of naval bombardment and had dropped over 155,000 tons of bombs on North Vietnam. We had expended less bombing tonnage than Johnson had during a comparable period. But because North Vietnam was now waging a conventional war and because I had given our commanders the authority to maximize the advantage of our air power, we succeeded in crippling North Vietnam's military effort.

Our most telling operation was the mining of North Vietnam harbors and the blockade of its coast. The port at Haiphong received an estimated 2.1 million tons of supplies a year, including over 85 percent of North Vietnam's military matériel and 100 percent of its oil. Once our mines were in place, not a single ship entered or exited the port. It was impossible to transfer these shipments to the railroads through China without an extended period of adjustment. In early June we received reports that over 1,000 railroad cars were backed up on the Chinese side of the border and that ammunition shortages were becoming acute. Hanoi's offensive had bogged down.

When I spoke at the Oxford Union in 1978, one of the British students asked whether I had any regrets about ordering the incursion into Cambodia. I replied that my only regret was that I had not done it earlier. I have the same regrets with regard to my May 8, 1972, decision. We should have begun bombing North Vietnam and mining its harbors at the time of our Cambodian operations in 1970. From a military standpoint, it would have been far better to strike at Hanoi's military strength in North Vietnam rather than waiting until its troops were moving through Laos and Cambodia or fighting in South Vietnam.

I did not act sooner for three reasons. First, as the violent reaction to the Cambodia incursions would prove, I believed it would be very hard to hold the country together while pursuing a military solution. I thought that adding the bombing and mining to the incursions would have been more than the traffic could bear. Second, I knew that winning a temporary respite from enemy actions would not by itself guarantee South Vietnam's survival. It was imperative that the United States be able to stay in Vietnam until our allies had developed the capability to defend themselves. Third, since our initiatives to open new relationships with China and the Soviet Union were only in their early stages, I feared that their chances for success would be snuffed out if we took such strong action against their North Vietnamese allies.

In retrospect, however, I would have to agree that a good case can be made by those who believe that we should have taken strong action against North Vietnam much earlier than we did.

In June, South Vietnam's counteroffensive began. For over two months the defenders of Anloc held out with phenomenal courage under a brutal siege. Every soldier had been a casualty at some point. Now, with the help of our bombing, they began to strike back. After two weeks of house-to-house fighting, they had cleared the city of enemy troops. By August the South Vietnamese Army had retaken the rest of Binh Long Province. On June 28, it attacked along the northern front. Ten weeks later, despite the monsoon rains, three South Vietnamese divisions had pushed six North Vietnamese divisions out of the provincial capital of Quang Tri.

North Vietnam had thrown the total weight of its armed forces into the spring offensive. Fourteen divisions and twenty-six independent regiments had invaded South Vietnam, leaving one division and four independent regiments in Laos and no regular ground forces at all in North Vietnam. Hanoi's armed forces were in tatters. Seventy-five percent of its tanks had been destroyed. Its ranks were now filled with sixteen- and seventeen-year-old soldiers. Some of its battalions had been ground down to fifty troops. Estimates put the number of their killed in action at over 100,000.

In the spring offensive of 1972, South Vietnam's army had held off the North Vietnamese onslaught without the assistance of any American ground combat troops. Our senior military commanders in Vietnam and Washington, many of whom had earlier questioned whether Vietnamization would succeed, now unanimously agreed that the South Vietnamese Army had proved that, if properly equipped and led, it could hold its own against North Vietnam's best troops.

We can never know whether the South Vietnamese could have won without the assistance of American air power. But we know for certain that we could not have won with our air power alone. Vietnamization had worked. Our ally had stopped the spring offensive on the ground, and our bombing had crushed it.

It was fashionable in academic circles to assert that the Vietnam War proved that military power no longer had any utility in international politics. But the exact opposite was the case.

For almost four years the North Vietnamese had stalled both our public and private peace talks. Now, after the United States and South Vietnam had decisively defeated North Vietnam's spring offensive, Hanoi for the first time began to negotiate seriously.

Hanoi's reading of American politics added an incentive to settle the war quickly. Because I was leading Senator McGovern by as much as thirty percentage points in the polls, the North Vietnamese probably concluded that I was almost certainly going to be reelected on November 7. They also probably believed that they might get better terms from me before the election than after it.

As a result, our private channel with the North Vietnamese became active in August. In late September they presented a new proposal during a two-day session of our secret talks. Although it was significantly more forthcoming than any of their past proposals, it was still unacceptable on the key military and political issues. It was clear that the next meeting, scheduled for October 8, would be decisive in determining whether they intended to reach a settlement before the presidential election.

When the talks reconvened, Hanoi made a proposal in which it capitulated on most of the major issues. The North Vietnamese abandoned their demands for a unilateral American withdrawal, a coalition government for South Vietnam, the overthrow of President Thieu, and a cutoff of our military and economic aid to Saigon. Hanoi's new proposal called for a cease-fire in place, which we had been offering since late 1970, followed by an American withdrawal and an exchange of POWs within sixty days. When we signed the Paris peace agreements in January 1973, some observers claimed that we could have reached an identical settlement in 1969. They ignore the fact that Hanoi *rejected* these very terms until October 1972.

Most of our remaining disputes were hammered out in another session of talks in mid-October. But on one major issue we could not budge the North Vietnamese from their position:

They refused to withdraw their forces from South Vietnam. All along they had asserted that the conflict was a civil war and refused to acknowledge explicitly that they had any troops in the South. Hanoi therefore rejected our repeated demands for their withdrawal on the grounds that they were not involved in the war.

We knew there was no way to force them to concede this point. It is an axiom of diplomacy that one cannot win at the conference table what one could not win on the battlefield. Although South Vietnam had reversed the tide of battle before the monsoons set in, the North Vietnamese continued to occupy large areas of South Vietnam along the demilitarized zone and in the central highlands. We had to consider how Hanoi viewed its options. We knew that if reaching a settlement required the North Vietnamese to give away territory that South Vietnam had been unable to take away, they would calculate that they were better off not concluding an agreement. If we had stood firm in demanding North Vietnam's withdrawal, there would have been no peace agreement.

In resolving the issue, we never conceded the legitimacy of North Vietnam's military presence in South Vietnam. Our tactic was to write a formulation that tacitly required the enemy to withdraw. We demanded that Hanoi pledge to stop the infiltration of men into South Vietnam. If the promise was kept, enemy forces in the South soon would have to withdraw or else wither away. When the North Vietnamese agreed to this, we set a timetable for signing a completed agreement by October 31.

On October 18, when Kissinger flew to South Vietnam to explain the agreement to the South Vietnamese, he ran into strong resistance from Thieu. After meeting with the entire South Vietnamese National Security Council and the ambassadors to the Paris talks, Kissinger reported that the South Vietnamese leaders were exhibiting a surprising awe of Communist cunning and a disquieting lack of confidence in themselves. It was clear that they were having great difficulty with the prospect of cutting the American umbilical cord. As Kissinger saw it, we were up against a paradoxical situation in which North Vietnam, which had in effect lost the war, was acting as if it had won, while South Vietnam, which had effectively won the war, was acting as if it had lost.

Thieu understandably wanted the agreement to require the North Vietnamese to withdraw their forces from his country. But his objections went deeper: He was profoundly insecure about what would happen after the United States withdrew. As a result, he proposed over twenty changes to the draft agreement, seven of which we knew the North Vietnamese would never accept. It now seemed inevitable that the October 31 deadline would pass without an agreement.

While negotiating with Thieu, we were also negotiating with the North Vietnamese over his reservations about the draft agreement. Hanoi, noting the difficulties we were having with Saigon, pursued a cleverly calculated strategy: On the one hand, its delegates agreed to virtually all of the technical points we raised in order to build a perfect negotiating record that, if publicized, would make it appear that South Vietnam was obstructing a settlement. On the other hand, through leaks and press interviews, they portrayed the agreement as a Communist victory. Their strategy sought to whipsaw Thieu between international and domestic public opinion. If he rejected the agreement, he would be attacked throughout the world for refusing what appeared to be fair terms. If he accepted it, he would be attacked within South Vietnam for caving in to what the Communists were presenting as terms favorable to them.

On October 26, the North Vietnamese sprang their trap by going public with the peace agreement, including our timetable for signing. Kissinger went ahead with a press conference he had scheduled that day to reassure the North Vietnamese that we were serious about reaching an agreement and to distract attention from Thieu's objections. In his opening statement, he said, "We believe that peace is at hand. We believe that an agreement is within sight, based on the May 8 proposals of the President and some adaptations of our January 25 proposal, which is just to all parties." News-media reports focused on the his statement that "peace is at hand." I knew immediately that our bargaining position with the North Vietnamese would be seriously eroded. Since we had publicly stated that we expected the negotiations to produce an agreement, there would be pressure on us to deliver—and that could be exploited to extract concessions from us.

Our critics claimed that Kissinger's statement was a ploy to win voters with the election less than two weeks away. This was not true. Polls indicated that our handling of the war in Vietnam was generally viewed as a positive issue for me and a negative one for McGovem, who was perceived as weak and even as favoring surrender. If we had hastily concluded an agreement in time for the election, it would have provoked charges of the worst kind of cynicism. It would not have won us new support from either side of the political spectrum: A suspiciously quick agreement would have led hawks to accuse us of selling out in order to meet a self-serving deadline, and doves to claim that I could have obtained the same terms in 1969.

I hit this issue head on in a televised campaign speech on November 2. I declared, "We are not going to allow an election deadline or any other kind of deadline to force us into an agreement which would be only a temporary truce and not a lasting peace. We are going to sign the agreement when the agreement is right, not one day before. And when the agreement is right, we are going to sign, without one day's delay."

We soon concluded that meeting the October 31 deadline was unrealistic. Thieu's unwillingness to agree to what I believed were the best possible terms was distressing. He seemed oblivious to the crucial issue. South Vietnam's survival did not depend on whether enemy troops occupied a few sparsely populated regions. It depended on whether the United States enforced the terms of the peace agreement, both with continuing aid and with a credible threat of military action. That would be possible only if Saigon retained the support of Congress. If we did not settle the war quickly, Congress would probably legislate an end to the war in January. If Congress concluded that South Vietnamese obstructionism had delayed an agreement, it would probably undermine our ability to come to the aid of our ally if necessary. Nevertheless, I was willing to give Thieu more time to come around.

The negotiations were scheduled to reconvene after the election. In the meantime, we found that both Saigon and Hanoi were playing a frustrating game with us. Our intelligence indicated that Thieu had told his generals to prepare for a cease-fire before Christmas, but he continued to pretend that he was willing to go it alone. Our intelligence also showed that Hanoi was preparing for military moves, but its delegates continued to affect a sincere desire to make peace.

On November 9, I sent Alexander Haig to consult with the South Vietnamese. I thought he was the best man to bring Thieu around because he would be able to talk to him as one respected military officer to another. He delivered a letter to Thieu in which I responded to the South Vietnamese objections to the October agreement. "We will use our maximum efforts to effect these changes in the agreement," I wrote. "I wish to leave you under no illusion, however, that we can or will go beyond these changes in seeking to improve an agreement that we already consider to be excellent." Haig stressed that if we did not reach a settlement before Congress reconvened in January, it would almost certainly cut off our aid to South Vietnam. He pressed Thieu relentlessly, but Thieu would not budge. He continued to restate his previous objections.

On November 14, I wrote another letter to Thieu. I reiterated that we would probably not be able to obtain all the adjustments he had requested. I pointed out that what was *said* in any agreement was what we would *do* in the event the North Vietnamese renewed their aggression. I added, "You have my absolute assurance that if Hanoi fails to abide by the terms of this agreement it is my intention to take swift and severe retaliatory action."

Meanwhile, the North Vietnamese had decided to try to take advantage of our differences with Saigon. Hanoi had come to two conclusions: that a lack of progress in the talks would be blamed on Thieu and that, if an agreement was not forthcoming, Congress would pull the rug out from under us. Therefore, its delegates started to stall.

On November 20, our talks reopened in Paris. Kissinger presented Thieu's proposed changes, as well as some of our own. Hanoi's delegates objected strongly. After several tough negotiating sessions, I concluded that if we were to reach an agreement, we would have to abandon most of Thieu's major demands. I instructed Kissinger to seek a settlement along the lines of the October agreement. But Hanoi now began to stonewall us. It hardened its positions on the unresolved issues and pulled back concessions it had made on some resolved questions. Having reached an impasse, we recessed the talks.

On December 4, when the talks reconvened, Hanoi turned even more obstinate. Its delegates not only categorically rejected every change we had requested, but also withdrew some that had already been agreed upon during the last round and introduced several new and unacceptable demands of their own. Kissinger reported to me, "There is almost no doubt that Hanoi is prepared now to break off the negotiations and go another military round. Their own needs for a settlement are now outweighed by the attractive vision they see of our having to choose between a complete split with Saigon or an unmanageable domestic situation." In the following days, although we succeeded in resolving some issues, the North Vietnamese reopened others. They gave us just enough each day to keep the negotiations going, but not quite enough to conclude an agreement. With the prospects for an agreement actually receding, Kissinger and I reluctantly concluded that the enemy had made a deliberate decision to prolong the war.

On December 13, we recessed the talks. I had decided that since Hanoi had made up its mind to continue the war, we had to make a move that would change its mind. We had to convince the North Vietnamese by our actions, not just by our words, that they were better off concluding an agreement on our terms than continuing the fighting. This meant stepping up the bombing of North Vietnam. On December 14, I issued an order to reseed the mines in Haiphong Harbor, to resume aerial reconnaissance throughout North Vietnam, and to bomb military targets in the Hanoi-Haiphong complex with B-52s. It was the most difficult decision concerning Vietnam that I made during my entire presidency. But I had no choice. I was convinced that if we did not compel the North Vietnamese to agree to our terms, Congress would force us to accept defeat by agreeing to a withdrawal in exchange for our POWs.

On December 17, we began the mining operation, and within twenty-four hours 129 B-52s flew bombing runs over North Vietnam. Over twelve days we sent B-52s on 729 missions and fighter-bombers on about 1,000, dropping a total of more than 20,000 tons of bombs. Our targets—which included communications facilities, railroad yards, power plants, airports, fuel depots, and the like—all had military significance.

Our bombing provoked hysterical outbursts from our critics. A newsmagazine wrote that "civilized man will be horrified at the renewed spectacle of the world's mightiest air force mercilessly pounding a small Asian nation in an abuse of national power and disregard of humanitarian principles." One newspaper wrote that it caused millions of Americans "to cringe in shame and to wonder at their President's very sanity." One columnist said the bombing was the action of "a maddened tyrant," and another stated that we had "loosed the holocaust." One senator said it was a "stone-age tactic." Another called it "the most murderous aerial bombardment in the history of the world" and "a policy of mass-murder that's being carried on in the name of the American people."

Seldom has so much heated rhetoric been so wrong. Our critics denounced our actions as the "Christmas carpet bombing." But they were wrong on both points: We did not bomb on Christmas day, and we never covered whole areas with a carpet of bombs, as had been the case with our bombing of German and Japanese cities during World War II. Our pilots struck only at specific military targets and had explicit orders

270

to avoid collateral damage to civilian areas—even if this exposed them to greater risks.

Our critics should have known better than to make the utterly false accusation that we were indiscriminately bombing civilians. Hanoi *at the time* had put the number of civilian fatalities at between 1,300 and 1,600. Regrettable though these accidental losses were, they did not approach the death tolls that resulted when the Allies deliberately bombed civilian targets in World War II. Over 35,000 civilians were killed in the triple raid on Dresden, over 42,000 died in six nights of bombing in Hamburg, and over 83,000 Japanese were killed in just two days when we fire-bombed Tokyo in 1945. If we had targeted civilian areas during the December bombing, North Vietnamese losses would have been a hundred times higher than they were.

Our bombing achieved its purposes. Militarily, we had shattered North Vietnam's war-making capacity. Politically, we had shattered Hanoi's will to continue the war. Admiral James Stockdale, one of our POWs who was awarded the Medal of Honor when he returned, later described the scene when the prisoners heard the explosions as the bombs began hitting their targets. He wrote that "cheers started to go up all over the cellblocks of that downtown prison. This was a new reality for Hanoi." He observed that the bombing took a heavy psychological toll on the enemy: "One look at any Vietnamese officer's face told the whole story. It telegraphed accommodation, hopelessness, remorse, fear. The shock was there; our enemy's will was broken." Our POWs knew that they were coming home, even if our editorial writers did not.

Hanoi quickly accepted our first offer to resume the talks. We had forced Hanoi to come back to the negotiating table to end the war through a fair settlement. On January 8, when our high-level negotiations reconvened, North Vietnam agreed to our basic terms within forty-eight hours.

On my sixtieth birthday, January 9, 1973, I received a cable from Kissinger informing me that all the outstanding issues had been resolved; only the formalities remained. When I heard the news, I should have been elated. Some White House staff members were puzzled that we did not raise a glass to toast "peace with honor" after America's longest war. But for most Americans Vietnam was a war without heroes, without victory parades, without celebrations. For many in the news media, the only heroes were the antiwar politicians, the antiwar demonstrators, and those who evaded military service rather than those who served.

There are those who believe that while war is an acutely traumatic and personal experience for soldiers who risk their lives on the battlefield, it is essentially an impersonal experience for a President who sends them into battle. A President, it is assumed, spends his time moving pins on a war map, reading reports on enemy body counts, and ordering the bombing of schools and hospitals. He is supposedly so obsessed with what happens to nations that he is oblivious to what happens to people.

But for Presidents, too, war is an intensely traumatic, personal ordeal. Like all Presidents, my four predecessors—Truman, Eisenhower, Kennedy, and Johnson—were men who cherished peace. Each one of them wanted to avoid going to war in Vietnam if at all possible. But they were hardheaded realists who knew that peace under communism has killed far more people than wars against Communists. And they recognized that a Communist conquest of Vietnam would be detrimental to American interests not only in Southeast Asia but also in the rest of the world.

I had been intimately associated with the history of Vietnam for twenty years. In 1953, as Vice President, I had made an official visit to the French colonial cities of Saigon and Hanoi. In 1954, I had participated in the National Security Council debate about whether to use American air power to prevent the fall of Dien Bien Phu. In 1956, I developed a close friendship with President Diem. I had great respect for him as a strong anti-Communist leader. I was deeply saddened when I learned of his assassination in 1963 and was shocked when I

heard that the United States had encouraged and master-
minded the coup that resulted in his death. In the mid-1960s,
I visited South Vietnam a number of times and developed a
deep respect for our fighting men. I also felt a strong affection
for the South Vietnamese people—a courageous nation that
was suffering the ravages of a cruel war waged by a ruthless
enemy who treated even women and children as legitimate
targets for terrorism, torture, and murder.

In 1969, when I became President, I wanted nothing more
than to end the war as quickly as possible, but in a way that
would both prevent the imposition of Communist repression
upon the South Vietnamese people and discourage other Communist aggressors from launching such wars in the future. I
had to deal with other great foreign policy issues during my
presidency, but a day never passed when the war in Vietnam
was not prominent among my concerns. I hated the Vietnam
war. But even more, I hated all wars. I knew that I must not
end the Vietnam War in a way that would lead to more and
larger wars in the future.

It was my responsibility to see the war from afar—and to
make the decisions that would hasten its end on an honorable
basis. But I also saw the war in intensely personal terms. I
spent hours on letters to the next of kin of our soldiers who
had been killed in action. No matter how hard I tried to give
them personal warmth, I was never satisfied with the final
product. It always seemed too cold. There were just no words
to express adequately the heartfelt emotions I experienced
when I heard about the death of an American who was killed
in the prime of life in the service of his country.

During the Christmas holidays each year, I called the next
of kin of our killed in action on a random basis. Usually, their
mothers answered the telephone. I called to give them a lift,
but frequently they ended up giving me a lift—probably without knowing how much I needed it. In their voices there was
no self-pity and no recrimination, only simple and eloquent
expressions of support for the actions I was taking to bring the
war to an end. I vividly recall a conversation I had shortly

before Christmas in 1971 with a widow whose only son had been killed in action. I could sense the loneliness and sadness in her voice and was deeply moved when she told me at the end of our talk that she went to mass every day and always said a rosary for me and my family.

Most Americans are now aware of the heroism of our prisoners of war. But the families who prayed for their return were also heroic. Mrs. Nixon and I met with members of the League of Families a number of times. It was an emotional and heartwarming experience to hear them express support for the administration's policies and reject the demands of antiwar politicians that we accept defeat and simply withdraw our forces in exchange for our POWs. I often marveled at how our nation could produce men of such courage and devotion to country as our POWs, but in a different way the wives and mothers who remained at home were even more courageous.

I knew that there were heroes in the Vietnam War. I was reminded of this whenever I presented the Medal of Honor and read the citation to its recipient or, if it was awarded posthumously, to the next of kin. The overwhelming majority of those who received the Medal of Honor came from modest backgrounds. Many would call them "common men." But when each was confronted with the ultimate challenge—risking his life to save the lives of other—she demonstrated that he only had to be tested to display uncommon qualities of extraordinary courage and patriotism.

All wars are alike in the personal tragedies that occur on the battlefield. What distinguished the war in Vietnam was the trauma we suffered on the home front. It was the most divisive foreign war in American history. It turned senators and congressmen who had been my friends for over twenty years into bitter adversaries when I was President. It turned many in the news media who previously prided themselves on being objective into viciously biased critics of the American war effort. Most journalists have always shown a liberal bias in their reporting, but during the Vietnam War their views were completely out of step with the country. In the presidential election of 1972, when I won with 61 percent of the vote, my antiwar opponent received 81 percent of the votes of the members of the national news media. Their antiwar views showed in their reporting. Equal credibility was granted to enemy propaganda and United States government statements; and while our statements were greeted with skepticism, North Vietnam's word was usually taken at face value. Secret documents were published whenever reporters could get their hands on them. Reporters considered it their duty to try to oppose government policy by whatever means were available. The Vietnam War started the tradition of "adversary journalism" that still poisons our national political climate today.

But what distressed me most was the effect of the war on our young people. I wanted the new generation of Americans, who had been taught to hate America during the 1960s, to learn to love and respect their country. I was proud that the voting age was lowered to eighteen years during my administration and that the military draft was ended in 1973. As Vice President, I had found that my public appearances before college audiences were, for me, among the most stimulating and satisfying ones that I made. I was unable to make such appearances during the war years as President because of security problems. I could still see them: young people by the thousands demonstrating against the war during the presidential campaigns of 1968 and 1972, along the route of the inaugural parade in 1969, and at every public appearance I made as President. One group of young antiwar protesters confronted me before I delivered a speech at a convention in colonial Williamsburg, Virginia. A young girl, who could not have been more than seventeen years old, broke through the Secret Service barricade. She came up to me, and screamed, "Murderer!" Then she spit in my face.

And I knew I would never forget the most profoundly depressing moment for me during the war years of my presidency: It was when I saw the pictures in the newspaper of the two girls and two boys who had been killed at Kent State University on May 4, 1970.

As I reflected on the war, my thoughts turned to Lyndon Johnson. Since leaving office, he had been dying of a broken heart emotionally. He died of a broken heart physically one day before we initialed the Paris peace agreements. The war in Vietnam had destroyed this intensely proud, strong, and patriotic President just as if he had been killed in battle. Over and over he had heard the obscene chant "Hey, hey, LBJ, how many kids did you kill today?" After four years of war, he finally gave up. He spent the last years of his life on his ranch in Texas, unmourned and unappreciated by hundreds of leaders in politics and business whom he had helped during his years in Washington. He had thought they were his loyal friends. But now that he could do nothing for them, they had deserted him.

Because he died before the public announcement of the conclusion of the Paris agreement, I later wondered whether he had learned that the war was over before his death. I was relieved to find that Bob Haldeman had talked to him by phone on January 15. In 1969, Johnson had told me that the sixteen bombing halts he had ordered in Vietnam had all been mistakes. He urged me not to make the same error. I assured him that I would not. In their conversation, Haldeman informed Johnson that all bombing had been stopped. He responded simply, saying, "Well, I know what that means."

My elation on hearing that the Vietnam War finally was ending was tempered most of all by a profound recognition of the opportunities we had lost during America's longest war. Over 50,000 lives had been lost. Over $50 billion had been spent. And over ten years had elapsed—time that could never be recovered. Vietnam paralyzed our efforts on many other fronts. I had initiated many new social and domestic programs during my presidency, but I had been able to make very little progress on them because so much of our resources had to be devoted to the war in Vietnam, and because the atmosphere had been so poisoned by the controversy over the war.

Thus, when I received the news from Paris, I reacted with relief rather than elation. I was determined to make up for those lost years. But I knew that the peace was fragile. I intended to take whatever actions were necessary to keep the peace so that our sacrifices would not have been in vain. I knew that the enemy would keep the peace only if he was convinced that the price of breaking it would exceed whatever gain he could make by doing so.

Was it all worth it? Our intervention had saved 19 million people from totalitarian tyranny for eighteen years—from 1954 to 1972. Our tenacity had made similar wars less likely in that period by deterring those who would launch them and by buying time for nations like Indonesia, Thailand, and the Philippines to build up their internal strength so they could resist attempts to turn them into another Vietnam. I knew all our gains depended on convincing Congress that simply concluding the Paris peace accords did not end our responsibilities. A peace agreement is only as good as the will of the parties to keep it. We knew we would have to demonstrate to the North Vietnamese that we had the will to enforce the peace agreement.

On January 27, 1973, almost twenty years after the French had lost the first Vietnam War, we had won the second Vietnam War. We signed the peace agreement that ended the war in a way that won the peace. We had redeemed our pledge to keep South Vietnam free. Now, to keep the peace, we had to take whatever actions were necessary to prevent a third Vietnam War.

HOW WE LOST THE PEACE

We won the war in Vietnam, but we lost the peace. All that we had achieved in twelve years of fighting was thrown away in a spasm of congressional irresponsibility.

When the Paris peace accords were signed in January 1973, a balance of power existed in Indochina. South Vietnam was secure within the cease-fire lines. North Vietnam's leaders—who had not abandoned their plans for conquest—were deterred from renewing their aggression. Vietnamization had succeeded. But United States power was the linchpin holding the peace agreement together. Without a credible threat of renewed American bombing of North Vietnam, Hanoi would be sorely tempted to prepare to invade South Vietnam again. And without adequate American military and economic assistance, South Vietnam would lack the power to turn back yet another such invasion.

Congress proceeded to snatch defeat from the jaws of victory. Once our troops were out of Vietnam, Congress initiated a total retreat from our commitments to the South Vietnamese people. First, it destroyed our ability to enforce the peace agreement, through legislation prohibiting the use of American military power in Indochina. Then it undercut South Vietnam's ability to defend itself, by drastically reducing our military aid. Within two years the balance of power swung decisively in Hanoi's favor. When the North Vietnamese Army was poised to launch its final offensive, South Vietnam's army was in its weakest condition in over five years, reeling from the effects of congressional budget cuts that had strapped it with severe fuel and ammunition shortages.

On April 30, 1975, with Soviet-built tanks rolling through the streets of Saigon, South Vietnam surrendered. Communist Khmer Rouge guerrillas had conquered Cambodia thirteen days before. Hanoi-backed Pathet Lao forces took over Laos a few days later. All the dominoes in Indochina had fallen.

But the end of the war did not bring the beginning of peace for the peoples of Indochina. Those who had warned during the war that a bloodbath would follow a Communist victory found their worst fears confirmed. Communist forces now executed or imprisoned those who opposed them as they imposed their new rule. Thousands of Vietnamese were killed in Hanoi's prison camps. Hundreds of thousands more drowned in the South China Sea as they fled in the pathetic flotillas of the "boat people." And over 2 million Cambodians— a quarter of the country's population—were killed in a brutal frenzy of Communist vengeance and destruction.

Nor did the war's end produce a more peaceful world. Our defeat in Vietnam paralyzed America's will to act in other Third World trouble spots and therefore encouraged aggression on the part of those who had made them trouble spots to begin with. Over the next five years, Soviet clients and proxy forces unleashed a geopolitical offensive that led to stunning reversals for the United States in virtually every region of the world.

The Agreement on Ending the War and Restoring the Peace in Vietnam was not perfect. But it was adequate to ensure the survival of South Vietnam—as long as the United States stood ready to enforce its terms.

Militarily, the agreement called for a cease-fire in place, followed by an American withdrawal and an exchange of prisoners of war within sixty days. It forbade both the United States and North Vietnam from sending more troops into South Vietnam. It permitted the United States and North Vietnam the piece-for-piece replacement—but only that—of military equipment and supplies used up after the cease-fire. It created two bodies—the Joint Military Commission and the International Commission on Control and Supervision—to verify the compliance of both sides.

Politically, it directed Saigon to hold consultations with Communist and other non-Communist political parties to set up a National Council of National Reconciliation and Concord. The council's principal task would be to organize free elections to select the government of South Vietnam. Also, to assist with national reconciliation, the United States pledged to contribute financial aid for postwar reconstruction throughout Indochina once the cease-fire was established.

When we presented the draft agreement to President Thieu in January 1973, he strongly objected to it. Antiwar critics always portrayed him as a puppet of the United States. That was never the case. Whenever he perceived a threat to the South Vietnamese national interest in our actions, he became obdurate. This was the situation with the Paris peace accords. He called it a "surrender agreement" and categorically refused to sign it. Even after we exerted enormous pressure on him, Thieu would not budge. Only when we declared that we would sign the agreement without him if necessary did he reluctantly consent to it.

I sympathized with Thieu and shared his concerns. I knew that the agreement contained serious weaknesses. But I believed that on balance it was sound. And I knew that, in light of the growing stridency of our opposition in Congress, we had no alternative to signing it.

I saw two critical problems with the settlement. First, it was almost certain that the two commissions created to monitor the cease-fire would not work. Delegates from North and South Vietnam sat on the Joint Military Commission. Representatives of Hungary, Poland, Indonesia, and Canada formed the International Commission on Control and Supervision. Complaints about cease-fire violations were to be filed with these commissions, and their members were to determine who was at fault. These provisions appeared reasonable on paper. But they had a fundamental flaw. All commission rulings on cease-fire violations had to be approved by a unanimous vote of its members. This meant that the North Vietnamese or their Hungarian and Polish allies would be in a position to block all actions Hanoi opposed.

However, I did not consider this a fatal flaw. Our high-altitude reconnaissance aircraft could photograph military convoys traveling along the Ho Chi Minh Trail and detect preparations for a major Communist offensive. If either of these became evident, I had no intention of waiting for a representative of Hungary or Poland to give his assent before I ordered retaliatory actions against North Vietnam.

The second problem was that the agreement did not force North Vietnam to withdraw its armed forces from South Vietnam. We had, however, insisted on several provisions that mitigated this weakness. North Vietnam was not permitted to send in additional military personnel and agreed to respect the demilitarized zone and the neutrality of Laos and Cambodia. If Hanoi fully complied, its forces in South Vietnam would be isolated, completely cut off from new supplies and reinforcements. Still, I had no illusions about whether the North Vietnamese would try to circumvent these terms.

That was Thieu's greatest fear. He had no doubt that the Communists would try to use the cease-fire to build up their forces for a renewed assault on his country, keeping their shipments of troops and supplies at a level low enough to avoid provoking an American response. I was aware of this danger. If Hanoi chose this strategy—as I believed it would—I would be put in a difficult position politically. Mobilizing support in Congress for a retaliatory strike would be much harder if Hanoi's cease-fire violation was merely a step-up in military shipments rather than an outright invasion. I thought this problem could be overcome. I was firmly determined not to grant the North Vietnamese the luxury of treading the thin line between mild encroachments and blatant violations.

I saw two ways of evaluating the peace agreement: how it looked on paper, and how it worked on the ground. If the North Vietnamese observed its written terms in good faith, the South Vietnamese would have no problems. But I knew that was unlikely. As a rule, Hanoi broke international agreements as soon as it signed them. I did not expect the Paris accords to be an exception. Therefore, to ensure that the terms were observed on the ground, I issued two guaranties to Thieu: We would continue to send enough military aid to maintain the balance of power, and we would respond swiftly to North Vietnamese attempts to subvert the terms of the agreement. South Vietnam would handle minor violations of the cease-fire, and the United States would retaliate against major ones. This was the least we could do for our ally.

Our military power was the principal disincentive to Hanoi's breaking the cease-fire. But the Paris agreement contained carrots as well as sticks. Our offer of reconstruction aid was potentially one of the most important provisions in the agreement. During our negotiations, Hanoi had routinely demanded that the United States pay massive war reparations. We categorically rejected these demands. But I believed that it was in our interest to offer reconstruction aid to both sides. North Vietnam was in shambles. It desperately needed aid. Its Soviet and Chinese allies—who had their own economic problems—were unlikely donors. Therefore, once our aid began arriving in North Vietnam, Hanoi's leaders would acquire a strong interest in having it continue. Our aid would become a powerful incentive for Hanoi to keep the peace.

During our negotiations with Thieu in January 1973, I was painfully aware of the fact that the Paris accords were a political necessity if we were to continue aiding South Vietnam. Congress was ready to vote us out of the war if we did not get an agreement. Our legislative analysts expected a major challenge to our Vietnam policy as soon as Congress reconvened. If we waited until the battle in Congress was joined, Hanoi was certain to stall the talks again. On January 2, 1973, the House Democratic Caucus voted 154 to 75 in favor of cutting off all funds for military operations in Indochina as soon as arrangements were made for the safe withdrawal of American troops and the return of our prisoners of war. This would have been an abject surrender to North Vietnam's most extreme demands. Two days later the Senate Democratic Caucus passed a similar resolution 36 to 12. We had run out of time.

It was imperative for us to conclude the Agreement on Ending the War and Restoring Peace in Vietnam. It was not perfect. It had some major weaknesses. I wished we could have negotiated a better one. But it was impossible for us to hold out for more favorable terms with Congress poised to legislate an end to our involvement on Hanoi's terms.

It was not our finest hour—but it was the *final* hour.

In early 1973, when we left South Vietnam, we left it in a strong position militarily. A stalemate existed on the battlefield: South Vietnam's army had an advantage in military strength; North Vietnam's forces countered this edge through an improvement in their overall strategic position. Our bombing of North Vietnam had ended with the cease-fire, and Communist troops continued to hold certain territories captured in 1972 that greatly complicated the defense of the rest of South Vietnam. But because it was militarily weak, Hanoi could not exploit its opportunities.

In January 1973, the military balance of power was decisively in South Vietnam's favor. Its army fielded over 450,000 troops, split about half and half between combat and support units. Its air force enlisted 54,000, and its navy 42,000. In addition, there were 325,000 troops in its Regional Forces and another 200,000 in its Popular Forces. North Vietnam's strength stood between 500,000 and 600,000 troops. About 290,000 were in North Vietnam, 70,000 in Laos, and 25,000 in Cambodia. Only about 148,000 combat troops were in South Vietnam—which gave our ally at least a four-to-one advantage on the battlefield.

We had tried to tip the balance of power toward the South Vietnamese by launching a massive resupply effort in late 1972. We undertook two operations—code-named Enhance and Enhance Plus—to replace equipment and supplies lost or expended during the 1972 offensive and to improve South Vietnam's combat capability before the cease-fire agreement limited our aid to one-for-one replacements. Our deliveries included 175mm guns for three artillery battalions; M-48 tanks for two armored battalions; 286 UH-1 helicopters; 23 CH-47 airlift helicopters; 22 AC-119K gunships; 28 A-1 fighter aircraft; 32 C-130A cargo airplanes; 90 A-37 light bombers; 118 F-5A fighters; and 23 EC47 electronic reconnaissance airplanes. North Vietnam was also sending net equipment and supplies to its forces in South Vietnam as fast as it could, but our efforts outdistanced Hanoi's by a wide margin.

South Vietnam's military advantage extended to all fronts. North Vietnam's forces had suffered catastrophic losses during their 1972 offensive. Along the northern front, although the battle lines were several miles below the demilitarized zone, Hanoi's army was pinned down trying to hold on to its gains. Some divisions were below 50 percent of their authorized strength. In the central highlands—where South Vietnam's army was weakest—Communist forces could not advance beyond their limited territorial enclaves and held no significant towns. In the area around Saigon, North Vietnamese units were in total disarray. With many units below 30 percent of their normal strength, they posed no serious threat to South Vietnamese troops or civilians. In the Mekong delta—where 50 percent of South Vietnam's people lived—North Vietnam's forces were in dire straits. Some regular units had dwindled to 15 percent of their full strength.

Hanoi faced a grim outlook. It had lost over 190,000 troops in 1972, yet had won very little territory. Saigon controlled all significant commerce, all important lines of communication,

and all population centers. Communist sources admitted that
South Vietnam ruled over 80 percent of its territory and 87
percent of its population. Hanoi told its forces in the South
not to expect a large-scale offensive for at least three to five
years. "Our troops were exhausted and their units in disarray,"
a North Vietnamese general later wrote. "We had not been able
to make up our losses. We were short of manpower as well as
food and ammunition, and coping with the enemy was very
difficult." Communist morale and combat effectiveness were
hitting an all-time low.

But that still did not mean that the North Vietnamese would
abide by the peace agreement. Hanoi's definition of a cease-
fire was that we cease and they fire.

We expected the North Vietnamese to make a last-minute
military push to seize control of as much territory and population as possible before the cease-fire took effect. This had
happened when an agreement seemed imminent in October.
It had failed then because their attack came two full weeks
before the prospective cease-fire and their forces were too weak
to hold on to their gains. In January both sides tried to seize
a few strategic points as the cease-fire approached. But as the
agreement was being initialed in Paris, North Vietnamese
forces launched a series of raids throughout South Vietnam
and continued it *after* the cease-fire was to have gone into
effect.

While Hanoi's regular units pinned down Saigon's in fixed
positions, Communist guerrillas took over hundreds of hamlets, raising their flag in the hope of asserting a claim on them
when the cease-fire lines were drawn. But their successes were
shortlived. South Vietnamese territorial forces struck back
quickly and effectively. Two weeks later the Communists had
suffered over 5,000 killed in action; and out of the 400 hamlets
they had attacked, only twenty-three were still reported as
contested. Saigon even expanded its control in some areas.

Antiwar critics charged that both Saigon and Hanoi were
violating the cease-fire because both were fighting. But they

overlooked the fact that one side was on the offensive and the other on the defensive. In their eagerness to absolve Hanoi by finding equal fault with Saigon, they failed to note that there was a difference between shooting first and shooting back.

Once its land-grabbing raids were repulsed, Hanoi began blatantly violating the prohibition on sending additional troops and supplies into South Vietnam. Both sides in South Vietnam were allowed to replace equipment destroyed or worn out after the cease-fire on a piece-for-piece basis. Arms transfers were to take place at designated entry points under the scrutiny of the International Commission on Control and Supervision. Hanoi disregarded these rules from the start. Checkpoints were never set up, because the North Vietnamese refused to establish them. In early February our reconnaissance aircraft sighted a convoy of 175 military trucks moving across the demilitarized zone and a column of 223 tanks driving down the Ho Chi Minh Trail toward South Vietnam.

Soon, North Vietnamese reinforcements and supplies were coming into South Vietnam at unprecedented rates, exceeding even those just before the 1972 invasion. By May 1973, Hanoi had shipped in over 35,000 troops and more than 30,000 tons of matériel.

Nor did Hanoi comply with other key provisions of the Paris peace agreement. It did not withdraw its troops from Cambodia and Laos or stop using their territories as a logistic base. It refused to free several hundred South Vietnamese prisoners of war. It obstructed the negotiations on creating the National Council of National Reconciliation and Concord, and thereby thwarted the plan for new national elections. It observed only those clauses in the agreement from which it benefited.

Despite the dedicated efforts of its Indonesian and Canadian members, the International Commission on Control and Supervision did nothing to prevent North Vietnamese cease-fire violations. Hanoi quickly demonstrated that it had no intention of cooperating with the commission in any way. Hungarian and Polish representatives acted as loyal proxies of the North Vietnamese. Since the commission required unanimous consent for all actions, the Communist-bloc members were able to veto all motions contrary to the interests of the North Vietnamese. Hanoi's delegates similarly stalemated the Joint Military Commission.

North Vietnam, not content with having paralyzed the machinery for international supervision, now sought to destroy it. On April 7, while flying over Quang Tri Province along Route 9 toward the Laos border, two commission helicopters were shot down by North Vietnamese forces. One crashed after being hit with a heat-seeking surface-to-air antiaircraft missile, killing all nine passengers and crew; the other was forced to make an emergency landing after being damaged by small-arms and machine-gun fire. It was a brutal warning from Hanoi: Anyone who sought to monitor North Vietnamese compliance with the cease-fire would be making a fatal mistake. No one missed the point. Canada soon announced its withdrawal from the commission on the grounds that its delegates were observing a war instead of supervising a peace.

While Hanoi brazenly broke key provisions of the peace agreement, a shocking double standard operated in news-media reports about cease-fire compliance. South Vietnam—which permitted international scrutiny of its actions—received devastating criticism whenever it undertook any military actions, even if they were taken in retaliation or reprisal. Hanoi—which shot down those seeking to monitor its behavior—received hardly even a slap on the wrist.

Among objective observers there was no doubt that it was Hanoi which was undermining the cease-fire. With direct reference to North Vietnam, Michel Gauvin, the departing head of Canada's delegation to the international supervisory commission, explained that they were leaving because of the failure of "some parties to cease-fire agreement to live up to their commitment."

Hanoi's blatant breach of the Paris agreement outraged me. I was determined to respond with force if its serious cease-fire violations continued. I was able to take several counteractions.

But two developments—the outcry over Watergate and the backlash against Vietnam in Congress—prevented me from doing more.

North Vietnam's cynical land grab in late January was disconcerting. But I still believed that the success of Vietnamization and the memory of the December bombing might lead the North Vietnamese to decide that peace, or at least a stable cease-fire, was in their interest. It was in our interest as well. Our POWs were still in North Vietnam. We needed to follow through on important issues in the peace agreement.

Kissinger met with North Vietnam's leaders in Hanoi in February 1973. All they wanted to talk about was when they would start receiving American economic aid. Kissinger pointed out that such aid depended on compliance with the peace agreement. He vigorously protested their failure to live up to their commitments. He also reopened critical unfinished business left over from the last negotiations: Both sides had pledged in the Paris agreement to work to bring about cease-fires in Laos and Cambodia. Little progress was made but Kissinger made it clear that our patience had its limits.

I knew that there could be no peace in South Vietnam unless Hanoi withdrew its forces from Laos and Cambodia. South Vietnam's survival ultimately depended not on whether it had a democratic government or a competent military but on simple facts of geography. Given that the fighting would take place in South Vietnam, control of Laos and Cambodia was crucial. Virtually every important military advantage—from holding the high ground to having internal lines of communication—would depend on who ruled these countries. If the North Vietnamese succeeded in turning either into a massive forward base for their army, the chances of South Vietnam surviving on its own would become slim.

In Cambodia, Hanoi was totally uncooperative with our efforts to work out a cease-fire between government forces and Communist Khmer Rouge guerrillas. After our bilateral diplomacy failed, Cambodian President Lon Nol made an appeal to the Khmer Rouge. He announced a unilateral halt to all offensive military operations, and we suspended both our tactical and our strategic bombing of enemy positions. Khmer Rouge leaders responded not with reciprocal restraint but with shrill declarations of the start of a new military offensive.

Cambodia's Communists enjoyed unprecedented military strength. During 1971 and 1972, North Vietnam had built up the Khmer Rouge forces. Hanoi's hope was that its client could score a quick victory against Phnom Penh and thereby isolate South Vietnam. Lon Nol had expanded Cambodia's army from 30,000 to 200,000 troops. But its forces were spread thinly, and their leadership and training were poor. In January 1973, Communist forces surrounded Phnom Penh, cutting off vital roads and blockading the Mekong River.

We could not afford to see Lon Nol's government fall, for to lose Cambodia was to lose South Vietnam. But there were few actions we could take. Congress had legislated severe limitations on our options. Since the Cambodian incursions in 1970, Congress had prohibited us from undertaking military operations with ground troops on Cambodian territory, from assigning military training personnel to the Phnom Penh government, from sending amounts of aid above a restrictive ceiling, or even from stationing more than 200 civilian advisers in the country at one time. We therefore chose our only remaining option: We resumed bombing Khmer Rouge positions.

Our bombing relieved the pressure on Cambodia's capital and alleviated the danger of an imminent collapse. It also won a breathing space for Lon Nol's army, which used the time to regroup its forces and improve their combat effectiveness. In May, when the Khmer Rouge guerrillas launched another all-out offensive, Cambodia's army turned them back. Our critics accused us of engaging in indiscriminate terror bombing, which they claimed slaughtered hundreds of civilians. But the record shows that our air strikes were directed against enemy military targets and were highly accurate.

As we continued to search for a way to stabilize Cambodia, we enlisted China's help. Chinese Prime Minister Zhou Enlai also wanted to prevent a North Vietnamese victory in Indochina. China wanted closer relations with the United States to counter increasing hostility from the Soviet Union. Therefore, it was directly contrary to Peking's interests for Moscow's clients in Hanoi either to achieve hegemony in Indochina or to humiliate the United States. As late as October 1973, Zhou reportedly told North Vietnamese leaders, "It would be best for Vietnam and the rest of Indochina to relax for, say, five or ten years."

Our talks with the Chinese focused on the possibility of finding a way to bring Sihanouk back into Cambodia's government to end the civil war. We had the elements necessary to strike a deal. We had significant influence over Lon Nol. China could pull the strings of the Cambodian Communists. Sihanouk, who was in exile in PeKing and serving as the nominal head of the opposition forces, would listen to Zhou's counsel. We soon put together a plan. Lon Nol would give Sihanouk a limited role in the government in exchange for an end to the fighting. Sihanouk and Khmer Rouge forces would settle the war in exchange for an end to our bombing.

Our air strikes represented the critical bargaining chip that made a Cambodian settlement possible. Zhou had to be able to tell the Khmer Rouge that the prospective halt to our bombing was a concession from us contingent on a settlement of the civil war. We thus had to make it clear that in the absence of a settlement we would continue our bombing, because otherwise the Khmer Rouge would have no incentive to negotiate an end to the war. When both Cambodian parties turned out to be responsive to our plan, we made steady progress and were on the verge of sealing a deal in mid-June.

Meanwhile, we had achieved a limited success in Laos. Hanoi was exploiting the cease-fire in Vietnam to improve the position of the Communist Pathet Lao in the civil war in Laos. Since January, while the North Vietnamese pledged to help bring about a cease-fire among the contending factions as stipulated in the Paris accords, the fighting had actually intensified. Laotian Premier Souvanna Phouma said that the Pathet Lao had launched a "general offensive" and he asked for our help. In mid-February, after the North Vietnamese captured a key town south of the Plain of Jars, I ordered air strikes against their positions using both fighter-bombers and B-52s. I also stopped the removal of our mines from North Vietnamese waters. As a result, within forty-eight hours a cease-fire in Laos was established.

Our efforts to extend the cease-fire to Cambodia and Laos were vitally important. But they did not address the central issue: North Vietnam's use of these countries to ship men and matériel into South Vietnam. In the spirit of the Paris peace agreement, we had stopped the bombing of North Vietnamese positions in Laos. But in violation of the letter of the accords, Hanoi did not withdraw its forces from the country. Now, without fear of American bombers, over 18,000 trucks and over 70,000 troops moved down the Ho Chi Minh Trail in a crash effort to resupply forces in South Vietnam before the monsoon rains made the area impassable in April.

There was a real danger that without an American response Thieu's worst fears would come true. But I was reluctant to retaliate militarily during the first two months of the cease-fire because I did not want to jeopardize the release of our POWs scheduled for March 27. We continued to seek compliance with the cease-fire through diplomatic efforts which culminated with a communiqué in June reaffirming the January accords. In April, I repeatedly threatened retaliatory actions if Communist cease-fire violations continued. But no such actions were taken. We neither renewed our bombing of North Vietnam nor attacked its forces moving through Laos. This was a major mistake.

Our restraint was not militarily significant. In April, since the dry season was almost over, there were few important targets left along the Ho Chi Minh Trail. But our failure to act promptly set a devastating political precedent: Hanoi's leaders found they could flaunt the terms of the Paris accords and get away with it.

Also, though I did not know it at the time, I had lost the last opportunity I would have to use American power to enforce the peace agreement. The possibility of retaliating against North Vietnam evaporated by the end of April 1973. It was not a failure of presidential will—I was willing to act—but an erosion of congressional support. Whenever I had spoken of retaliation, a tremor of opposition rippled through Congress, and with each recurrence it had grown more intense. In May I no longer could have mustered the votes necessary to back up my strong words with strong actions—and Congress would in any case soon strip me of the authority to do so.

Antiwar senators and congressmen launched a frontal assault on our policy in May and June. Initially, their target was legislating a halt to our bombing in Cambodia. But soon they raised their sights to a prohibition of all direct and indirect American military actions in or around Indochina. They also sought to forbid the sending of reconstruction aid to North Vietnam. When they succeeded with both efforts, Congress had withdrawn both the carrots and the sticks built into the agreement. Hanoi as a result had no reason to comply with its terms.

During the debate over the bombing cutoff, our critics constantly questioned whether we sincerely wanted peace and repeatedly demanded that we resolve the conflict in Indochina through diplomacy alone. Senator Ted Kennedy, who was a principal sponsor of the measure, said, "If we really want peace in Cambodia—and ceasefire arrangements for all of Indochina—then we should be sending our diplomats to help negotiate these arrangements, instead of sending our B-52s to bomb." It was sadly ironic that Kennedy, whose brother had committed the United States to the defense of the free countries of Indochina, was leading the fight to abandon them.

Our critics refused to recognize that the cause of the fighting in Cambodia was not our bombing but the aggression of the Khmer Rouge and their North Vietnamese allies. Our side had declared a unilateral cease-fire. Our enemies responded with a renewed offensive. Our choice was either to bomb or to accept defeat in Cambodia—which would quickly lead to defeat in South Vietnam.

Worse still, antiwar critics were naïvely ignorant of the fact that diplomacy cannot succeed without power to back it up. Diplomacy involves our getting another country to take certain actions against the wishes of its leaders. Foreign leaders who oppose our course of action are seldom brought along by reason and persuasion alone. If it is a minor dispute with a pliable adversary, diplomatic prodding may suffice. If it is a military confict with an implacable foe—as it was in Indochina—diplomacy is helpless unless combined with direct military pressure. Nothing would convince Congress of this simple fact of international life in 1973. Simple facts had somehow lost their persuasive impact.

Our problems with Congress were doubly frustrating because all our diplomatic efforts to end the civil war in Cambodia were absolutely dependent on the continuation of our bombing. Our ability to hold back the antiwar opposition in Congress fell apart in June. We needed supplemental funds to continue the bombing in Cambodia. Congress not only refused to give us the necessary appropriations but also began to attach amendments to spending bills that would prohibit the use of any money for the bombing.

When the first bill with this amendment reached my desk on June 27, I vetoed it. In my veto message, I informed Congress that I had taken this action "because of my grave concern that the enactment into law of the 'Cambodia rider' to this bill would cripple or destroy the chances for an effective negotiated settlement in Cambodia and the withdrawal of all North Vietnamese troops as required by Article 20 of the January 27 Vietnam agreement." I could only allude to our diplomacy with China because secrecy was absolutely necessary for success.

This veto outraged the antiwar opposition in Congress, but they were unable to override it. Senator Mansfield then declared that it was his intention "to attach similar riders to every other possible piece of legislation." His first target was a continuing resolution that had to be signed so that funds would be available to keep the government running. "If the President does not want to stop the bombing in Cambodia but does want to stop the government from functioning," Mansfield warned, "that is the President's responsibility."

Some of our supporters in Congress urged that I accept a fixed date for the cessation of our bombing. I was highly reluctant to go along with such a compromise. For one thing, it would destroy our secret diplomatic initiative with the Chinese. But it was becoming clear that the antiwar majority in Congress would soon be able to impose its will. After all, our critics were debating not about *whether* to cut off the bombing but about *when* to do so—immediately or on a compromise date fixed with the White House—and they were gaining strength. I therefore approved a measure that permitted the bombing in Cambodia to continue for forty-five days.

On June 30, I signed into law the bill containing the bombing cutoff. The amendment read: "None of the funds herein appropriated under this Act may be expended to support direct or indirect combat activities in or over Cambodia, Laos, North Vietnam, and South Vietnam or off the shores of Cambodia, Laos, North Vietnam, and South Vietnam by United States forces, and after August 15, 1973, no other funds heretofore appropriated under any other Act may be expended for such purposes." This defeat stripped me of the authority to enforce the peace agreement in Vietnam—and gave Hanoi's leaders a free hand against South Vietnam.

Congress sought to add further restrictions on the President's ability to use military power by passing what became known as the War Powers Act. It stipulated that the President must consult with Congress before intervening with our forces in an armed conflict. As commander in chief, the President after such consultation could continue the intervention for sixty days without congressional approval and another thirty days if he certified in writing that the safety of our fighting men required it. If the Congress did not then authorize his actions by a declaration of war or other legislation, our forces would have to be brought home.

On October 24, I vetoed the War Powers Act because I believed that it was an unconstitutional encroachment on the powers of the President. I also knew that it would gravely undermine our ability to act decisively in an international crisis. Nevertheless, Congress voted to override my veto on November 7. When it did so, it also laid to rest any fears Hanoi might have had that another invasion of South Vietnam would provoke an American response.

There were two underlying reasons for the mounting congressional challenge to my Vietnam policy. In April 1973, Watergate had become the successor to the Vietnam War as the rallying cry for antiadministration critics. Some of my closest aides resigned under a darkening cloud of serious allegations and scurrilous innuendo. Watergate became an obsession in Washington. It not only began to consume much of my time and concentration, but also steadily chipped away at my executive authority to act in other areas as well.

Watergate alone, however, was not enough to destroy my ability to enforce the Paris peace agreement. Our growing difficulties in Congress were rooted in a profound backlash against our involvement in the war, which antedated our Watergate problems. This backlash was already evident when antiwar resolutions came perilously close to passage in 1972 and when, three months before Watergate became a major issue, the House and Senate Democratic Caucuses voted overwhelmingly in January 1973 in favor of withdrawing our troops in exchange for our POWs.

The antiwar sentiment was largely limited to Indochina. While some media critics irresponsibly charged that I called an alert of United States forces during the Yom Kippur War in October 1973 solely to divert attention from Watergate, there was overwhelming support in the Congress for the massive airlift and other military actions I took to save Israel. But Vietnam was different. Without Watergate, we would have faced the same opposition to our use of military power to enforce an agreement that would bring peace to Vietnam.

I was caught off-guard by the intensity of this backlash. It was inconceivable to me that, after sacrificing over 55,000 lives in a twelve-year struggle to win a just peace settlement in Vietnam, we would casually cast away what our men died to achieve. I knew that those who had violently opposed our involvement in the war would not support our policies even after our withdrawal. But I did not foresee any major difficulty in raising support to enforce the peace agreement, which would require actions involving relatively little expense or risk to American lives compared to those during the war.

We could not find strong support for our policy in any quarter. During the war, doves did not dare cut off funds for the war, because it would have meant abandoning our men in the field. I miscalculated how they would respond after the settlement. I thought their opposition to our policy would end with the war's end. Instead, it increased. With the return of our troops, the last restraint on their attack was removed. Those who opposed us during the war had constantly been calling for us to give peace a chance, yet after we negotiated a fair though fragile peace, they refused to give it a chance.

Hawks supported the American war effort initially. But its length had taken its toll. As the war became more unpopular, they tired of the struggle and kept a low profile politically. I could still count on their votes during the war, and most remained true to our cause afterward. But none was willing to lead the charge on Capitol Hill.

An unexpected combination—fierce opposition from the doves and quiescent passivity from the hawks—enabled the antiwar measures to win the approval of Congress in 1973. These removed the last threat to the North Vietnamese of an American retaliation—and this, in turn, destroyed our last chance to achieve a peaceful resolution of the war in Vietnam.

The North Vietnamese wasted little time in seizing this opportunity. In October 1973, Hanoi's leaders sent orders to its military commanders to start going on the offensive. It was the beginning of the third Vietnam War.

When the cease-fire began, the South Vietnamese held a numerical edge on the battlefield. But the numbers overstated the case. One huge disadvantage operated against our ally: Its forces were on the defensive. All fighting took place in South Vietnam; no threat existed to North Vietnam. This meant the tactical and strategic initiative passed to Hanoi. Its leaders could choose when, where, and how to attack. Thus, South Vietnam's generals had to spread out their forces to protect the entire country.

North Vietnam adopted a brilliant strategy to further compound Saigon's strategic problems. Communist forces were organized to create two separate threats to the South Vietnamese. Hanoi had irregular units trained to take over villages and hamlets in the countryside through guerrilla tactics, and regular units designed to overrun South Vietnam's defenses through conventional warfare. Saigon's leaders thus were caught in a dilemma. If they increased their emphasis on maintaining regular forces to handle the conventional threat, the countryside would be vulnerable to the guerrillas, thereby risking the gains in pacification. If they shifted their resources to handle the guerrilla threat at the expense of their regular forces, South Vietnam would become vulnerable to defeat by installment—that is, the North Vietnamese could mass their strength sufficiently to overwhelm our ally's positions one by one.

South Vietnam had never had much room for error in this perilous game of balance. It had survived the offensive in 1972 through mobility and air power. We had calculated then that South Vietnamese forces were several battalions short of what was needed to turn back a full-strength attack from North Vietnam. That was why they suffered their early reversals. But two things turned the tide. First, Saigon stabilized the battle by shifting its airborne reserves between fronts as circumstances dictated. Then we stepped in with our air power to destroy North Vietnam's massed forces. Had South Vietnam not had both mobility and air support, it would have been questionable whether they could have prevailed against the 1972 offensive.

After the cease-fire, I knew that South Vietnam would be secure only as long as North Vietnam was not permitted to recoup its losses. Hanoi would have no difficulty keeping up the guerrilla threat. Saigon had to devote much of its strength to countering this or else lose the countryside. Thus, if Hanoi were allowed to restore its decimated regular forces along the front lines, South Vietnam would face the same shortfall in military strength that it did before the offensive in 1972.

As we had feared, North Vietnam dedicated itself to the task of rebuilding its forces in South Vietnam during 1973. Wisely seeking to create a smoke screen to obscure its violations of the provisions in the peace agreement prohibiting such a buildup, Hanoi launched a political offensive to rally the South Vietnamese people to its cause and a major international propaganda effort to blame Saigon for all cease-fire violations. While the former failed miserably, the latter succeeded in totally hamstringing the South Vietnamese. If Saigon had tried to interrupt or interdict Hanoi's buildup, the uproar in Congress would have been deafening.

Meanwhile, the Communists undertook an enormous effort to upgrade their system for sending supplies into the South. They built a string of antiaircraft-missile installations to prevent surveillance or attack on their positions by Saigon's air force; a set of huge oil-storage facilities in South Vietnam's northern provinces of Quang Tri and Thua Thien; a paved highway and an oil pipeline running from their bases south of the demilitarized zone to their headquarters north of Saigon; and a modern radio network stretching throughout the territories they occupied. Within twelve months, Hanoi had added over 12,000 miles of roads to its logistics network and had reduced by two-thirds the time needed to transport troops in North Vietnam to the front lines over 1,200 miles away in South Vietnam.

Hanoi also engaged in a massive reinforcement of its forces in South Vietnam. Before the cease-fire, when our air force and navy made regular strikes against the Ho Chi Minh Trail, North Vietnam had never attempted a buildup on this scale. Communist forces traveled in small numbers and only at night. Now, unhindered by our bombing, immense convoys—numbering over 300 trucks—rolled along the Ho Chi Minh Trail in broad daylight. Thousands of trucks arrived every week with new stocks of supplies, equipment, and ammunition. New antiaircraft regiments, artillery units, and tank battalions came in as well. North Vietnam's military strength in the South grew ominously. It sent in over 75,000 combat troops, bringing its ranks up to about 170,000. It increased its tank strength fivefold to over 500 and upped its number of heavy artillery pieces from 170 to over 250.

The fact that Hanoi had never before dared to conduct such a rapid large-scale buildup demonstrated how important and effective our bombing of Laos had been. It also pointed out how disastrous it was that Congress had prohibited us from resuming the bombing.

It was deeply frustrating to watch as Hanoi steadily built up its forces in South Vietnam. Within a year of the cease-fire, Hanoi restored the military position it had held before the spring offensive in 1972. South Vietnam would again face a serious threat of renewed invasion—only now without our air support to back up its forces on the ground.

While North Vietnam rushed troops and supplies to the front lines, Congress slashed the amount of military aid budgeted for South Vietnam. In a period of two years—from the eve of the cease-fire in January 1973 to the eve of the final Communist offensive in January 1975—we witnessed a complete reversal of military superiority from Saigon to Hanoi.

We had promised in the Paris peace accords to replace all arms, munitions, and war matériel destroyed or expended by South Vietnamese forces after the cease-fire. That was a pledge the antiwar majority in Congress refused to fulfill. They cut the level of every aid package for South Vietnam proposed by the administration and reduced aid from $2,270 million in fiscal year 1973 to $1,010 million in fiscal 1974 and $700 million in fiscal 1975.

Antiwar senators and congressmen argued that our military assistance was "fueling" the war and that reducing aid to Saigon would bring it to an end—as if South Vietnamese troops were in the North and not the other way around. It was reminiscent of an incident that occurred during the Constitutional Convention: It was proposed that there be a constitutional limit on United States armed forces of 3,000 troops, whereupon George Washington was overheard to whisper that the Constitution perhaps should also deny hostile foreign powers the right to invade the country with more than 3,000 men. When Congress cut American aid to South Vietnam, it neglected to slow the flow of Soviet aid to North Vietnam.

Inflation compounded the effect of our aid reductions. Estimates of South Vietnam's military requirements—and thus financial needs—were worked into our program budget months before equipment and supplies were actually bought. Prices often skyrocketed in the meantime. South Vietnam, where inflation ran at 65 percent in 1974, needed more money to pay its troops. Prices for military supplies increased an average of 27 percent. Oil cost 400 percent more because of OPEC's 1973 embargo. Budget figures were never adjusted to compensate for these price increases. Therefore, there was a lot more bang for the buck in our budget estimate than on the battlefield.

Our estimates also did not take into account the intensity of the continuing Communist attacks after the cease-fire was to have taken effect. Military planners had expected the cease-fire to result in a 70 percent drop in ammunition usage, but this turned out to be overoptimistic. Based on the expectation of diminished fighting, a budget ceiling of $1,126 million was set for assistance to Vietnam and Laos in fiscal 1974. In December 1973, after increased fighting seriously depleted South Vietnam's stocks of ammunition, our defense planners sought a $494 million increase in the budget.

In January and February 1974, when this request began running into trouble on Capitol Hill, South Vietnam's army was forced to impose severe restrictions on the use of ammunition for the rest of the year. Patrolling soldiers accustomed to re-

ceiving ten grenades now were given only one. Isolated outposts were restricted to firing to two or three mortar or artillery
rounds when challenged. Artillery units were permitted to fire
only after targets had been clearly identified. Harassing and
interdiction fire were prohibited. Morale and combat effectiveness plunged. But this rationing was necessary to slow a
dangerous trend that had developed: South Vietnam was using
up ammunition faster than it was being shipped in.

When Congress rejected our appeal for additional funding
in April 1974—only three months before the beginning of the
fiscal year—South Vietnam's supply situation turned critical.
Our defeat in the budget battle meant that for months the
supplies flowing through the pipeline to South Vietnam would
slow to a trickle.

Stocks of ammunition totaling 177,000 tons in January 1973
had plummeted to 121,000 tons in May 1974 despite significant savings achieved through the strict restrictions on its use.
In April, supplies of shells for the army's most critical weapon,
the 105mm howitzer, were sufficient for only fifty-two days of
fighting—less if the war intensified. About 35 percent of its
tanks and 50 percent of its armored personnel carriers and its
aircraft stood idle for lack of spare parts. During the summer,
stocks of many critical items—such as tires, radio batteries,
and M-16 rifle barrels—dipped below safety levels. Because
of strict fuel-conservation rules, only 55 percent of the army's
vehicles could be operated. The South Vietnamese Army's
mobility—the key to its victories against the 1972 offensive—
had vanished.

Congressional budget cuts cost South Vietnamese lives because our ally's ability to get medical help to casualties on the
battlefield deteriorated. In 1974, stocks of critical supplies—
such as blood-collection bags, intravenous fluids, antibiotics,
and surgical dressings—dwindled to dangerous levels. There
were no supplies at all for about 50 percent of the medical
items on the army's stockage lists. No insect repellent was
available for soldiers as the monsoons arrived in the malaria-

ridden zones of the northern provinces. Shipments into medical supply depots had fallen from 24,000 metric tons in March to 8,000 in May.

However painful the hardships South Vietnam endured during fiscal year 1974, those of fiscal 1975 were certain to be several times worse if the United States did not send adequate economic and military assistance. In September 1973, a $1,450-million proposal had been drawn up by our Defense Attaché Office in Saigon. In May 1974, we won the initial round of the budget battle in the House, but our prospects looked grim in the Senate.

As Congress debated the fiscal 1975 budget, Major General John E. Murray, the head of the United States Defense Attaché Office in Saigon, sent a prophetic cable. "In the final analysis," he wrote, "you can roughly equate cuts in support to loss of real estate." He then set out what was the best our ally could do with various levels of aid:

(a) $1.126 billion level—gradual degradation of equipment base with greatest impact in out-years. Little reserve or flexibility to meet a major enemy offensive in FY 75.

(b) $900 million level—degradation of equipment base that will have significant impact by third or fourth quarter of FY 75. No reserve or flexibility to meet offensive in FY 75.

(c) $750 million level—equipment losses not supportable. operations ("O") funds would not support hard-core self-defense requirements. Any chance of having Hanoi see the light and come to conference table would be sharply diminished. If enemy continues current level of military activity, RVNAF [South Vietnam's armed forces] could only defend selected areas of country.

(d) $600 million level—write off RVN [South Vietnam] as a bad investment and a broken promise. GVN [Government of Vietnam] would do well to hang on to Saigon and Delta area.

On September 23 and 24, 1974, the House and the Senate approved only $500 million in actual military assistance for South Vietnam. Antiwar congressmen and senators had written off our ally.

When I resigned from the presidency on August 9, 1974, I was profoundly frustrated with the situation in Vietnam. In concluding the Paris peace agreement, I had considered two conditions absolutely necessary to make it work: We had to maintain a credible threat of American retaliation against an invasion from North Vietnam and provide a continuing flow of military aid to South Vietnam sufficient to maintain the balance of power. Both were undermined in Congress.

It had been Thieu's nightmare, and mine, that North Vietnam would succeed in exploiting the peace in order to prepare for war. Our greatest fear was that Hanoi would rearm its forces while holding on to its positions in Laos, Cambodia, and South Vietnam. As I left office, I knew that Congress already had let this happen and would not let President Ford reverse it.

I was shocked by the irresponsibility of the antiwar majority in Congress. South Vietnam was a small country that depended on the United States for help in order to survive against a brutal onslaught from a totalitarian power. Senators and congressmen who demanded that our South Vietnamese allies stand alone were being totally unfair. None would expect South Korea to be able to deter an attack from North Korea without the presence of 50,000 American troops. None would expect the countries of Western Europe to hold off the Soviet Union without the help of 300,000 of our troops and a threat of American nuclear retaliation to back them up. None would expect Israel to be able to survive attacks from its enemies without massive military assistance from the United States. Yet they were unwilling to allow us to retaliate against a North Vietnamese invasion or even to provide the South Vietnamese with enough ammunition for their guns.

I could understand their desire to put the Vietnam War behind us. But I could not understand why they seemed so

303

determined to see South Vietnam conquered by North Vietnam. Whatever their intentions, that was the effect of their actions.

"By limiting our military assistance," argued one senator during the budget debate over aid for South Vietnam, "we do signal ally and adversary alike that it is time to negotiate." Hanoi did not share this interpretation of the meaning of Congress's action. Instead, when the North Vietnamese politburo and general staff conferred in October 1974, they interpreted Congress's actions as a green light for their next invasion.

General Van Tien Dung, commander of North Vietnam's forces in South Vietnam, described the conference in his memoirs. Hanoi's top brass opened the meeting with an evaluation of the military situation. They observed that Saigon's troops were "growing weaker militarily, politically, and economically every day" and that Hanoi's forces were now "stronger than the enemy in the South." They noted that they had "set up strategic positions linking North and South, had increased our forces and stockpiles of matériel, and had completed the system of strategic and tactical roads." And given the decline in American assistance to Saigon, they concluded that the United States was "meeting difficulties at home and abroad" and that "its ability to give political and military aid to its protégés was declining every day."

Dung wrote that there was a heated discussion of one key question: "Did the Americans have the ability to send troops back into the South when our large attacks led to the danger of the Saigon army's collapse?" He noted that all "paid special attention to the fact that since they had signed the Paris Agreement on Vietnam and had been forced to withdraw from South Vietnam, the Americans had grown more confused and were in greater difficulty than before." Inflation, recession, energy shortages, and Watergate all handicapped the United States. Communist party First Secretary Le Duan concluded, "Now that the United States has pulled out of the South, it will be hard for them to jump back in." Congress, in his view, was abandoning Saigon and would never intervene to save Thieu's government.

Hanoi's war council decided to launch a major offensive in 1975. In November it sent a directive giving the word to its military commanders in the South. "Enemy air and artillery capability [is] now limited as a result of reductions in U.S. aid. In short, the enemy is declining militarily and has no chance of regaining the position they held in 1973. On the other hand, our position is improving. We are now stronger than we were during the Tet Offensive in 1968 and the summer of 1972. We now have ample amounts of money, weapons, and equipment which makes it possible for us to initiate a sustained attack on a wide front."

North Vietnam, now armed to the teeth, was poised to strike. Its readiness was a result of a massive resupply effort by the Soviet Union and China. In 1973, while Congress was cutting aid to South Vietnam, North Vietnam received 2.8 million metric tons of imports from its Communist allies, an amount 50 percent larger than that of 1972 and 10 percent higher than the record set in 1971. And in 1974, Hanoi imported over 3.5 million metric tons. In November 1974, when President Ford met with the Soviets in Vladivostok and the Chinese in Peking, he asked for greater restraint on their part. But neither slowed the flow of arms.

Hanoi's rearmament had not been inevitable. Initially, its Communist allies had not been eager to give more aid, because we had made it clear to them that doing so would damage their new relationships with the United States. When Hanoi's leaders complained about the level of resupply, the Soviets and the Chinese dragged their feet, offering some new aid but with strings attached. Moscow and Peking demurred, saying that it was a hopeless and wasteful effort to keep sending arms that would later be destroyed through American bombing. But after Congress cut off the possibility of future bombing in June 1973, there was no longer any reason for restraint. Moscow and Peking had been willing to help us contain Hanoi—but only if we were determined to do so as well.

During 1974, with the benefit of its new supplies, North Vietnam prepared to renew its offensive. It built up its forces and logistics system in South Vietnam while conducting a series of strategic raids designed to make marginal improvements in its positions. By December, Hanoi had arrayed a heavily armed, 185,000-man expeditionary force against South Vietnam's thin lines of defense. Once again Saigon's shortfall of regular combat battalions was sharply evident. But unlike the situation in 1972, our ally did not have the mobility to redeploy its forces quickly, because of budget cuts in Congress, and did not have the air cover of American bombers, because of the bombing cutoff legislated by Congress.

As the dry season began in December 1974, South Vietnam faced the looming danger of being overrun after a North Vietnamese breakthrough. On December 13, after initiating several diversionary strikes, the North Vietnamese began the assault on Phuoc Long Province about fifty miles north of Saigon. It moved in two divisions, a tank battalion, an artillery and an antiaircraft regiment, and several local sapper and infantry units. South Vietnam's forces were comprised of two battalions of the Regional Forces and two platoons of the Popular Forces. Although these units were putting up a heroic resistance, the weight of superior numbers took its toll. Saigon deployed some reinforcements, but outposts had to be abandoned one by one under barrages of artillery fire sometimes as heavy as 3,000 rounds per day. Soon, South Vietnamese forces were unable to return fire. By January 6, 1975, Phuoc Long Province had fallen—the first Communist conquest of a provincial capital since 1972 and of a full province since 1954.

When the news reached Hanoi, North Vietnamese leaders were holding a series of strategy-planning meetings. Le Duan advocated a bolder military attack, with a two-year timetable for total victory. He argued that the failure of the United States to respond in any way demonstrated that we would not intervene even with our air power to prevent the defeat of Saigon. He called for a "widespread attack in 1975 to create conditions for a general uprising in 1976 to liberate all of South Vietnam."

But he was advising this option simply as the minimum. "If opportunities present themselves early or late in 1975," he added, "South Vietnam should be liberated this year."

On the eve of their battle for survival, our South Vietnamese allies were in their weakest condition in over five years.

Congressional cuts in military assistance for fiscal year 1975 had an immediate effect on South Vietnam's armed forces because they needed to ration their fiscal 1974 appropriations even more strictly if they were to have any hope of getting through the following year.

Our $700 million aid package actually amounted to only $500 million because Congress now forced our ally to foot the bill for shipping and other expenses. South Vietnam's needs for ammunition *alone* were $500 million *at 1974 prices*. Its army received only about 50 percent of what it required, and its air force only about 30 percent. Its fuel supplies would be so tight that it could afford to operate only 49 percent of its vehicles. Over 200 aircraft had to be put into storage. And any significant troop movements required the approval of the corps commander.

Our pledge to replace, piece for piece, all equipment destroyed or worn out during the cease-fire went out the window. By June 1974, South Vietnam had lost 58 ships. It received no replacements. It had lost 281 aircraft, but received only 8 primitive, propeller-driven Cessna 0-1's in return. Furthermore, South Vietnam could afford only 33 percent of the spare parts it needed. Over 4,000 vehicles and aircraft stood idle awaiting repair.

This had a serious detrimental effect on air support. South Vietnam's air force, knowing that no replacements or spare parts were available, could not afford to take any risks when attacking enemy positions. Bombing and strafing became far less effective as a result.

Availability of ammunition required severe restrictions on its use. South Vietnamese commanders in the field were begging their superiors for more as the fighting intensified. A comparison of the available supplies from July 1974 through February 1975 with the actual consumption rate under the intensive fighting during 1972 led to grim conclusions. In 1972, South Vietnam's army had fired an average of 2.8 rounds per day from its 81mm mortars, 25.0 rounds from its 105mm howitzers, and 16.2 rounds from its 155mm howitzers. But now there were, respectively, only 1.1, 6.2, and 4.9 rounds per day available for these weapons. Less than a third of the firepower used by South Vietnamese forces in 1972 would be available to them during 1975.

In February 1975, stocks of critical ammunition were far below the sixty-day safety level. South Vietnam had a thirty-one day supply of munitions for the 5.56mm rifle, twenty-five days of the fragmentation grenade, twenty-nine days of the 40mm grenade, twenty-seven days of the 60mm mortar, thirty days for the 81mm mortar, thirty-four days for the 105mm howitzer, and thirty-one days for the 155mm howitzer. This constituted a crisis of the first order. Even if the combat rates stayed at the levels of late 1974, the fact was that South Vietnam would simply run out of all ammunition in May 1975.

The availability and quality of medical care for South Vietnamese casualties plunged. Wounded soldiers could not count on evacuation helicopters. Stocks of basic medical supplies were depleted to such critical levels that strict conservation measures were ordered. It was even necessary to wash bandages, surgical dressings, intravenous sets, rubber gloves, and hypodermic needles and syringes so they could be reused.

When these shortages made it painfully clear that Saigon urgently needed more military assistance, President Ford asked Congress for a $300 million supplementary appropriation for South Vietnam. He also requested another $222 million for Cambodia—which had even worse supply shortages.

These requests were the bare minimun necessary for our allies to survive.

None of these events went unnoticed in the North Vietnamese war councils. Hanoi's leaders could not believe their good fortune as the antiwar majority in Congress did their work for them.

"Nguyen Van Thieu," General Dung later wrote, "had to call on his troops to fight a 'poor man's war.' " He observed that the "decrease in American aid had made it impossible for Saigon troops to carry out their combat and force-development plans" and noted that there was a 60 percent drop in South Vietnamese fire support and a 50 percent reduction in mobility. "This situation," he continued, "forced them to change over from large-scale operations and deep-penetration helicopter and tank assaults to defense of their outposts, digging in and carrying out small search operations."

As North Vietnam started its final offensive, he wrote, the most significant point was that "as we increasingly took the initiative and grew stronger, the enemy grew weaker and more passive every day."

After its victory in Phouc Long, Hanoi ordered an attack on Ban Me Thout, the capital of Darlac Province in the central highlands. On March 10, three North Vietnamese divisions advanced on the city. South Vietnamese defenses were manned with only one regiment of regular troops and three battalions of territorials. General Dung later wrote that his forces had advantages of 5.5 to 1 in infantry, 2.1 to 1 in heavy artillery, and 1.2 to 1 in tanks and armor. Yet despite these odds, South Vietnam's troops did not cut and run—they stood and fought. It was a hotly contested battle. Antiaircraft fire and intense fighting at the city's air strip made sending in reinforcements impossible, and the relentless hammering of enemy artillery soon forced the South Vietnamese to fall back. In the end, Ban Me Thout fell in less than 24 hours. But it was because the South Vietnamese were lacking not valor but numbers. When Hanoi's forces had taken the city, its streets were strewn with the bodies of hundreds of South Vietnamese soldiers killed in action.

With the fall of Ban Me Thout, North Vietnamese forces held the western approaches to Saigon. President Thieu therefore called a meeting of his military strategists and commanders at

Cam Ranh on March 14. He did so with a heavy sense of pessimism. On March 12, the House Democratic Caucus had voted 189 to 49 against the Ford administration's request for $300 million in supplemental appropriations, and the next day the Senate Democratic Caucus had affirmed this verdict 38 to 5. Thieu knew, as did Hanoi, that there was no way to overcome those majorities. He now had to recognize the painful fact that his forces could no longer afford to defend the entire country.

Thieu told his commanders that he was switching to a strategy of "light at the top, heavy at the bottom." He explained that the government was going to withdraw forces from the central and northern provinces to reinforce its defenses in the Saigon area and the Mekong delta, where most of the country's population lived. It was a desperate gambit—but as North Vietnam's offensive took shape, South Vietnam was in desperate straits.

At the Cam Ranh conference, Thieu took his first step toward implementing his new strategy: He ordered the abandonment of the central highlands. He knew this meant that the Communist forces in the region would sweep to the coast and thereby divide the country. But he also knew that his two divisions there could not hold out indefinitely against Hanoi's four unless major reinforcements were sent in. None were available. Cuts in military aid had left South Vietnam without any reserves. Therefore, he reluctantly told his generals to withdraw South Vietnam's forces from Pleiku and Kontum and redeploy them for a counterattack to retake Ban Me Thout.

Thieu's strategic withdrawal was more easily ordered than executed. North Vietnamese forces had interdicted all major roads running eastward from Pleiku and Kontum. South Vietnamese troops would take a severe pounding if they tried to punch through along Route 19 or 14. Thieu therefore decided to have them take Route 7B, an old logging road that had not been used in years. This turned out to be a disastrous mistake. No one took the time to find out if Route 7B was usable. Not until it was too late did the South Vietnamese discover that the road had been overgrown with brush and was missing an important bridge.

On March 15, as South Vietnamese soldiers prepared to pull out, Pleiku City and Kontum fell into chaos. No one had the slightest intention of being left behind. A mass exodus of their entire populations—over 200,000 people—made it impossible to conduct an orderly military retreat. As civilians got mixed into the ranks of soldiers, progress slowed. Poor road conditions soon brought the march down to a snail's pace.

Although the surprise withdrawal at first threw General Dung off-balance, he quickly recovered. On March 18, a full division attacked the convoy at the town of Cheo Reo, where a key bridge was out, and succeeded in cutting Saigon's forces in half. Military and civilian losses were heavy. Cheo Reo was littered with corpses. South Vietnam's remaining forces pressed toward the coast, limping along as North Vietnamese units struck at them repeatedly. On March 25, Saigon's ragged columns reached the coast. Out of the eighteen battalions that started out on the withdrawal, only three managed to finish it.

In March 1975, when South Vietnam had no longer had any room for error, President Thieu had made an enormous one with this hastily arranged withdrawal. It was a tragic mistake—although probably an academic one given the votes of the Democratic Caucuses—that precipitated the collapse of South Vietnam.

After vacillating about whether to withdraw his best forces from the northern front to defend Saigon, Thieu realized that there was no alternative to this after the disaster in the central highlands. His plan called for his northern forces to retrench in coastal enclaves around Hue and Danang. North Vietnam's offensive in the area, which began simultaneously with the attack on Ban Me Thout, had made little progress. But as South Vietnam's best forces prepared to withdraw on March 18, the area's commanders were forced to redeploy their troops in tighter lines of defense.

No one was under any illusions about how difficult the maneuver would be. A strategic retreat is a perilous operation under the best of circumstances. South Vietnam's northern commanders now had orders to pull back under the worst of conditions, as the growing intensity of enemy attacks jeopardized their ability to establish a new line of defense. On March 19, North Vietnamese tanks rolled across the cease-fire lines. Quang Tri Province soon had to be abandoned. Thousands of refugees fled the Communist advance and streamed south toward Hue. Then, when pressure mounted on Hue, over a million refugees set out for Danang.

As the front deteriorated, what came to be known as the "family syndrome" set in. Because the war required South Vietnam's soldiers to spend years in the service, they were allowed to have their families live near their posts. Now, hundreds of troops were abandoning their units to get their wives and children to safety. As chaos set in, three divisions evaporated almost overnight.

On March 25, Hue fell to the North Vietnamese. Danang quickly came under attack from over 35,000 Communist troops. As Saigon tried to evacuate whatever organized military units remained, mass hysteria seized the city. Over 2 million people milled in the streets, looking for family members or trying to find transportation to escape to the south. Thousands waded into the sea in a desperate struggle to reach barges and fishing boats offshore. Among them was the commander of South Vietnam's northern army, who had striven valiantly until the last moment to salvage his disintegrating forces. On March 30, almost exactly ten years after American troops first landed on its beaches, Danang was overrun by the North Vietnamese.

Within less than a month, Thieu's forces had lost half of South Vietnam's territory. But they had little to show for it. Thieu's strategy of withdrawing from the north to concentrate on the defense of the south had utterly failed. Its success was absolutely dependent on whether South Vietnam's forces could be pulled out *intact*. After the disastrous withdrawal in the central highlands and the panic-stricken collapse of the northern front, Thieu's plans resulted in just a handful of organized military units reaching the Saigon area.

Meanwhile, Cambodia was in its last hours. On March 16, the United States Embassy had started to evacuate its nonessential personnel. Ever since Congress had cut off our bombing in 1973, Communist Khmer Rouge had had free run of most of the country. Their forces had encircled Phnom Penh and now were on the verge of strangling it. Artillery barrages were deliberately fired at crowded refugee camps. Stories circulated about brutal atrocities committed in Communist-occupied territories. But the United States did little to alleviate the situation. Congress had imposed restrictions on aiding Phnom Penh that were even more draconian than those on helping Saigon. On April 16, with supplies and ammunition running out, Phnom Penh capitulated to the Khmer Rouge.

Our Saigon embassy did not begin its evacuation until April 4, because it was feared that if the South Vietnamese realized we were pulling out, their resistance would crumble. The delay had consumed precious time, however. Now, although the United States would be able to pull out all of its personnel and dependents it would be impossible to get out all the South Vietnamese civilians who had worked for us over the years and who faced a serious risk of being executed immediately after the Communist took power. In the final days, American helicopters shuttled thousands from the embassy roof to our ships offshore. But many thousands more were left behind.

Hanoi was now throwing everything it had into the offensive. From September 1974 through March 1975, North Vietnam had sent over 120,000 additional combat troops into South Vietnam. With Saigon on the ropes, Hanoi went for the knockout punch. In April it hurled in another 58,000 troops. Saigon was dazed. No one expected defeat to come so quickly. Thieu, whose counterattack on Ban Me Thout had long ago become fantasy, now sought to regroup his forces to defend a truncated South Vietnam. But with North Vietnamese reinforcements piling into his country, events overtook his every

313

move. Almost as soon as he proposed a new line of defense, it became unfeasible to defend.

On April 9, the final significant battle of the third Vietnam War began at Xuan Loc. It looked like a total mismatch on paper. But Xuan Loc's defenders put up fierce resistance despite the enemy's huge superiority in numbers. North Vietnam's forces ravaged the ranks of South Vietnam's troops with some of the heaviest artillery barrages in the entire war.

On April 10, as the North Vietnamese offensive swept across South Vietnam, President Ford went before a joint session of Congress to request emergency assistance for our allies. He asked for $722 million in military aid and $250 million in economic and humanitarian aid. In light of the gravity of the situation, he also requested that Congress respond no later than April 19. It was an act of great political courage, because he knew that seeking assistance for Saigon would win him no friends in Congress.

When Ford later met with leaders of Congress, he ran into strong opposition to helping Saigon. "I will give you large sums for evacuation," said one senator, "but not one nickel for military aid." Another said, "I will vote for any amount for getting Americans out. I don't want it mixed with getting Vietnamese out." They were willing to give money to retreat but none to avoid defeat. Since the 1974 elections, antiwar majorities controlled the House and Senate more firmly than ever. A flurry of hearings were held, but Ford's request never came to a vote on the floor. It died in committee.

Meanwhile, South Vietnamese soldiers at Xuan Loc were repulsing multiple assaults in hand-to-hand combat, with over 1,200 enemy troops left dead on the battlefield. North Vietnam's forces hammered away at our ally's positions with thousands of rounds of artillery. South Vietnamese lines held back the onslaught until April 15, when the tattered remains of their units finally fell back, unable any longer to continue the fight.

With the fall of Xuan Loc, there was little left to stop the North Vietnamese Army's advance along the road to Saigon. Other battles were being fought all around South Vietnam, but on April 20 an eerie stillness settled over the country for almost a week as all eyes turned to see what would happen in Saigon. Over 120,000 North Vietnamese troops in sixteen divisions surrounded the capital and were preparing for a massive, three-pronged attack on its 30,000 defenders. It was clear that, except for the paper work, the third Vietnam War was over.

On April 21, President Thieu resigned with the hope that a successor would be able to spare Saigon from total destruction in a final battle. He was soon replaced with General Duong Van Minh, who intended to open negotiations with the enemy. It was a hopeless undertaking. Saigon had nothing left to bargain with. Hanoi, sensing imminent victory, was interested not in conversation but in conquest.

On April 30, 1975, with South Vietnamese forces totally demoralized, North Vietnamese tanks rolled into the streets of Saigon. At this point, it would have been the height of futility to resist Hanoi's invading armies. After one armored unit crashed through the gates of the Presidential Palace, General Minh and his government were taken prisoner. A North Vietnamese soldier scrambled onto a balcony to wave the flag of the victors. Soon it was flying all over Saigon.

South Vietnam, after courageously resisting Communist aggression for twenty-one years, had surrendered.

In the presidential campaign of 1972, Senator George McGovern claimed that South Vietnam would collapse within seventy-two hours of the final withdrawal of American troops. But it did not collapse then. It did not collapse when Congress took away threat to Hanoi of an American retaliation in 1973. It did not collapse when Congress sharply reduced its military and economic aid in 1974. It did not collapse until 1975, when all hope of future American aid was lost. For over two years, South Vietnam held off the hordes of invaders from the North.

Our news media portrayed the soldiers of the Army of the Republic of Vietnam as cowards. Americans remember the images of desperate troops clinging to the skids of evacuation helicopters or racing with refugees to see who could escape

315

the fighting the fastest. In fact, some South Vietnamese units did fall apart under fire in 1975. That has happened to all armies, including our own, in all wars. But it is important to recognize that it is asking a lot of a soldier to fight bravely when his ammunition is rationed and the enemy's is not.

If the media's story were the whole story, South Vietnam would not have survived as long as it did. But it was not. The record shows that South Vietnam's troops fought bravely in many battles right up to the end. In 1973, they fought well in Chau Doc, Quang Duc, Quang Nam, Quang Tri, Tay Ninh, Binh Long, Phouc Long, Din Duong, and Hua Nghai provinces. In 1974, they fought well in Kien Tuong, Dinh Tuong, Hau Nghia, Tay Ninh, Binh Duong, Bien Hao, Long Khanh, Quang Tin, Kontum, Darlac, Quang Nam, Quang Ngai, Thua Thien, Binh Tuy, Phouc Long, Choung Thien, Ba Xuyen, Vinh Binh, Vinh Long, and An Xuyen provinces in South Vietnam and in Svay Kieng Province in Cambodia. In 1975, despite desperate supply shortages and catastrophic military reversals, South Vietnamese units fought heroically in battles in Quang Nam, Binh Dinh, Pleiku, Kontum, Binh Tuy, Tay Ninh, Kien Tuong, Chuong Thien, Dinh Tuong, Phu Bon, Quang Duc, Darlac, Klanh Hoa, Long An, Binh Long, Binh Duong, Long Khanh, Binh Thuan, Ninh Thuan, Phouc Tuy, and Hao Nghai provinces. For almost two years, no provincial capital was lost to the North Vietnamese.

Objective military analysts have stated that South Vietnamese soldiers were, man-for-man, better fighters than the North Vietnamese. They lacked nothing in spirit. Our ally suffered more killed in action in the years after our withdrawal than we did during the entire war. Its soldiers proved willing and able to fight against enemy troops—but it was too much to expect them to fight against impossible odds.

Congress turned its back on a noble cause and a brave people. South Vietnam simply wanted the chance to fight for its survival as an independent country. All that the United States had to do was give it the means to continue the battle. Our

South Vietnamese friends were asking us to give them the tools so they could finish the job. Congress would not, so our allies could not.

"Indochina Without Americans: For Most a Better Life" read the headline of an article in the *New York Times* on the eve of the fall of Cambodia. That encapsulated one side's argument about the morality of our intervention in the war in Vietnam. Those who opposed our actions had hammered on the theme that no greater evil could be visited upon the people of Indochina than the war we were waging. Those who supported our efforts had argued that a Communist peace would be more brutal than an anti-Communist war. In April 1975, the world would finally find out which side had been right.

Since February 1974, reports had circulated in the West about the intentions of the Khmer Rouge. Kenneth Quinn, a State Department Cambodia expert, wrote that the leaders of the Cambodian Communists were fanatics who were planning to carry out a "total social revolution." All vestiges of the past were to be considered "anathema and must be destroyed." It would be necessary to "psychologically reconstruct individual members of society." This meant "stripping away, through terror and other means, the traditional bases, structures, and forces which had shaped and guided an individual's life" and "rebuild him according to party doctrines by substituting a series of new values."

Khieu Samphan and Pol Pot, the principal leaders of the Khmer Rouge, wasted no time implementing their plan. On April 17—the day Cambodia fell—the forced evacuation of Phnom Penh was begun. Three million people were herded into the countryside at gunpoint. No one was exempt. Soldiers opened fire on anyone lingering in the streets and even cleared the sick and dying out of the city's hospitals. Our first look at the new Khmer Rouge government did not show the just order that antiwar leaders had envisioned. It was a grisly picture of desperate doctors and nurses who were forced to roll their

317

critically wounded patients out of Phnom Penh on their hospital beds, with bottles of intravenous plasma and serum still suspended above them. By nightfall, the city's 20,000 wounded had been sent into the jungle and toward certain death.

That was only the beginning. Similar evacuations were conducted in all Cambodian cities. Wanton executions soon followed. Khmer Rouge soldiers immediately killed army personnel, government employees, intellectuals, teachers, students, and anyone who was seriously ill. In Siem Reap, over 100 patients were murdered in their beds with knives and clubs. In Mongkol Borei, after carefully planting land mines throughout a field, the Communists forced 200 army officers to walk into it. In Do Nauy, Khmer Rouge troops crucified one colonel on a tree after beating him and cutting off his nose and ears; it took him three days to die. And after these executions, the wives and children of the victims were led off to be killed.

Living conditions killed hundreds of thousands more. Over 4 million Cambodians who were evacuated from cities and towns were now scattered across the country to implement the government's plan to build New Villages. It was not a carefully considered policy to develop the countryside but a barbaric plan that would lead to a horrendous death toll. It boiled down to simply dumping city dwellers into desolate jungle tracts to carve out their homes and eke out an existence with nothing more than their bare hands.

Cambodia, which had been the rice bowl of Indochina before the Communist victory, now experienced a famine. A manual worker normally needed between 500 and 800 grams of rice a day to survive. The standard ration for civilians exiled in the countryside was 90 grams of rice a day, and their food supplies sometimes ran out completely. Weakened through malnutrition, the population was ravaged by disease. Yet, while the Cambodian people starved, Communist officials and soldiers had all the rice, meat, and fish they wanted. This was corruption on a scale that did not come close to being matched even by the most grotesquely distorted charges of malfeasance against Lon Nol's government.

Surviving in the New Villages meant foraging for food in the jungle. Soon, all the fish, field crabs, and snails in surrounding areas were depleted. Villagers then became desperate. "We ate whatever we saw the oxen eat, figuring it couldn't harm us," said one refugee. "Our main diet was a very bitter fruit, which we had to soak in water before we could eat it. We also ate the bark of a tree. We'd first scrape it, then boil it in water before we could eat it." Algae, leaves, locusts, grasshoppers, lizards, snakes, worms, and termites became the sustenance of those exiled into the New Villages. Villagers in one area saw their skin turn yellow and began to vomit blood after they ingested inedible grasses and vines.

"We weren't allowed to complain about the food," one survivor explained, "because the Khmer Rouge said, 'If you're not happy, we'll take you to a place where there is more than enough to eat.' They meant the rice paddy where they executed people who were dissatisfied."

Complaining about inadequate food was not the only capital offense under the Khmer Rouge. Married couples were prohibited from engaging in prolonged conversations. This was punishable on the second offense with death. Communist officials conducted public executions reminiscent of those held under Ho Chi Minh's land-reform program. Victims were led off to a field prepared in advance to serve as a mass grave. Villagers were gathered around to witness the spectacle. Children were forced to watch as their parents were decapitated or stabbed, bludgeoned, or tortured to death. It was a barbaric ritual repeated thousands of times throughout Cambodia. These killing fields later turned into sunken pits as the hundreds of bodies buried underneath began to decay.

It has been estimated that Khmer Rouge policies killed over 1.2 million Cambodians in 1975 and 1976. Over 100,000 were executed in the first wave of terror. Over 20,000 died while fleeing the country. Over 400,000 were killed in the mass exodus from Cambodia's cities. Over 680,000 were executed or

319

died of disease or starvation in the New Villages in the countryside. The Communists did not let up their murderous pace. By December 1978, when Phnom Penh fell to Vietnam's invading armies, it is estimated that between 2 million and 3 million Cambodians had died at the hands of those who had called themselves "liberators."

When the North Vietnamese conquered South Vietnam in April 1975, their own reign of terror followed quickly. Hanoi conducted widespread executions to take its revenge against Saigon's defeated government and armed forces and to secure its totalitarian rule. This attracted little attention because more killings took place in rural than in urban areas. But Nguyen Cong Hoan, who served as a National Liberation Front agent and then as a member of the National Assembly of the united Communist Vietnam before fleeing the country in 1977, was in a position to know about Hanoi's executions. He said that the death toll reached into the tens of thousands.

South Vietnam's people were worse off by every measure after Saigon became Ho Chi Minh City. Antiwar critics charged that under Thieu South Vietnam was governed by a hopelessly corrupt regime. It is true that there was some corruption—but there was also substantial freedom. Under Thieu, elections were held with international observers present, and opposition Buddhists almost won control of the National Assembly. There was freedom of religion for all faiths. There were economic freedoms. South Vietnam became a prosperous small developing country. There was some freedom of the press. South Vietnam had three television stations, twenty radio stations, and twenty-seven daily newspapers, all of which were free to express dissenting views within certain bounds.

Now there are no political, religious, economic, or press freedoms. There are no free elections. There is ruthless repression of religion. More Buddhist monks have committed suicide through self-immolation under the Communists than under Diem and his successors combined. Southern Vietnam has become an economic disaster area. Vietnam now has one television station, two radio stations, and two dailies—all of which pump out government propaganda.

There are those who held that there was no difference between authoritarian and totalitarian governments. But in the case of Vietnam it was not a question of distinguishing among shades of gray—rather of seeing a difference between night and day.

Hanoi developed three ways of dealing with those it considered enemies.

First, the Communists built a Vietnamese gulag—a string of prisons stretching across the country. After their victory, North Vietnamese forces quickly arrested all individuals who could possibly lead opposition groups. This included not only all former military officers, political figures, and government leaders but also virtually the entire South Vietnamese intelligentsia. Among those jailed were the organizers of the Buddhist peace movement in Saigon, the leader of the anti-Thieu opposition in the National Assembly, the head of the group that had protested against government corruption in 1974 and 1975. Even some members of the National Liberation Front found themselves behind bars when they dared to express views that differed from Hanoi's.

Prison conditions are inhumane. Doan Van Toai, a political dissident who had spent years in South Vietnamese prisons, later described the conditions he found when he was incarcerated in those of the Communist Vietnamese: "I was thrown into a three-by-six-foot cell with my left hand chained to my right foot and my right hand chained to my left foot." His food consisted of a mixture of rice and sand. "After two months in solitary confinement, I was transferred to a collective cell, a room fifteen feet wide and twenty-five feet long, where at different times anywhere from forty to one hundred prisoners were crushed together. Here we had to take turns lying down to sleep, and most of the younger, stronger prisoners slept sitting up. In the sweltering heat, we also took turns snatching a few breaths of fresh air in front of the narrow opening that was the cell's only window. Every day I watched my friends die at my feet."

Nguyen Van Tang, a Communist who had been jailed for fifteen years by the French, eight years by Diem, six years by Thieu, and who is in Hanoi's jails today, was able to put prison conditions into perspective. He said, "My dream now is not to be released; it is not to see my family. My dream is that I could be back in a French prison thirty years ago."

It is estimated that Hanoi's prisons today hold between 200,000 and 340,000 Vietnamese. Official Vietnamese statements assert that no more than 50,000 have ever been jailed. But in 1978, Prime Minister Pham Van Dong gave the lie to his own government's assertion when he said that he had "released more than 1 million prisoners from the camps."

Second, Hanoi sends those it considers potentially disloyal to what it calls New Economic Zones. Among these potential opponents are all relatives of those detained in its prison system and all class enemies, such as former capitalists. They are exiled to desolate stretches of terrain where their task is to clear the land and to dig irrigation canals. Living conditions are primitive. Food is scarce. Disease is rampant. Premature death is common. It is estimated that over 1 million Vietnamese have been consigned to the New Economic Zones.

Third, the Communists caused the exodus of over 1.2 million people in the tragic flotillas of the boat people. In the spring of 1978, when Hanoi decided that Vietnam's ethnic Chinese might constitute a threat to its rule because of the conflict with China, it systematically expelled them, driving hundreds of thousands into the treacherous waters of the South China Sea on almost anything that would float. Hundreds of thousands more Vietnamese followed them in a desperate gamble to escape life under communism. Observers estimated that half— 600,000 people—drowned at sea.

In order to secure its grip on power, Hanoi has found it necessary to destroy the South Vietnamese nation. Before Hanoi's leaders could rule they had to ruin. It was unprecedented to see deeply nationalistic Vietnamese fleeing their nation.

"Our people have a traditional attachment to their country," wrote Nguyen Cong Hoan. "No Vietnamese would willingly leave home, homeland, and ancestors' graves. During the most oppressive French colonial rule and Japanese domination, no one escaped by boat at great risk to their lives. Yet you see that my countrymen by the thousands and from all walks of life, including a number of disillusioned Viet Congs, continue to escape from Vietnam."

As the plight of the Cambodian and Vietnamese peoples became publicized in the late 1970s, many antiwar figures reacted in horror to the consequences of their own policies. In 1974, Senator McGovern had argued that the Cambodian people "should he left to settle their own differences." His policy prevailed in Congress. In August 1978, to his credit, he called for the State Department to recommend that an international force be assembled to "knock the Cambodian regime out of power."

A generous view of the antiwar movement's position would be that there was no way they could have known what would happen in the wake of our defeat. But it *was* known—and they should have known.

It was no secret that Ho Chi Minh killed hundreds of nationalists in 1946 and over 50,000 peasants after coming to power in North Vietnam in 1954.

It was no secret that the National Liberation Front assassinated over 35,000 local South Vietnamese leaders and systematically used terror tactics against civilians.

It was no secret that Communist forces killed nearly 5,000 people in their month-long occupation of Hue during the Tet Offensive.

It was no secret that Hanoi's forces *deliberately* killed far more civilians by shelling them as they fled the fighting in Quang Tri during the 1972 offensive than our bombers *accidentally* did during their attacks on North Vietnam in December 1972.

It was no secret that Communist Khmer Rouge forces fired artillery shells into refugee camps in Phnom Penh and were

323

carrying out brutal atrocities in the areas under their occupation in 1973 and 1974.

Those in the antiwar movement might not have known about these facts. If so, however, it was a kind of willful ignorance. Their vicious brand of self-righteousness had grotesquely twisted their moral sense. It blinded them to a profound but simple truth: It is the essence of moral responsibility to determine *beforehand* the consequences of our action—or our inaction.

Today, after Communist governments have killed over a half million Vietnamese and over 2 million Cambodians, the conclusive moral judgment has been rendered on our effort to save Cambodia and South Vietnam: We have never fought in a more moral cause. Assertions in the antiwar news media that life in Indochina would be better after our withdrawal served to highlight in a tragic way the abysmally poor level of their reporting throughout the war. But of all their blatantly inaccurate statements over the years, none was more hideously wrong than that one.

"If wise men give up the use of power," de Gaulle once said, "what madmen will seize it, what fanatics?"

When we abandoned the use of power in Indochina, we also abandoned its people to a grim fate. When the American ambassador to Cambodia, John Gunther Dean, was about to be evacuated from Phhom Penh, he offered Lon Nol's closest colleague, Sirik Matak, asylum in the United States. The former Premier responded in a letter:

Dear Excellency and Friend,

I thank you very sincerely for your letter and for your offer to transport me toward freedom. I cannot, alas, leave in such a cowardly fashion. As for you, and in particular your great country, I never believed for a moment that you would have this sentiment of abandoning a people which has chosen liberty. You have refused us your protection, and we can do nothing about it.

You leave and my wish is that you and your country
will find happiness under this sky. But mark it well, that
if I shall die here on the spot and in the country I love,
it is too bad, because we are all born and must die one
day. I have only committed this mistake of believing you.

Sisowath Sirik Matak

It was a fittingly noble, if tragically sad, epitaph for his country,
his people, and himself. He was among the first whom the
Khmer Rouge executed.

After we abandoned the use of power, it was seized by the
North Vietnamese and Khmer Rouge Communists. Our defeat
was so great a tragedy because after the peace agreement of
January 1973 it was so easily avoidable. Consolidating our
gains would not have taken much to accomplish—a credible
threat to enforce the peace agreement through retaliatory
strikes against North Vietnam and a sufficient flow of aid to
Cambodia and South Vietnam. But Congress legislated an end
to our involvement. It also legislated the defeat of our friends
in the same stroke.

A lesson that our adversaries should learn from our intervention in Vietnam is that the United States, under resolute
and strong leadership, will go to great lengths and endure great
sacrifices to defend its allies and interests. We fought in Vietnam because there were important strategic interests involved.
But we also fought because our idealism was at stake. If not
the United States, what nation would have helped defend
South Vietnam? The fact is that no other country would have
fought for over a decade in a war half a world away at great
cost to itself in order to save the people of a small country
from Communist enslavement.

One lesson we must learn from Vietnam is that if we do not
exercise power for the good, there are plenty of men like Ho
Chi Minh, Le Duan, Khieu Samphan, and Pol Pot who will
gladly exercise it for evil purposes. Our armed intervention in
the Vietnam War was a not a brutal and immoral action. That
we came to the defense of innocent people under attack by

totalitarian thugs is no moral indictment. That we mishandled it at times in no way taints the cause. South Vietnam and Cambodia were worthy of our help—and the 3 million people who were killed in the war's aftermath deserved to be saved. Our abandonment of them in their moment of greatest need was not worthy of our country.

Another lesson we must learn is that in the real world peace is inseparable from power. Our country has had the good fortune of being separated from our enemies by two oceans. Others like our friends in Indochina, did not enjoy that luxury. Their enemies lived just a few miles away up the Ho Chi Minh Trail. Our mistake was not that we did too much and imposed an inhumane war on peace-loving peoples. It was that in the end we did too little to prevent totalitarians from imposing their inhumane rule on freedom-loving peoples. Our cause must be peace. But we must recognize that greater evils exist than war.

Communist troops brought peace to South Vietnam and Cambodia—but it was the peace of the grave.

THIRD WORLD WAR

The Third World war began before World War II ended. Saigon's fall ten years ago was the Soviet Union's greatest victory in one of the key battles of the Third World war. No Soviet soldiers fought in Vietnam, but it was a victory for Moscow nonetheless because its ally and client, North Vietnam, won and South Vietnam and the United States lost. After we failed to prevent Communist conquest in Vietnam, it became accepted dogma that we would fail everywhere. For six years after Vietnam, the new isolationists chanted "No more Vietnams" as the dominoes fell one by one: Laos, Cambodia, and Mozambique in 1975; Angola in 1976; Ethiopia in 1977; South Yemen in 1978; Nicaragua in 1979.

Since President Reagan took office in 1981, America's first international losing streak has been halted. But the ghost of Vietnam still haunts the debate over aid to the government of El Salvador and to the anti-Communist contras in Nicaragua. If we fail to halt Soviet support of aggression in our own hemisphere, we will have little hope of doing so when our interests are threatened in other parts of the world. We must purge ourselves of the paralyzing sickness of the Vietnam syndrome if we are to avoid other defeats in the battles of the Third World war.

Nobody wants another Vietnam. Because they fear that any U.S. intervention in Third World countries might lead to another Vietnam, the new isolationists contend that the United States has no strategic interests in the Third World that would justify the use of our military power, and that we should limit our role to foreign aid programs and diplomatic imtiatives. They are wrong.

We must be concerned with what happens in the Third World because of the enormous strategic and economic stakes involved. Two-thirds of the world's people live in the developing countries of Asia, Africa, the Middle East, and Latin America. Those countries have natural resources that are indispensable to the industrial nations of the West. United States trade with Third World countries last year was $175 billion— equal to our trade with Western Europe and Japan combined.

We must be concerned because it would be the height of immorality to stand by and allow millions of people to suffer the fate of the people of Vietnam and other Third World countries that have had repressive totalitarian regimes imposed upon them.

We must be concerned because the greatest threat to peace today is in the Third World. Since the end of World War II, there have been 120 wars in which 10 million people have been killed. Except for the Falklands in 1981 and Greece in 1947, all of these wars began and were fought in the Third World. British military strategist B. H. Liddell Hart's famous maxim is "If you want peace, understand war." If we want peace, we must also understand the Third World, because it is there that an incident is most likely to occur that would lead to war between the United States and the Soviet Union.

In considering the possible threats to peace in the world, the least likely is that the Soviet Union would launch a nuclear strike with their SS-20 missiles on Western Europe. Apart from the risk of retaliation, a Europe in ruins is not an attractive military prize. As Michael Howard puts it in *The Causes of*

Wars, the Soviet Union is now a status quo power in Europe. In the Third World, however, the Soviet Union has been, even during the heyday of detente, and will continue to be an anti-status-quo power. It accepts the postwar national boundaries of Europe as formalized by the Helsinki Agreement, but it continues to support what it calls "national liberation movements" in the Third World.

We have no interest in gaining domination over Third World nations, but we have a powerful interest in preventing the Soviet Union from doing so. If we have any doubt of the strategic importance of the Third World, the Soviet Union's actions should remove them. The men in the Kremlin are not philanthropists, and they are not fools. They are spending billions of rubles on fomenting and supporting revolutions in Third World countries and subsidizing the bankrupt economies of the regimes they have helped put in power. Except for Afghanistan, where they are attempting to suppress a counterrevolution against a Soviet puppet regime, Moscow has gained domination over nine Third World countries since 1974 without committing any troops to combat.

The question is not whether we should play a role in the Third World, but how we can do so without suffering another Vietnam. We must first examine the types of conflicts we confront.

The Korean War in 1950 demonstrated that a conventional attack across a border of a non-Communist country would bring immediate and united reaction from the United States and our UN allies. This is the least likely kind of attack we will face in the future.

Since Korea, the Soviets have gone under and around borders in a variety of ways. North Vietnam, with Chinese and Soviet logistic support, waged guerrilla war against South Vietnam until 1972, when the North Vietnamese launched a massive conventional attack across the demilitarized zone.

In Cuba and Nicaragua, the Soviet Union encouraged and eventually captured broad-based revolutionary movements in the guise of supporting so-called wars of liberation.

In Angola and Ethiopia, the Soviet Union backed up Communist leaders with Cuban proxy troops who helped them gain or retain power.

In El Salvador we are witnessing a technique similar to that used in Vietnam—a guerrilla insurgency without broad-based popular support and with no chance to survive, much less prevail, without the logistic support it receives from Nicaragua, the Soviet Union, and Cuba.

Sometimes the Soviets spark a revolution. Other times they capture one already in place. Either way the Soviet Union wins and the West loses another battle in the war for the Third World.

Never in history has there been a conflict as broad-based and as pervasive as the Third World war. It challenges us to rethink all of our time-tested assumptions about the nature of war and aggression. If we insist upon preparing for today's war by mounting yesterday's defenses, we are doomed to defeat. Today the important battles are not along borders but in remote villages and small countries whose names few Americans have heard. In pinpointing aggression, it is no longer enough to look for the smoking gun; now we must look for the hidden hand. We must become more aware of the role the Soviets and their surrogates play in instigating and supporting insurgencies against non-Communist governments.

We must begin by disabusing ourselves of some popular misconceptions about how to deal with conflicts in the Third World.

At one extreme there are those who insist that if we are strong enough militarily, we will be able to meet and defeat any challenge we face. It is true that our overwhelming nuclear superiority was one of the factors that enabled us to stop Communist aggression in Korea. But with that superiority gone, the fact that we have far more accurate and powerful nuclear weapons today than those we had during the Korean War is irrelevant in Third World conflicts. Great nations do not risk nuclear suicide to defend their interests in peripheral areas. And superior conventional forces will not prevail against an enemy who wages unconventional war. Helping a government stop a violent revolution militarily without helping it deal with the economic conditions that helped spawn the revolution would buy only a short-lived victory. After one revolution was put down, another would take its place.

At another extreme are those who say that poverty is the problem, and that instead of providing military aid to ensure security, we should provide economic aid to promote progress. They are only half right, and therefore all wrong. I recall the year 1947, when President Truman asked for military and economic aid to Greece and Turkey to meet the threat of Soviet-supported Communist guerrillas in Greece. Along with those of other congressmen, my office was flooded with hundreds of postcards reading, "Send food, not arms." We resisted the pressure and voted for the Truman program. If we had sent food only and not arms, Greece would be Communist today. The lesson of the Greek experience is that in the short run there can be no progress without security. But we must also recognize that in the long run there can be no security without progress.

Still others naïvely contend that diplomacy is the answer to armed conflicts in the Third World. Diplomacy cannot succeed without military power to back it up. For example, when President Carter ruled out the use of force at the outset of the Iranian hostage crisis, he weakened the effectiveness of diplomacy to resolve it. The pathetic failure of the League of Nations and the United Nations to play a significant role in keeping peace or ending wars is striking proof of the impotence of diplomacy without power.

There is too much of a tendency to see all Third World conflicts as part of the larger conflict between East and West. While the Soviet Union profits from most of them, it is not responsible for all the conflicts in the world. As one observer has pointed out, their policy is to trouble the waters and then fish in them.

A strategic consensus against the Soviet threat in the Middle East and the Persian Gulf may prove useful in some conflicts;

but without the Soviet Union playing a role at all, there would still be war between Iran and Iraq, and fighting between Israelis and Arabs. The most violent and dangerous forces in the Mideast are not Communist revolutionaries taking orders from Moscow but Moslem fundamentalist revolutionaries egged on by Khomeini and Qaddafi.

It is an illusion, however, that if the Soviet Union does not play a role in a Third World conflict, our interests are not threatened. The Soviets do not have to fight to win. Whether they fight or not, wherever we lose, they win. Khomeini's revolution in Iran had nothing to do with communism or the Soviet Union, but this does not mean that the Soviets did not benefit from it. When the Shah of Iran was driven from power, the United States lost its strongest ally in the Mideast. Had he remained in power, the war between Iran and Iraq and even the invasion of Afghanistan by the Soviet Union might never have taken place. Because a strong, dependable, pro-Western regime was replaced by an unpredictable, extreme, anti-Western one, the balance of power shifted against us and toward the Soviets. The Shah's downfall, like the fall of South Vietnam, was in part the result of the failure of the United States, his longtime ally, to back him when he needed it most. As a result, in each case the Soviets scored an important victory in the Third World war.

Instability is the Soviet Union's most powerful ally in the Third World war. Soviet leaders scan the globe for potential trouble spots, places where people are groping for a better way or suffering through episodes of unrest, and then find ways to make those bad situations worse. While the Soviet Union is not behind all violent revolutions, it is first in line to pick up the pieces when they are over. Instability—both the fact of it and the fact that the Soviet Union profits from it—threatens our interests, wherever it occurs in the world.

We must develop strategies to meet the Soviet offensive at three different levels: when a non-Communist nation is under attack by a Communist insurgency; when a Communist regime has already won power; and when a non-Communist nation is at peace before a revolution begins.

When a Soviet-supported guerrilla war or revolutionary war is already under way, we must not make the mistakes we made in Vietnam. Defeat can be a powerful positive force if we learn the right lessons from it, just as victory can be a destructive negative force if we learn the wrong lessons from it.

In 1969, I realized that after our experience in Vietnam the American people would be very reluctant to commit American forces to another war in the Third World. For that reason, I formulated the Nixon Doctrine. It states that in the future, unless a major power intervened in a Third World conflict, the U.S. should not commit its combat forces. We should provide military and economic aid to the target countries equal to that provided to the insurgents by the Soviet bloc, but the country under attack should have the responsibility for providing the men for its defense. If after being adequately trained and armed to defeat an insurgency a country still lacked the will and capability to fight and win, our doing the fighting for them would at best provide only temporary success. Once we left, the enemy would take over. We should never again make the mistake we made in Vietnam. The policy of Vietnamization should have been initiated at the beginning of the war rather than four years later after the United States had committed over 500,000 troops to the battle.

Some misinterpreted my announcement of this doctrine as a signal that the United States was beginning a total withdrawal from Asia and the rest of the world as well. But the Nixon Doctrine was not a formula for getting America *out* of the Third World; it provided the only sound basis for America to stay *in* and to continue to play a responsible role in helping our friends and allies defend their independence against Communist aggression.

In our military training programs, we should avoid another mistake we made in Vietnam: restructuring our allies' forces on the American model and thereby developing great capability for fighting a conventional war but very little for fighting a guerrilla war. Armies must be equipped and trained to meet the threat they are facing. Money could be spent in far better way than in having a country like El Salvador equip itself with high-performance fighter aircraft for use against guerrillas who have no air force.

A third mistake many Americans made in the last years of the Vietnam War was failing to see that in Third World conflicts our choice is usually not between our allies and someone better but between our allies and something far worse. Liberals today frequently call for the United States to break its ties with rightwing dictators. Otherwise, they claim, we will be guilty of supporting the world's most flagrant violators of human rights. They are wrong. By any measure the most repressive governments are those of the Communists. The record is clear. Cubans are worse off under Castro than under Batista. The Vietnamese are worse off under the Communist Le Duan than under Thieu. Cambodians were worse off under Pol Pot than under Lon Nol. When non-Communist regimes were in power, the United States could at least exert some pressure to increase adherence to human rights in those countries. Now it can do nothing. We must never take a course of action that results in the fall of a government that permits some freedom and the victory of one that permits none. If there is one profound lesson to be learned from the aftermath of the Vietnam War, that is it.

Finally, we must not make the mistake of helping our allies fight the insurgency and ignoring the source of the insurgency. That is why it makes no sense to provide economic and military assistance to El Salvador without bringing pressure to bear on Nicaragua and other Soviet-bloc countries that are providing arms for the insurgents.

Helping a country prevent a Communist regime from gaining power is difficult. It is even more difficult to help anti-Communist forces in countries where the Communists have already gained power. It is tempting to boldly proclaim that we will help anyone anywhere who fights against a repressive Communist regime, but we must recognize the limits of what we can do. We must not make the tragic mistakes we made in Hungary in 1956 and at the Bay of Pigs in 1961, where we encouraged revolutions against Communist regimes and then failed to support our friends when they came under attack from superior forces. The test should be whether there is some reasonable chance for success. The anti-communist Savimbi forces in Angola, for example, would meet this test. The freedom fighters in Afghanistan also deserve support, especially because this is the only leverage we have on the Soviets to mitigate their repression in that country.

The Soviets cannot have it both ways. If they have a right to support Communist "liberation" forces in non-Communist countries, we have an even greater right to support true liberation forces in Communist countries. In Nicaragua we should help the contras as long as the Sandinistas continue to support the guerrillas in El Salvador. A more difficult question arises if the Nicaraguan government agrees to discontinue that activity. In that case, we will be justified in continuing aid to the contras only if we are prepared to see it through in the event that they come under attack from superior forces.

The successful operation in Grenada served three important purposes: It rescued Americans whose lives were in danger; it removed the possibility of another Soviet base being constructed in the Caribbean; and most important, it erased some of the feeling of impotence we developed after the fall of Saigon. But while Grenada demonstrated that we could still do something on the world stage, it did not prove that we could do everything. Public support for the Grenada operation was high because it was over quickly, casualties were light, and the immediate provocation—the threat to American lives—was clear. Overcoming 600 lightly armed Cubans on the beaches of Grenada is a far different task from the one we would confront if we had to fight 50,000 Sandinistas, armed with Soviet heavy weapons, in Nicaragua.

But while it would be dangerous to assume that Grenada proved we could do everything, it is even more dangerous to assume that because we failed in Vietnam, we will fail everywhere. We must not allow our failure in Vietnam to blind us to the stark reality that without military power and the will to use it surgically and selectively in crucial Third World battles, we will lose the Third World war.

The reluctance of our military leaders to be bogged down in another Vietnam is understandable. It is not surprising that current military doctrine rules out the commitment of our military forces unless the following conditions are met: The actions must be "vital to our national interests" or those of our allies; we should commit forces only as a last resort; when we commit our troops, we must do so with the sole object of winning; the war must be winnable in that we have the means to achieve our goal of victory; and we must have assurance of support by Congress and the public.

No one can question these conditions if they are properly defined. But some go so far as to contend that our vital interests are involved only if there is an attack on our allies in Europe and Japan, a threat to our oil supplies in the Persian Gulf, or a threat against our close neighbors to the south. They are wrong. Our vital interests are affected by what happens in other parts of the world as well.

Israel is a case in point. Most military experts would agree that our interests would be affected if there were a threat to Saudi Arabia and the oil supplies of the West. On the other hand, Israel has virtually no oil. It is smaller than the state of Massachusetts. Only 4 million of the 100 million people who live in the Mideast live in Israel. It is not a formal ally of the United States. It could therefore be argued that Israel is not one of our *vital* interests. Yet when Israel has been attacked, every American President has made it clear that we would use military power to prevent Israel's defeat. Our interest in Israel's survival extends beyond the profound moral issues involved and the fact that Israel is an island of democracy in a sea of authoritarian states. Israel's regional presence and substantial military capability make its survival an important interest of the United States. And we cannot ignore the fact that the Soviet

Union is providing virtually unlimited arms to some of Israel's enemies.

Although it might not technically qualify as a vital American interest, most Americans understand both the moral and strategic reasons for our steadfast support of Israel. In the Third World war there will be other small countries where our interests, and the interests of the people of those countries, may be served by U.S. assistance in their efforts to resist Communist aggression. If we define our vital interests too narrowly solely out of fear of getting involved in another Vietnam, we run the risk of abandoning millions of people to totalitarianism and, eventually, of losing the Third World war.

No one can quarrel with the proposition that we must not use military force unless we have the means to achieve our goal of victory. But we must recognize that where our interests are clearly involved, we must take risks to protect them. Every military operation cannot be a sure thing. The United States is a great power with worldwide responsibilities. We will not prevail against an enemy willing to take any risk to achieve victory if we are unwilling to take some risks to prevent defeat.

The same principle applies to international terrorism. Some urge restraint in retaliating against terrorism because of the admittedly significant risk of casualties among civilians, hostages, and our military personnel. But while we cannot act in every instance of terrorism, we should always act decisively when we know who is responsible and where they are. Otherwise we give carte blanche to these international outlaws to strike again. If one group of terrorists succeeds in intimidating the United States, others will be encouraged to try, and more lives will undoubtedly be lost as a result. Swift, timely retaliation, even if there is some risk to innocent people, will mean that other terrorists will be less likely to threaten and kill innocent people in the future. Repeated threats to retaliate that are not followed by action are counterproductive. A President of the United States should warn only once.

Terrorism, whether undertaken by states, political groups, or individuals, is one of the most insidious and deadly aspects of the Third World war. The Soviet Union and its proxies use terrorism to wage covert war against the West and its friends and allies. It is also a tactic that our enemies use to try to drive the United States out of the Third World. We were forced out of Lebanon not by another country but by suicidal terrorist bands whom we could barely identify and whose sponsors remain out of our reach. Our military forces can only fight an enemy they can see. All the military power in the world is useless against shadows. If the United States wants to continue to play a role in the Third World, it must attack terrorism at its source. We must hold those who inspire it and pay for it accountable for their actions.

The most powerful weapon the terrorists have is the civilized world's parochial approach to combating them. If Americans are taken hostage, the world considers it solely an American problem. If most of the passengers of a hijacked jet are Kuwaitis, the hijacking is considered primarily Kuwait's problem. When a car bomb explodes in the streets of Paris, we leave it up to France to respond. By reacting in this narrow-minded way, we play into the terrorists' hands. Terrorism today is an international challenge to international order, and it requires an international response.

The Soviet Union's record in fueling international terrorism is well known. But it is not the only nation that does so. Khomeini's Iran and Qaddafi's Libya are both international outlaws that openly praise, protect, and incite those who commit terrorist acts. Such state-supported and sponsored terrorism is one of the most dangerous threats to peace in the world.

Dealings within and between nations depend on order. Diplomats must be able to travel, and embassies must be able to keep their doors open, without fear of assassinations and attacks, and businessmen must be able to go about their business without fear of being kidnapped. Terrorism breeds fear; fear breeds insularity and suspiciousness; and these inevitably will serve to drive nations apart. When that happens, the whole world will suffer the consequences.

In most cases of state-sponsored terrorism, military reprisals, though tempting, are impractical. But what has been most pathetic about the civilized world's response to terrorism is that it has made so little use of the wide array of choices short of military action available to it. Terrorism is a way to divide and conquer—but only if its victims allow themselves to be divided. When terrorists act against one nation, other nations should respond as if it is an attack on them all—because, in essence, it is. The first impulse of other nations should not be relief that they *were not* the victims but outrage that someone *was*.

The civilized world must develop a unified policy for dealing with terrorism. All nations that are potential victims should pool and share intelligence-gathering and communications resources. When military retaliation is appropriate, they must be prepared to act together. Most important, they must recognize that even nations that support terrorism depend on their victims. While neither Iran nor Libya could survive without selling oil, the rest of the world could survive without Iranian and Libyan oil. In the past, economic and diplomatic sanctions and quarantines have been justifiably criticized for being ineffective. They were ineffective, however, primarily because too few nations participated.

Terrorists will not be deterred by UN resolutions or expressions of outrage by leaders and legislatures. But they may be deterred once they realize that by using terror they will spark the wrath of all nations that do not want to exist in a world riven by a tiny minority who have resorted to violence in pursuit of their objectives. We will only eliminate terrorism if we choke it off by drawing the dark curtain of international condemnation around its sponsors. And actions will speak louder than words. Unless they are willing to live peacefully in the community of nations, we cannot allow them any of the privileges of membership.

. . .

Wars cannot be waged without the support of the Congress and the people. But there are times when the Congress and the people may not recognize our vital interests in Third World conflicts. Leaders should lead and not just follow uninformed public opinion. It is their responsibility to educate the people and the Congress about where our vital interests are and then gain support for whatever military actions may be necessary to protect them. Leaders who do only what opinion polls indicate uninformed voters will support are not true leaders, and if America follows them, it will cease to be a great nation. Trotsky once wrote, "You may not be interested in strategy, but strategy is interested in you." Uninformed people may not be interested in affecting what goes on in the Third World, but what goes on in the Third World is interested in affecting them.

We should be selective insofar as our involvement in Third World conflicts is concerned. As Frederick the Great observed, "He who attempts to defend everywhere, defends nothing." Simply because we are the major free world power does not mean we have a responsibility for everything that goes wrong in the world. Qaddafi's invasion of Chad was an example. The French had far more assets in Chad than we did, and they very appropriately assumed the responsibility for countering Qaddafi. That they have found him a difficult nut to crack does not mean that we could or should have done any better. But as Vietnam so clearly demonstrated, victory by a Soviet proxy in one Third World conflict encourages Soviet adventurism and leads to more aggression in other parts of the Third World. Therefore, no instance of Soviet aggression anywhere in the Third World should go unchallenged by the West.

Our goal should always be to use force as a last resort. But the capability and the will to use force as a first resort when our interests are threatened reduces the possibility of having to use force as a last resort, when the risk of casualties would be far greater. Vietnam highlighted the importance of blocking aggression early. Winston Churchill made the point that World War II was an unnecessary war because it could have been prevented by timely action against Hitler when he launched his conquests of smaller countries. But at the time European leaders did not consider them vital to their interests.

Everyone agrees that we should never commit our forces to a losing cause. But *win* must be properly defined. We are a defensive power. We are not trying to conquer other countries. That is why we must have a policy in which we will fight limited wars if they are necessary to achieve limited goals. We *win* if we prevent the enemy from winning. The world has probably seen its last conventional war between major powers. In the end the world conflict will probably be decided by the outcome of unconventional, limited wars. A President must not be faced with the option of either waging total war or accepting total defeat.

In the wake of Vietnam, however, Congress has tried to force Presidents to make exactly that choice by passing measures that drastically curtail their ability to use limited and unconventional military power. The War Powers Act makes it impossible for a President to act swiftly and secretly in a crisis and permits Congress to pull our troops out simply by doing *nothing*—by failing to pass either a resolution for or against the President's action. The Foreign Assistance Act limits aid to governments that do not have squeaky-clean human rights records. Had it been in force during World War II, it would have prevented us from assisting our ally, the Soviet Union, against Hitler. The Clark Amendment of 1976, which forbade covert aid to the freedom fighters in Angola, gave Cuba and the Soviet Union the green light for *their* covert activities in Angola and around the world. The Boland Amendment of 1982 paved the way for the disastrous decision by Congress to cut off all covert aid to the contras fighting the Sandinistas in Nicaragua.

These measures require a President to wage war under Marquis of Queensbury rules in a world where good manners are potentially fatal hindrances. The Soviets observe no rules of engagement except for the one that says winning is everything. No one suggests that we should become like them in order to prevail. It was Nietzsche who wrote, "Who fights with crocodiles becomes one." But we must also remember that he who does not fight will be devoured by crocodiles.

There are no limits on the Soviets' power to invade, overthrow, and undermine any non-Communist government or to arm, strengthen, and encourage any aggressive Communist government. Hamstringing our power to respond in such instances invites further aggression. Futhermore, sometimes we must assist governments that are fighting Communist aggression even if their human rights records do not meet our standards. With our assistance and influence, their people will have a chance to have some human rights; under the Communists, they will have none. And we must face up to the reality that covert war is a fact of life in the Third World. If every shipment of arms to an anti-Communist government or group requires a full-blown congressional investigation, the arms will never leave the dock, and our friends will come up empty-handed. The Soviets and their surrogates, meanwhile, will fight harder and win faster in country after country, just as they did during the late 1970s.

The outstretched hand of diplomacy will have a very weak grip unless a President holds the scepter of credible military power in his other hand. The pace and the nature of events in the modern world make it more important than ever for a President to have the ability to make expeditious use of the full range of our military and intelligence forces when the situation calls for it. He cannot wait on the 535 members of Congress to make these quick, tough decisions for him. Events will not wait for us to respond. As Charles de Gaulle observed shortly before his death, members of parliaments can paralyze policy; they cannot initiate it. Congressional leadership means leadership by consensus, and consensus leadership is no leadership. By the time a consensus has formed, the time to act has passed. Congress is a deliberative body; its wheels grind slowly, often maddeningly so. A President, however, must look, think, and then act decisively.

The War Powers Act and the other measures that limit a

President's latitude are lingering symptoms of the Vietnam syndrome, manifestations of the fear of our own strength that swept America following our failure in Indochina. Those days are now past. If we are to hold our own in the crucial battles of the Third World war, the President and Congress should join together in an effort to remove these self-defeating restrictions from the lawbooks.

Avoiding another Vietnam and yet trying to help a non-Communist nation defeat a Communist insurgency—or to help anti-Communists where Communists have already won power—is very difficult. The surest way to prevent another Vietnam is to act before the fighting breaks out. When all is quiet in the Third World, it does not mean that all is well. We need an early warning system for finding potential Third World hot spots. Once we identify them, we must offer an active, workable alternative to the status quo at one extreme and to communism on the other. We need to practice preventive political medicine before the patient is infected with an incurable revolutionary virus.

This is a battle we can wage on our turf—where we are strongest and the Communists are weakest. Ironically, in the long run the Communists lose when they win in the Third World, because Soviet socialism does not work. The Communists have gained power in eighteen countries since the end of World War II. In not one did they gain a majority of the vote in a free, democratic election. In not one do they dare to have one. Immediately after World War II, the Communist idea had appeal in the Third World precisely because the people did not know what it would produce. Now they know. Communism no longer has appeal to the masses. It promises peace and produces war. It promises liberation and produces tyranny. It promises justice and produces gulags. It promises progress and produces poverty. But while communism no longer has appeal to the masses, it has a powerful appeal to leaders. It offers a means to gain power and to retain it. The Communists will continue to try to expand their empire, but they can succeed only because of the power of their arms and not the power of their ideas.

The major geopolitical development since the end of World War II has been that the Communists have lost the ideological battle in the world. But the fact that they have lost this battle does not mean that the West has won it. The 3.5 billion people who live in the Third World have an average per capita income of $600, compared with $10,000 in the United States. Their societies are divided between the very rich and the very poor. The people of these countries want change. The only question is whether change will come by peaceful means or by violence, whether it destroys or builds, whether it leaves totalitarianism or freedom in its wake. For people who want change, it is no answer to offer the status quo. If there is no hope for peaceful change, violent change is inevitable.

There is too much of a tendency to look for scapegoats for the problems of Third World countries. Some blame their lot on the legacy of colonialism. Others contend that exploitation by the West's huge multinational corporations is responsible for the Third World's economic backwardness. Others charge that the West's niggardly aid policies and restrictive trade policies have caused Third World countries to lag behind in their development.

The real answer is that the economies of most Third World countries are sick, and they cannot recover without a proper diagnosis of the illness. Since the end of World War II, people in newly independent countries have suffered under incredibly bad governments—most of them corrupt, many of them repressive, very few of them democratic. Tinhorn dictators skimmed off billions of dollars in graft to feather their nests. Demagogues like Sukarno and Nkrumah built monuments to themselves rather than leaving a legacy of progress for their people. Socialist ideologues have imposed economic policies that discouraged private investment and, in the name of equality, have reduced millions of people to sharing poverty rather than participating in progress.

Their lot is not our fault, but it is our responsibility. The people of these countries have terrible problems. The Communists at least talk about the problems. Too often we just talk about the Communists. This is not worthy of America. America is a great country. We became great not by just being against what was wrong but by being for what was right. We must make it clear to the people of the Third World that we would be concerned about their plight even if there were no Communist threat; that we are not for the status quo in which millions languish in poverty; that we are not just *against* the Communist way that would make things worse but *for* a better way in which others may share in our progress toward a more free, just, and prosperous society.

We have left the impression that we become actively involved in the Third World only when our interests are threatened by Communist aggression. We must now develop policies that address *their* interests. Even if there were no Communist threat, millions of people would justifiably demand reforms to lift the burdens of poverty, injustice, and corruption that have been their lot for generations. In addressing these concerns, we will serve the interests of the people of the developing world and serve our own interests as well by depriving the Communists of the issues they exploit to gain power and impose a new tyranny.

Until now, we have moved to put out fires of revolution after they start. We must learn to keep them from igniting in the first place. We have learned to project power around the world at a far greater level than any nation in history. We must learn to project progress just as dramatically. We must seize the opportunity to make a peaceful revolution in the Third World now or confront the necessity of dealing with violent ones later.

For forty years the Soviet Union has been on the offensive, promising struggling people the impossible: instant justice, instant prosperity, sudden destruction of oppressive old institutions and establishment of fairer new ones. In turn we have offered money and democracy. Unfortunately, democracy is more easily talked about than practiced, and money is more

easily stolen or wasted than it is used for the kind of fundamental economic development that Third World countries
need. When it has come to inspiring people with a vision of
the future that contrasts with the squalor of the present, the
Communists have won hands down. Their vision is a mirage,
but a mirage is better than nothing.

The answer to the false promise of the Communist revolution
is to launch a peaceful revolution for progress in the Third
World. We and our allies must be as bold and generous in
helping Third World countries down the road to economic
progress as the U.S. was in helping Europe and Japan recover
after World War II.

This new initiative would not be a Third World Marshall
Plan. The Marshall Plan was officially called the European
Recovery Program. What is needed in the Third World is not
a recovery plan for nations with advanced economies but a
start-up plan for nations with primitive economies. The aid
must be structured in such a way that those who receive it
will have a strong incentive to adopt political and economic
policies that promote both progress and justice. The people of
the Third World must be given something to fight for, not just
against.

This is a competition in which we have an enormous advantage over the Soviet Union. Since the end of World War II,
the United States has provided $160 billion in foreign aid to
its former enemies, to its allies, and to Third World countries.
In that same period, the Soviet Union has provided only $20
billion. Yet while Congress generally votes overwhelmingly
for more defense spending, foreign aid has invariably been cut
below the amounts requested by Presidents since the end of
World War II. We spend 7 percent of our gross national product
on defense and two-tenths of 1 percent on economic aid. This
means that we are spending thirty-five times as much in preparing for a war that will probably never be fought as we are
for programs that can help us win a war we are losing.

The time has come to reassess our priorities. I am not sug-
gesting that we should support the well-intentioned but soft-

headed proposals for a massive transfer of wealth from rich nations to poor. This would only create a permanent under-class of pauper nations seeking handouts. We should share not our wealth but the means to achieve wealth. The Reagan administration's Caribbean initiative and the Kissinger Commission's recommendations for aid to Central America point to the direction we should take.

With the industrial nations only now beginning to recover from the recent worldwide recession, the last thing they are thinking about is more foreign aid. This is true despite the fact that in the last twenty years foreign aid has fallen substantially when measured as a percentage of gross national product. In 1960, seventeen of the largest non-Communist industrial nations gave one-half of 1 percent of their combined GNPs for foreign aid; by 1981, it had fallen to a third of 1 percent. Nations are fed up with seeing their money wasted on ill-conceived, poorly planned, and badly executed projects in the Third World. They are also discouraged by the lack of progress. For example, during the 1970s, personal income in black Africa, excluding oil-rich Nigeria, actually decreased despite billions of dollars in aid. The fact that Ethiopia's Marxist dictator Mengistu Haile Mariam spent $110 million on an obscenely lavish anniversary celebration last year while millions of Ethiopians were starving to death has disillusioned even the staunchest supporters of foreign aid programs.

Many abroad and in the United States have understandably concluded that foreign aid is not worth the investment. As far as traditional government-to-government aid is concerned, they are right. Much of it is wasted, especially when it is handed over with no strings attached. Often officials in a developing country are too proud to take advice from foreigners about how to spend the money, while the bureaucrats in the donor countries are too poorly informed or too sensitive to Third World officials' tender egos to offer advice, lay down conditions, or follow up on a grant once it has been made. But just as a bank does no favor to a borrower by making him a bad loan, we do not help a Third World country when we provide aid that subsidizes socialism, the status quo, corruption, or repression.

The debate over U.S. foreign aid is waged between two extremes. Some say we should cut government-to-government aid and increase private investment. Others insist that more government-to-government aid, rather than more private investment, is the answer. In fact, neither will work without the other. Government-to-government aid should be used as fertilizer to prepare the ground for private investment and thus for economic growth. Aid must be conditioned on the recipient country's willingness to adopt policies that will attract more private investment, because private investment brings with it something government aid does not: the technical expertise and training programs that will produce real progress for the recipient country's economy.

Private investment has an additional advantage: It is not limited by budget restraints in the donor country. Its only limitation is the investment climate of the recipient country. We must base our policy on the recognition of the fact that our strength, both at home and abroad, is not what we do through government but what we do through the private sector.

We should also explore how we can do more, through modification of personal and corporate income taxes, import and export tariffs, and other devices to encourage American businesses to do more business abroad.

Part of the intellectual flotsam of the 1960s and 1970s was the notion that the multinational corporation was an international outlaw, sucking cheap labor and natural resources out of the Third World and giving nothing in return. In fact, big business has already done a great deal to spur economic development in the Third World. It should be encouraged to do more.

Fear of foreign competition and loss of jobs is contributing to rising support for protectionism. While this is admittedly a painful immediate problem, in the long run we gain by having more prosperous countries in the Third World. Our two best customers in the world are Japan and Canada—both highly developed countries.

No matter how much aid the West provides, it undercuts itself by establishing trade policies that hurt Third World countries. Some nations, including the United States, discourage economic development by imposing tariffs on finished or partially finished goods from a country but not on the raw materials from the same country that go into those goods. The West also hurts the Third World, in which 70 percent of the poorest people depend on agriculture to live, by price supports for domestic crops that otherwise might well be imported. Eliminating policies such as these will cause short-term hardship at home, but will enhance the prospects for economic growth in the Third World, and in so doing make all of us more prosperous and secure in the long term.

To launch an effective program for economic progress for the Third World is a formidable task. Our goal cannot be achieved unless several conditions are met. First, we must restore bipartisanship in foreign policy. The great foreign-affairs initiatives of the postwar years—the Greek-Turkish aid program, the Marshall Plan, the rebuilding of Japan—were bipartisan initiatives. Bipartisanship in foreign policy was one of the major casualties of the Vietnam War. It is crucially important that our Third World initiative begin as a bipartisan effort and stay that way. Economic development does not happen overnight, but a change of attitude in a democracy often does. Unless we decide at the outset that our effort to win the Third World war will not be a political football, there will always be the danger that in the future a President or the Congress, eyeing the next election, will punt and give the ball back to the other side.

The United States cannot afford to have its leadership bitterly divided over our policy for dealing with conflict in the Third World. On the one hand, hawks emphasize the importance of defending American interests and of helping Third World governments that are fighting the spread of communism.

On the other hand, doves emphasize the importance of helping only those governments that respect human rights and that strive for economic development with equity. Both sides are only half right.

If the hawks and doves take a hardheaded look at the political facts of life in the Third World, they will find themselves seeing eye-to-eye with one another. For doves this means ending their romance with the idea of revolution. Too often this has led them to lavish uncritical praise on anyone who claims to act in the name of the people, no matter how violent or destructive his actions may be. Revolutions seldom produce democracy, and in the post-World War II period revolutions from the left never have. This does not mean that we must never support a revolutionary cause or that we should turn our backs on those striving for political and social reform. It does mean that we need to be patient with countries whose systems are imperfect, and that we should be skeptical of those who claim they will produce the millennium overnight. While democracy works for the nations of the West, instant democracy is neither possible nor desirable for most of the Third World.

Hawks must also reexamine their position. They must recognize that there are economic and political causes of revolution. The United States could regain its military superiority over the Soviet Union and still lose the Third World war. We must disabuse ourselves of the notion that national strength is measured solely by military power and that simply by having enough of it we can feel secure. Doves must recognize that to stay on the sidelines and to fail to do what is necessary to prevent the victory of a repressive Communist regime is immoral. Hawks must understand that using the specter of the Communist threat to justify the status quo or repression by the right is also immoral.

Second, it is essential that foreign economic issues be given equal status and consideration with political and military issues in the office of the President. Some will contend that foreign economic policy receives the attention it deserves because of its position on the organizational charts of the National Security Council and the State Department. This is not true. Highsounding titles do not give power and influence. Only direct access to the President does.

In the NSC, political and military issues receive first priority; economic issues have been and continue to be treated as second-priority matters. In the State Department, economic officers, with very few exceptions, are second-class citizens. The fairhaired boys in the Foreign Service who go to the top and become ambassadors are political officers. It is therefore no surprise that, with a few notable exceptions, the quality of economic officers is lower than that of political officers.

Foreign economic policy is an orphan, with second-level bureaucrats in the State, Commerce, and Treasury departments squabbling over custody. This is why economic policy decisions are often at odds with political decisions, particularly where East-West trade issues are involved.

During World War II, the United States recognized the importance of economic power by setting up a Board of Economic Warfare. Today we need a Foreign Economic Policy Board to concert the use of our economic power in the Third World war. It should be given the same status as the National Security Council. It should answer directly to the President, because only he is able to knock heads together when the bureaucrats in the various agencies involved with foreign economic policy engage in Washington's favorite sport, fighting for turf. Policies governing trade, foreign aid, loans, and support of international lending agencies must be coordinated to serve American foreign policy interests. A process must also be established for enlisting the cooperation of the private sector in serving those interests. It makes no sense for the government to cut off aid to hostile nations while American banks continue to make huge loans to those same nations.

Third, this is a task for all of the industrial nations of the West, not just the United States. Europe's GNP exceeds ours, and Japan's could equal ours by the end of the century. Japan spends two-tenths of 1 percent of its GNP on foreign economic aid, as does the United States. But we spend 7 percent of our GNP on defense, compared with nine-tenths of 1 percent for Japan. We can understand Japan's political problems, which make it difficult to spend more than 1 percent of its GNP on defense. But as the second richest nation in the free world, Japan should pay for the free ride it is getting on the military front by a corresponding increase in its economic assistance to Third World countries.

Our diplomatic initiatives should include a major effort to enlist the Soviet Union in joining us in cooling crises in the Third World. While this may seem unrealistic since the Soviet Union stirs up many of the crises and profits from most of them, we must not overlook the fact that they have other priorities as well. They want nuclear-arms control as we do. What destroyed any chance of Senate approval of SALT II was not the alleged flaws in the agreement but the Soviet invasion of Afghanistan. There is no way the Senate will approve any agreements in the future for arms control when the Soviet Union is blatantly supporting revolutions that threaten our interests in areas like Latin America and the Mideast.

While the Soviets want the world, they do not want war. A conflict in the Third World that involved the interests of both the United States and the Soviet Union could escalate into world war. And as a major nuclear power, the Soviets are concerned about the proliferation of nuclear weapons, just as we are, and about the possibility that an international outlaw like Qaddafi might acquire such weapons.

Therefore, while they will continue to proclaim their support for wars of national liberation, they will stop short of any action that could escalate into a suicidal world war. When a nation has to make a choice between ideology and survival, survival always comes first. We should challenge the Soviet leaders to peaceful competition in the Third World. If they can produce progress for people and not just power for Third World dictators, we say, "Welcome to the club."

. . .

I do not underestimate the cost or complexity of launching a peaceful revolution for progress in the Third World. But we have the economic resources. We have the skilled manpower and the brainpower. Our national interest requires it. There is only one nagging question. British strategist Sir Robert Thompson once wrote, "National strength equals manpower plus applied resources times will." Do we have the will to undertake such a bold initiative? Americans don't like to play a role on the world stage. Vietnam eroded our will to do so. But America is a great nation. Great nations must be mature enough to accept the fact that you do not win all the time. Defeat is never fatal unless you give up, and America must never give up. We must not turn away from our responsibilities in the world. If we refuse to play a major role, the rest of the free world will be at the mercy of totalitarian aggressors.

We must continue to play that role, not just for others but for ourselves. A world one-third rich and two-thirds poor will never enjoy real peace. America cannot be at peace in a world of wars. Where freedom is destroyed anywhere, it is threatened in America. We cannot have a healthy American economy in a sick world economy. By providing more economic aid now, we reduce the possibility of having to provide more military aid later.

I believe the American people are ready to accept this challenge. Defeatism, indifference, and malaise are not American characteristics. Optimism, compassion, and high-spiritedness are. We are a people who are never satisfied with the status quo. Americans are always striving for something better. We must put those qualities to work beyond our borders. We must be as impatient with the status quo in the Third World as we are at home.

The best way to slow down and eventually halt the locomotive that propels the Communist offensive in the Third World war is to deny it fuel. If a program for progress gives people in target countries the promise of a peaceful revolution, those who are trying to incite violent revolution will run out of gas.

In the past, being against Communist aggression has been reason enough to mobilize public opinion in support of American foreign policy. Our self-interest in this great initiative is obvious. But Americans will respond even more enthusiastically if the case is presented in idealistic terms.

In World War I, being against the Kaiser and German militarism was a powerful incentive for our war effort. But Woodrow Wilson's greatest contribution to our eventual victory was that he presented our effort in idealistic terms. We were fighting "a war to end wars," a war "to make the world safe for democracy."

In World War II, Hitler and Hirohito made very convenient enemies to be against. But Roosevelt and Churchill inspired the people of the free world by presenting in idealistic terms not just what we were fighting *against* but what we were fighting *for*—for the Four Freedoms and eventually a new world organization that would initiate an era of peace.

Throughout our history our greatest Presidents have called upon Americans to participate in great causes—causes that were bigger than themselves, bigger than America, as big as the whole world itself. Thomas Jefferson said, "We act not for ourselves alone but for the whole human race." Lincoln proclaimed, "We shall nobly save or meanly lose the last best hope of earth." Theodore Roosevelt declared, "Our first duty as citizens of the nation is owed to the United States, but if we are true to our principles we must also think of serving the interests of mankind at large." Speaking at Independence Hall on July 4, 1913, Woodrow Wilson said, "A patriotic American is never so proud of the flag under which he lives as when it comes to mean to others as well as to himself a symbol of hope and liberty."

Appeals to our highest ideals have never failed to move Americans to support great causes. To make the world safe not only for ourselves but for others is a great cause. Even greater is the challenge to give millions of people in poor nations a chance to share the blessings of freedom and progress we enjoy.

Our defeat in Vietnam was only a temporary setback after a series of victories. It is vital that we learn the right lessons from that defeat. In Vietnam, we tried and failed in a just cause. "No more Vietnams" can mean that we will not *try* again. It *should* mean that we will not *fail* again.

AUTHOR'S NOTE

Winston Churchill once remarked that history would treat him kindly because he intended to write the history. This book was not written to preempt historians. It was written because both during and after the war, as President and private citizen, I found that television and newspaper coverage of the Vietnam War described a different war from the one I knew, and that the resulting misimpressions formed in the public's mind were continuing to haunt our foreign policy. In these pages, I have set down the story of the war as I saw it, with the advantages and disadvantages that follow from this perspective.

This is the sixth book I have written, and the fifth that I have written since leaving the presidency. It is a book about which I have especially keen feelings. Its roots go back more than thirty years, to my first visit to Vietnam in 1953. But the intensity of my feeling about it stems from having been the President who inherited the Vietnam War at its peak and had to end it, and having then seen the peace that was won at such cost thrown away so cavalierly. The lessons of Vietnam are, to me, very personal ones. The analysis of events that I have given here is, of course, my own, derived from my own experience, study, and observation. Those who may disagree with its conclusions should direct their disagreements at me. However, there are others whose contributions I particularly want to acknowledge.

In the preparation of this book, I have drawn not only on my own experience, but also on scholarly and archival sources. In addition to the memoirs of the principal actors, among the most useful of these have been John Barron and Anthony Paul's *Murder of a Gentle Land: The Untold Story of Communist Genocide in Cambodia;* Larry Berman's *Planning a Tragedy: The Americanization of the War in Vietnam;* Peter Braestrup's *Big Story: How the American Press and Television Reported and Interpreted the Crisis of Tet 1968 in Vietnam and Washington;* Michael Charlton and Anthony Moncrieff's *Many Reasons Why: The American Involvement in Vietnam;* Hoang Van Chi's *From Colonialism to Communism: A Case History of North Vietnam;* Louis A. Fanning's *Betrayal in Vietnam;* Marguerite Higgins's *Our Vietnam Nightmare;* Colonel William E. Le Gro's *Vietnam from Ceasefire to Capitulation;* Guenter Lewy's *America in Vietnam;* Stephen J. Morris's "Human Rights in Vietnam Under Two Regimes"; Douglas Pike's *Viet Cong: The Organization and Techniques of the National Liberation Front of South Vietnam;* Norman Podhoretz's *Why We Were in Vietnam;* Francois Ponchaud's *Cambodia: Year Zero;* Sir Robert Thompson's *Peace Is Not at Hand;* Robert F. Turner's *Vietnamese Communism: Its Origins and Development;* and General Cao Van Vien's *The Final Collapse.*

For their contributions to my thinking on the issues involved in the Vietnam struggle, I want to thank the many members of my administration, and others, with whom the effort to deal with the war and its aftermath were shared. Many friends and associates offered information and counsel as I wrote this book, but I would especially like to express my appreciation for their advice to the late Ellsworth Bunker, who served as United States ambassador to Saigon from 1967 to 1973; General Edward G. Lansdale, who spent many years as an adviser to our allies in South Vietnam; and Stephen B. Young, who worked in our pacification program and now serves as dean of Hamline

Law School. For their specific help with this book, I also want to thank four people in particular: Dolores Dynes, for her devoted work in preparing the manuscript; Carlos Narvaez, for his diligence in searching out research materials; and, for their exceptionally able, astute, and dedicated assistance, Marin Strmecki—who served as principal research and editorial coordinator—and John H. Taylor, my administrative assistant.

—R.N.

Saddle River, New Jersey
December 31, 1984

RICHARD NIXON

Born in Yorba Linda, California, Richard Nixon attended Whittier College and the Duke University School of Law. After serving in the navy during World War II, he was elected to the United States House of Representatives in 1946, where he soon became known for his role in the Alger Hiss case. He was elected to the Senate in 1950, and became Dwight Eisenhower's vice-presidential running mate in 1952. As vice-president, he stood up to anti-American rioters in Venezuela, debated Khrushchev in Moscow, and briefly headed the government when Eisenhower suffered a heart attack. In 1960, he ran for the presidency against John Kennedy. In a hard-fought campaign, he narrowly lost, and his political career was seemingly finished.

In 1968, however, he became an early presidential favorite when Lyndon Johnson dropped out of the race, and he emerged victorious over Hubert Humphrey and George Wallace in a hotly contested election. As president, Nixon became the first American leader ever to visit Communist China, and he put forward a bold policy of détente with the Soviet Union. Combining tough military action with a tough negotiating stance at the peace table, he was ultimately able to begin to bring

America's involvement in Vietnam to an end and to secure the release of U.S. prisoners of war.

In 1972, he won a landslide reelection victory against George McGovern. Two years later, he resigned from office.

Since that time, Nixon has written seven books, and has met and consulted with many world leaders. He lives with his wife Pat in Saddle River, New Jersey.

THE RICHARD NIXON LIBRARY
AND BIRTHPLACE

The Richard Nixon Library and Birthplace at Yorba Linda, California, opened to the public in 1990, and is the first presidential library to be both constructed and operated without federal dollars. Its exhibits, including the former President's fully restored birthplace home situated on the same spot where his father built it, trace his life and career from birth to the present.

The Richard Nixon Library Editions

Six Crises
Updated with a New Introduction

Richard Nixon's first book, a bestseller when first published in 1962, examines the turning points of Nixon's early public career—from the Alger Hiss case and the Checkers speech to the kitchen debate with Khrushchev and the presidential campaign against Kennedy in 1960. It provides a remarkable self-portrait of Nixon as congressman, senator, and vice-president.

"Nixon pours out a story of intense fascination. . . . Fair, precise and relentlessly self-analytical."

—San Francisco Chronicle

RN: The Memoirs of Richard Nixon
Updated with a New Introduction

Richard Nixon's bestselling autobiography is an intensely personal examination of his life, public career, and presidency. With startling candor, Nixon reveals his beliefs, doubts, and behind-the-scenes decisions, shedding new light on his landmark diplomatic initiatives, political campaigns, and historic decision to resign from the presidency.

"Informative, explicit, even suspense-ridden . . . An important source for students of the Nixon presidency."

—The New York Times Book Review

ORDER NOW! NO-RISK 14-DAY FREE TRIAL

Simon & Schuster Inc.
200 Old Tappan Road
Old Tappan, NJ 07675
Mail Order Dept.

Please send me _____ copies of *Six Crises*.
ISBN# 0-671-70619-5; $12.95
Please send me _____ copies of *RN*.
ISBN# 0-671-70741-8; $17.95

_____ Save! Enclose full amount per copy with this coupon. Publisher pays postage and handling; or charge my credit card.
_____ MasterCard _____ Visa

My credit card number is_____ Card expires_____

Signature_____

Name_____

Address_____

City_____ State_____ Zip Code_____

The Richard Nixon Library Editions

The Real War
Updated with a New Introduction

In this landmark 1980 bestseller, Richard Nixon presents a trenchant analysis of American strategic shortcomings and a prescription for renewed strength. Nixon's tough-minded views became a blueprint for Reagan's military buildup and strategic initiatives—which some believe ultimately paved the way for the current thaw in East-West relations.

"Provocative . . . striking . . . says publicly what many foreign policy specialists probably believe but dare not reveal, and its world view has an inner consistency that forces every reader to examine his assumptions."

—The New Republic

Leaders
Updated with a New Introduction

Drawing on his personal acquaintance with virtually every major world leader since the Second World War, Richard Nixon brings to life the men and women who have shaped modern history, revealing both their strengths and their shortcomings. The leaders profiled range from Winston Churchill, Nikita Khrushchev, and Konrad Adenauer to Charles de Gaulle, Golda Meir, and Zhou Enlai.

"A veritable primer on leadership."

—National Review

ORDER NOW! NO-RISK 14-DAY FREE TRIAL